ROBERT FEKE

Colonial Portrait Painter

Library of American Art

ROBERT FEKE

Colonial Portrait Painter

By Henry Wilder Foote

Kennedy Galleries, Inc. · Da Capo Press
New York · 1969

Library of Congress Catalog Card Number 72-75357

Published by
Kennedy Galleries, Inc.
20 East 56th Street, New York, N.Y. 10022
and
Da Capo Press
A Division of Plenum Publishing Corporation
227 West 17th Street, New York, N.Y. 10011

ROBERT FEKE

LONDON : HUMPHREY MILFORD

OXFORD UNIVERSITY PRESS

ROBERT FEKE (THE EARLY SELF-PORTRAIT)

ROBERT FEKE

Colonial Portrait Painter

BY HENRY WILDER FOOTE

1930
CAMBRIDGE
MASSACHUSETTS
HARVARD UNIVERSITY PRESS

PRINTED AT THE HARVARD UNIVERSITY PRESS
CAMBRIDGE, MASS., U. S. A.

TO

THE HONORED MEMORY OF

MY FATHER

A LOVER OF NEW ENGLAND

A DILIGENT STUDENT AND FAITHFUL

INTERPRETER OF HER HISTORY

THIS BOOK IS DEDICATED

PREFACE

ROBERT FEKE, the best colonial portrait painter in America before Copley, has waited more than a century and three quarters for a biographer. Although the late Professor Poland, in a brief pamphlet printed a quarter of a century ago, put into consecutive form for the first time the few known facts regarding him, and Mr. Bayley gives a summary outline of his career in the recently printed *Five Colonial Artists of New England*, no attempt has hitherto been made to set forth a detailed study of his career or to catalogue his paintings. The present book is the result of a growing interest which has given pleasure to my leisure moments for a good many years, in the course of which I have slowly accumulated a body of information about Feke not to be found elsewhere. If to some who may take up this book I seem to have gone with unnecessary detail into the story of his antecedents, or into minor incidents in his life, my excuse is that I have endeavored to include every item of the scanty records which may enable us to discern what manner of man he was. If to others I seem to have indulged too largely in conjecture, I can only say that, until further documents come to light, we are dependent upon surmise and inference regarding his whereabouts and activities during the greater part of his life. It is only now and then that some brief item in an obscure record or a rare signed and dated portrait gives definite information as to where he was and what he was doing. Enough has been ascertained, however, not only to give us some idea of the man, but also to picture him in the colonial life of the first half of the eighteenth century.

I am indebted to many persons for assistance in preparing this study. I should be ungrateful not to thank particularly

Mr. Frank W. Bayley of Boston for frequent advice and for help in locating portraits; the staff of the Frick Art Reference Library in New York for many valued courtesies; and Mrs. Rutherford Sherman Elliott, who has greatly assisted my researches at the Newport Historical Society. Mr. Charles K. Bolton of the Boston Athenaeum has read the manuscript of Chapter I; Professor G. L. Kittredge has read Chapter II; Mr. John Hill Morgan has read Chapter X and has helped me at other points; and members of my own family have read parts of the manuscript, offering helpful criticisms. Many other friends have given clues or have gone out of their way to open doors for me which have led to fresh glimpses of the elusive figure of Robert Feke. To all these helpers I offer heartfelt thanks.

I have myself seen every one of the extant pictures attributed to Feke in the following pages. Perhaps I may make the whimsical claim of being the only person, except the painter himself, who has ever seen them all. In some instances, which I have noted, the attribution may be open to question, but generally, even where his signature is lacking, his characteristic style bears witness to his work, and its testimony can often be corroborated by information regarding the age and residence of the subject of the portrait. In selecting the illustrations I have for the most part chosen pictures which either have never been reproduced before or which have appeared in publications which are not readily accessible to the student of colonial art. This policy has involved the omission of most of the best known of Feke's paintings, such as the later portraits of the Bowdoins and the portraits of General Waldo, Benjamin Franklin, and "Pamela Andrews." But these pictures have all been reproduced several times, and they, and a dozen others, are to be seen in Mr. Bayley's book. Since all of Feke's paintings cannot be reproduced without unduly swelling the size and cost of my book I have felt that students would be

better served by showing a limited number of pictures hitherto
little known or wholly overlooked. The chief exceptions to this
policy are the early self-portrait, which is obviously appropriate
for use as a frontispiece, and the portrait showing Isaac Royall
and his family, which I have used because of its importance as a
turning point in Feke's career. In the descriptive catalogue the
inquirer will find information which will guide him to reproductions of most of the other pictures listed.

I am indebted to Harvard University for the photograph
of the inscription on the back of the Royall portrait, which I
saw and deciphered before the photograph was taken, but which
has now been hidden by the relining of the picture.

The following persons and institutions have generously given
me permission to reproduce portraits which they own:

Owner	*Subject*
Mr. Vincent Astor	Mrs. Charles Willing
Miss Edith Bangs	Mrs. John Channing, No. 2.
The Misses Bullock	Robert Feke
	Mrs. Robert Feke
Bowdoin College	James Bowdoin II
Mr. Thomas B. Clarke	Miss Williamina Moore
	Miss Ruth Cunningham
Miss Fannie Travis Cochran	Dr. Josiah Bond
Mr. Robert F. Cox	"Phiany" Cocks
Mr. W. E. C. Eustis and the Heirs of	John Channing, No. 1
F. A. Eustis	Mrs. John Channing, No. 1
Dr. Henry M. Fisher	Tench Francis, No. 2
Mr. George Hewlett	Josiah Martin
	Mrs. Josiah Martin
Harvard University	Isaac Royall
Mrs. Ben P. P. Moseley	Mrs. Barlow Trecothick
Mrs. Fannie B. N. Mercer	William Nelson
Newport Historical Society	Isaac Stelle
	John Gidley
Mrs. Leonard Opdycke	Mrs. Ralph Inman, No. 2
Pennsylvania Academy of the Fine Arts	Miss Mary McCall
Rhode Island Historical Society	Rev. John Callender

Owner	*Subject*
Mrs. R. M. Saltonstall	Richard Saltonstall
Sears Academy of Art	Unknown Man with Spaniel
Mrs. Sidell Tilghman	Tench Francis, No. 1
	Mrs. Tench Francis, No. 1
	Mrs. James Tilghman
Mrs. Vanderbilt	Rev. Thomas Hiscox
Mr. Robert C. Vose	Robert Auchmuty
Mr. E. Shippen Willing	Edward Shippen
	Mrs. Tench Francis, No. 2

I am grateful to the owners of these and other portraits, who, without exception, have given me permission to inspect their pictures, and have often given me, or permitted me to secure, photographs. Often these owners have added a touch of gracious hospitality to the stranger who came among them taking notes. It seems almost like a breach of that hospitality to attribute to Feke some of these portraits which the owners, clinging to family tradition, firmly believe to be by other painters, usually attributing them to Copley. I regret the disapproval, or the pain, which my inability to accept the tradition may, in some cases, cause, but I have not differed from them without good reasons, and, in such a study as this, the primary obligation of the writer is to use his unbiased judgment in stating what the historical evidence seems to indicate to be the facts.

Since at present no definitive life of Feke can be written nor complete catalogue of his works compiled it is inevitable that some errors should creep into this book, and that unlisted pictures should be discovered. I shall be grateful to readers who call my attention to any erroneous statement, to omissions of facts I should have known, or to portraits which I have not seen.

H. W. F.

July, 1930

SUPPLEMENTARY NOTE

AFTER this book had gone to press two more portraits attributable to Feke were brought to my attention, as well as an important article on Feke which appeared in *The Antiquarian* for October, 1930.

The first portrait depicts Foster Hutchinson (1724–1799), son of Thomas and Sarah Foster Hutchinson, who was graduated from Harvard in 1743, was justice of the Superior Court of Massachusetts, and who died in Halifax, whither he went in 1776 as a loyalist. The portrait (H. 50 inches, W. 40 inches) is signed "R. F. Pinx 1748," and was painted in Boston. It represents a handsome young man standing half-front, his right shoulder towards the spectator, his face turned right nearly full front. He wears a wig, a brown coat and a white satin waistcoat trimmed with wide gold braid. The background shows a landscape, with a high, arched stone bridge of European type over a small stream. The picture is a fine specimen of Feke's work. It is now owned by Thomas B. Clarke, Esq., who purchased it recently from a family in Providence, R. I., in which it had descended.

The second picture is a bust portrait (H. 30 inches, W. 25 inches), with spandrels at the lower corners. A paper pasted on the back reads: "Captain William Stoddard. Born 1719, Died 1778. The portrait was painted when he was twenty-one years old. The scar on cheek was received while engaged in a fight with Indians. Bayonet holes made by American soldiers, who, entering his home, and finding him absent, took this method of showing their disapproval of his sympathies with the Tories." The portrait depicts a young man with brown eyes, level eyebrows, and a boyish face, with a scar on his left cheek. He is shown three-quarters front, with his right shoulder towards the spectator, his face turned right nearly full front. He wears a white wig, a dark brown coat, a light brown waistcoat, and ruffles. The portrait is unsigned, but strongly resembles Feke's earlier work, before his technique was fully developed. It was purchased in October, 1930, by Mr. Robert C. Vose of Boston, from owners in Newport to whom it had descended.

The article in *The Antiquarian* is entitled "Robert Feke, First Painter to Colonial Aristocracy," and is by Theodore Bolton and Harry Lorin Binsse. It includes fifteen illustrations and a list of forty-eight pictures attributed to Feke, and gives the best account of the painter which has appeared since Professor Poland's pamphlet. All the pictures which the authors have reproduced or listed are discussed in this book, except the genre picture, noted below, and one which they list as "Young Girl, Mrs. Gardner Greene," which I believe to be by J. Theus. I find myself unable to accept the dates which they assign to several portraits, and it should be added that there are a number of minor inaccuracies in both the article and the list of portraits.

SUPPLEMENTARY NOTE

The authors have found in the *Town Records* of Oyster Bay, Long Island, a few items about the painter's father not included in the following pages, and the record of a survey, dated December 12, 1730, made by "Robart Feke Jur" and another man, proving that at that time the painter was working as a surveyor in his home town. Their most important discovery is a genre picture "representing what seem to be fanciful Turkish smugglers loading a vessel at night, against a background of Roman ruins. It is an interesting piece of work thoroughly in the fashion of its period, showing marked Flemish influence, especially in the animals and figures. It was possibly copied from an engraving." The picture is said to be signed "R. Feke," and to have been recently found in England. I have seen only the reproduction of this picture in *The Antiquarian*. If it be indeed Feke's work it suggests the possibility of further interesting discoveries regarding his career. We do know from the evidence of both Hamilton (pages 61–64) and Smith (pages 87–88) that Feke painted pictures other than portraits, and that he copied "The Judgement of Hercules" from an engraving. Unless this picture was also done from an engraving it would indicate considerable first-hand acquaintance with Dutch or Flemish art.

The authors of the article cited have also noted the indebtedness of Feke, in the Royall portrait, to Smibert's picture of Dean Berkeley's family, which I have discussed on page 42.

H. W. F.

October 20, 1930.

CONTENTS

LIST OF ILLUSTRATIONS

INTRODUCTION

FOR more than one hundred years after the death of Robert Feke his name well-nigh disappeared from the knowledge of his fellow-countrymen. It lay buried in neglected records; it was questioningly read by the very few who had the curiosity to note it upon the rare portraits which he signed; it appeared at the bottom of Okey's engraving of Rev. Thomas Hiscox which was published in 1773 and was reproduced in a denominational magazine half a century later; it was given in an obscure notice in the *Newport Mercury* in 1804 as that of the long dead husband of Mrs. Eleanor Feke. When Dunlap published his *History of the Arts of Design in America* in 1834, although he had a good deal of information about other colonial portrait painters, he would have omitted Feke as altogether unknown had not Mr. J. Francis Fisher informed him of the existence in Philadelphia of a portrait signed by Feke.

So far as I am aware Okey's engraving and its lithographic reproduction, the item in the *Mercury*, and the three-line notice in Dunlap, are the only places in which Feke's name occurs in print before the appearance in Dawson's *Historical Magazine* for 1859–60 of three letters about him.[1] The first of these letters was from the above-mentioned Mr. Fisher, giving a little more information about some of Feke's Philadelphia portraits and asking for details about the painter's life and work. He was answered in the next issue of the *Magazine* by two writers signing themselves "S. F." and "J. G. S.," who communicated a few facts about Feke's life as handed down by family tradition, embellished with

[1] Dawson's *New York Historical Magazine*, III (November, 1859), 348, and IV (January, 1860), 20, and 281.

dubious, legendary and conflicting details. These letters are our primary source of information about him, and since Dawson's *Magazine* is not easily accessible, they are reprinted in Appendix A.

Following their appearance Feke's name was included in various biographical dictionaries,[1] but in every case the accounts of him are merely uncritical summaries of the information given in the letters, so that all are incomplete and inaccurate, some of them grossly so. The only fresh items of information brought to light between 1860 and 1900 were obscurely printed in a history of Rhode Island which was a commercial rather than a scholarly compilation.[2] Even Goodspeed and Bayley, in their 1918 edition of Dunlap, were content with a footnote giving a very brief summary of his career, though they included reproductions of Feke's portrait of Hannah Flagg and of his own early self-portrait.

It was not until the late Professor Poland of Brown University read his paper on Feke in 1904 to the Rhode Island Historical Society that any fresh information was brought to light.[3] Starting with the letters in Dawson's *Historical Magazine*, Poland made a series of important discoveries. He unearthed the facts of Feke's descent; evidence of family intercourse with Newport, Rhode Island, before 1729; the record of Feke's marriage, of the

---

[1] *Book of Artists*, Tuckerman, 1867.
Dictionary of American Biography, Drake, 1872.
Biographical Encyclopedia of Representative Men of Rhode Island, 1881.
Cyclopedia of Painters and Painting, Champlin-Perkins, 1888.
National Cyclopaedia of American Biography, VIII (1899), 425.
Dictionary of Painters and Engravers, Bryan, 1903.
Outlines of the History of Painting, E. von Mach, 1906.
Allgemeines Lexikon der bildenden Künstler, Thieme und Becker, Vol. XI, 1915.
Dictionary of American Painters, Sculptors, and Engravers, Mantle Fielding, 1926.

[2] *History of the State of Rhode Island*, brought out in 1878 by Hoag, Wade & Co. It contains a crude lithograph of Feke's late self-portrait, and mentions the loss by shipwreck of Feke's eldest son, John.

[3] *Robert Feke, the Early Newport Portrait Painter, and the Beginning of Colonial Painting*. A paper read before the Rhode Island Historical Society, April 5, 1904, by William Carey Poland, Litt.D., Providence, 1907.

marriage of his aunt Abigail Feake, and of the marriages of his daughters; the names of his children; and the records of his wife's death and those of his children. He was well acquainted with the Newport background of Feke's life, and he was able to make an intelligent criticism of the legendary features reported in the letters, and, by shrewd surmises, to present for the first time something like a real sketch of Feke's career. Every student of colonial painting in America is permanently indebted to Poland for this groundwork of ascertained facts. The following study would have been impossible without his work as a basis. I have discovered a few fresh items, but reference to his sources has enabled me to draw somewhat more extended inferences from them. The criticism to be made of Poland's essay is that it is somewhat rambling and that his limited acquaintance with Feke's portraits deprived him of important evidence. He cites by name but thirteen of them and had seen only six, whereas nearly seventy have now been more or less certainly identified, some of which have an important bearing on his career.

The most important contributions to our knowledge of Feke, since Professor Poland's paper, have been those of the late Lawrence Park. His studies for his great work on Gilbert Stuart gave him a wide acquaintance with colonial portraiture. He became an enthusiastic admirer of Feke's work, and his trained judgment enabled him to attribute to Feke a number of unsigned portraits which had been ascribed to other painters. He also wrote three brief but valuable criticisms of individual portraits, which are cited in the following descriptive catalogue.[1] Had he lived he would perhaps himself have produced a life of Feke, done with wider knowledge and more adequate equipment than are mine.

[1] For notes by Lawrence Park on Feke's portraits, see *Art in America and Elsewhere*, VII, 216–218 (portrait of General Samuel Waldo); Vol. XII, No. 1 (portrait of Benjamin Franklin); *Bulletin of the Cleveland Museum of Fine Arts*, No. 5, June, 1919 (portrait of Charles Apthorp).

Early in the present century two contemporary references to Feke first appeared in print. The earlier and more important is in Hamilton's *Itinerarium*, privately printed by William K. Bixby of St. Louis. The second is in *Hannah Logan's Courtship*, edited by Albert Cook Myers, Philadelphia, 1904. In 1921 Mrs. Maud Howe Elliott read a paper before the Newport Historical Society in which she discussed the location of Feke's residence in Newport.[1] All these references are discussed in the following study. Mr. Frank W. Bayley has included Feke in his recently published book, *Five Colonial Artists of New England*, giving the best summary of Feke's life which has hitherto appeared, and reproducing seventeen of his best portraits, some of which have not been reproduced before. And Suzanne La Follette in her *Art in America* (1929) includes a summary of his career and a well-grounded estimate of his place among the early American painters. A few additional, but unimportant, notes about Feke, of recent date, have appeared in museum bulletins or in magazine or newspaper articles, and are referred to hereafter in footnotes, or in the descriptive catalogue.

The following study of Feke, therefore, is based primarily upon the letters in the *Historical Magazine*, Poland's pamphlet, and Lawrence Park's articles, supplemented by reference to the early records of marriages and deaths, of wills and deeds in Newport, and by careful study of the portraits which, with more or less certainty, can be ascribed to Feke's brush, and which are, in truth, the most important documents in tracing his career.

It will be observed that the foundation of known facts concerning Feke is still very slender. We really know very little about him — not even the exact dates of his birth and death. No scrap of his handwriting appears to have survived. We know his signature only as it is painted upon a few pictures. Of his portraits

---

[1] *Bulletin of the Newport Historical Society*, No. 35, January, 1921.

only about seventy are known to exist. Any study of him at present must, therefore, be largely based upon hypothesis and conjecture. Further researches may at any time bring more evidence to light, and it is reasonable to suppose that there are still in existence a good many undiscovered pictures by him. Though his career as a painter was brief when compared with those of Smibert, Copley, and Stuart, he might easily have produced at least twice as many pictures as are yet identified as his. Some, no doubt, have perished, besides those of his own kinsfolk, burned with the family residence in Oyster Bay a few years after his death, but many others must still remain in the hands of descendants of his sitters, or lie neglected in attics. If this study helps to bring to light further information concerning the man and his work, it will have fulfilled its purpose.

ROBERT FEKE

CHAPTER I

THE BEGINNINGS OF ART IN THE COLONIES

IN ORDER to understand the place of Robert Feke in the history of colonial painting it is necessary very briefly to sketch the slow and tentative development of art in the American colonies before the middle of the eighteenth century.

The subject is one about which until recently very little accurate information has been available. The first three generations of settlers were too much occupied by pressing necessities to give heed to such matters, even had they been more disposed than was the case to take an interest in them. In the eighteenth century, when a considerable artistic development took place, there was no thought of making any careful records either of artists or of their works. The Revolution displaced many of the families which had then risen to the social and economic level which had led them to acquire family portraits, and after the Revolution the heritage of colonial days was out of date and the strong democratic tendencies made unfashionable anything which savored strongly of claims to aristocratic descent. By the time a reviving interest in pre-Revolutionary history awakened in the nineteenth century, the very names of most of the early painters had been forgotten. In New England the surviving portraits of the colonial days were either looked upon as somewhat grotesque curiosities, or were ascribed to either Smibert or Copley, the two painters whose names were clearly remembered, while in the South family portraits were indiscriminately attributed to Lely or Kneller, with little regard to the period in which the subjects lived or to the question of whether they had ever visited England.

A widespread notion is still prevalent that the Puritans of
New England had a peculiar aversion to all forms of art. This
idea is based chiefly upon the tradition of bare austerity of life in
early New England, and upon the destruction of statues, stained
glass windows, and other ecclesiastical forms of art which went on
in England during the Civil Wars. It is quite true that the Puritans, both in the home country and in the colonies, were strongly
opposed on religious grounds to much of the art which the Church
of England had inherited from Rome, because of its association
with forms of religious thought which they had rejected, and that
both from necessity and from conscientious motives they sought
plain simplicity of life. But that Puritanism was not inherently
antagonistic to things beautiful is made clear by the life of John
Milton, a fervent lover of beauty as well as the greatest poet of
the English-speaking world between Shakespeare and the beginning of the nineteenth century. And, deplorable as was the destruction wrought during the Civil Wars, the Puritans have been
charged with a good deal more of it than is their due. More or
less damage of that sort is inevitable in any warfare; much was
wantonly done by disorganized soldiery on both sides; and much
of the loss of precious objects through neglect during the following century is now ascribed to the Puritans, though it occurred
long after their brief period of domination. And the total amount
of destruction of ecclesiastical buildings or their fittings which
can legitimately be charged to the Puritan element in England is
trifling in comparison with the destruction wrought a century
earlier by Henry VIII as head of the church. The orgy of con-
fiscation and destruction carried out under his orders, and to the
great profit of himself and his courtiers, met with little outspoken
opposition because he was in a position to suppress protests with
a strong hand, and the great families enriched by the spoils had
small desire in later generations to inquire into the sources of
their wealth.

The failure of the colonists anywhere on the Atlantic seaboard to develop anything more than rudimentary forms of art for nearly a century after the first settlements, was the result of their economic condition and their isolation from cultural contacts rather than of their race, their religious views, or their supposed native indifference to beauty. The French Catholics who settled Quebec have developed no arts of consequence, though belonging to a supposedly artistic race and to that form of Christianity which was the nurse of art for many centuries. Their failure is the more conspicuous because the early French explorers were often accompanied by draughtsmen capable of making drawings which could be reproduced to embellish their narratives. It was not, however, in the French Catholic colonies but in those settled by Protestants that the later development of art came about, and more conspicuously among the English than among the Dutch, although among the Dutch settlers of New Amsterdam there were two or three painters capable of good work, who were followed by other American-born artists of Dutch descent early in the eighteenth century, whose work is just beginning to be studied. Finally it was not in the South but in Puritan New England and Quaker Philadelphia that the impulse towards creative work in the arts and crafts first appeared with any lasting vitality.[1]

The emigrants from England to the Massachusetts Bay Colony were almost wholly recruited from the university-trained clergy, the sons of small landed gentry, and the yeomanry, trades-

[1] The "difficult beginnings [of American Art] were not among the cavaliers of the South nor the Dutch of New York . . . but among the Puritans of New England and the Quakers of Philadelphia." — Isham, *History of American Painting*, p. 3.

"It is not strange that the portraits by the early New England painters should be crude and forbidding, but it is strange that alone in New England an orderly development of art can be found." — Morgan, *Early American Painters*, p. 5.

"It is in the South that the least development of an art indigenous to America is to be found." — *Ibid.*, p. 7.

men, and lesser mercantile classes of England. There were very few either of the aristocracy or of the lowest classes; the great majority were of the upper and lower middle classes.[1] Many of them were men and women in fairly good circumstances, accustomed to skilled craftsmanship, and some of them were able to bring with them a few valued possessions — a piece of furniture; bowls, porringers, and plates of pewter; a silver salt-cellar; or a chased silver cup like that which John Winthrop owned and gave to the First Church in Boston. None of the emigrants, however, possessed any great store of such articles; they were commonly obliged to sell most of their possessions in England in order to meet the cost of their outfitting and voyage; and the ships in which they crossed the ocean were too small and crowded to permit many bulky articles of adornment or luxury being brought to this country. The conditions of life in the colonies during the first century after settlement necessitated hard labor of the most practical kind. The pioneers had to fell the forests, clear the fields of stones, and build roads, houses, and small mills; in a word, give their whole time and strength to the labor of establishing themselves in the wilderness. They had neither the surplus money nor the leisure needed for those forms of expression which issue in art.

When the rough pioneering work was done, however, and prosperity began to make life easier, and when trade with the West Indies and Europe developed profitably in the eighteenth century, the first thing which those who prospered did was to provide for their families better houses and more satisfactory furnishings. They showed no aversion to beautiful things, provided they were also convenient and serviceable. Their dwellings and meeting-houses were simple and practical, but as beautiful as their means permitted. In Puritan New England a few skilled

[1] C. K. Bolton, *Portraits of the Founders* (Boston, 1919), p. 13.

craftsmen appeared before the seventeenth century had ended, and many more in the eighteenth century, making beautiful furniture and silverware, the articles of daily use which an increasingly prosperous community naturally first seeks to embellish. The finest craftsmanship of this early period is to be found in the silver utensils which have survived. Some, at least, of the skilled workers in this material must have been trained in England, where the goldsmith's art was maintained at a very high level from the sixteenth to the eighteenth centuries. There was no comparable development in the southern colonies. A comparatively small number of rich planters there did, indeed, import many fine things from Europe, but neither the slave system of the plantations nor the depressed economic status of the poorer whites was conducive to the development of skilled craftsmanship in any such degree as was the community life of the more northern towns.

An interest in painting naturally came later. It should be remembered that the art of portraiture was not widespread in England in the first half of the seventeenth century, when the earliest settlers came. Art in England, as elsewhere in Northern Europe before the Reformation, had been either ecclesiastical or the luxury of kings and great nobles. Portraiture, as such, was hardly known to the English before Holbein painted Henry VIII and drew the lords and ladies of his court. Van Dyck was court painter to Charles I; Lely to Charles II; and Kneller to James II, William III, and Queen Anne. Holbein, Van Dyck, Lely, and Kneller were all born on the Continent and came to England in adult life. Although Samuel Cooper (1609–72) and William Dobson (1610–46) were English-born there were no great English portrait painters before the rise of Reynolds, Gainsborough, and Romney, all of whom began painting in the seventeen-forties. Even then portraiture was still largely limited to the aristocratic and the wealthy, although in steadily increasing measure less well-known or now forgotten "limners" sought to follow and spread the fashion set by the Court.

It is obvious that comparatively few of those who in the seventeenth century migrated to this country, even to Virginia, belonged to the very limited class in the England of that period who were in a position to have their portraits painted. So far as that is concerned, even today portraits by artists of recognized standing are a luxury for the well-to-do. Save the few instances in which the artist paints his kinsfolk or friends as a labor of love, only those among us have their portraits painted who either have considerable wealth or have attained such a degree of distinction that other people are glad to pay for their pictures. The rest of us are content with photographs, just as our ancestors in the eighteenth and early nineteenth centuries were perforce content with black paper silhouettes. It may well be doubted if as many people today in any of our larger cities, in proportion to the population, have their portraits painted as was the case in the decade between 1740 and 1750 when Smibert and Feke were painting in New England; or a little later when Copley and Benjamin West were at work in Boston, New York, and Philadelphia. In a word, the reasons why there was not more painting in the colonies before the second quarter of the eighteenth century were largely economic and social. Before that time no community in America, north of the vice-regal courts at Lima and Mexico City, was able to give a portrait painter either much, if any, training for his work, or a sufficient number of commissions to enable him to support himself without resort to other sources of income for the greater part of his time.

In view of these facts it is rather surprising that there should still be in existence in this country about one hundred and forty portraits of persons who came hither from Europe before the year

1701,[1] and that there should be more in New England than in either the Middle or the Southern States. A few are portraits of officials temporarily resident here, but most of them represent permanent settlers. A few were painted in England before the emigration of the subject. A few others were done when the person painted returned to Europe, the most famous example being that of Sir Richard Saltonstall, who, according to tradition, was painted by Rembrandt in Holland in 1644. The remaining portraits are by painters, mostly unknown, working in this country. It is no less surprising to discover that approximately four hundred portraits are known of persons who were born in the colonies before the eighteenth century began.[1] Most of them are the work of artists regarding whom we can find only occasional scraps of information.[2]

The earliest portrait known to have been painted in America is that of Governor Richard Bellingham, painted in Boston, dated 1641, and signed "W. R." The present owner, Mr. Thomas B. Clarke of New York, believes that "W. R." was William Read, an Englishman who settled in Weymouth, Massachusetts, in 1635, who lived in Boston from 1646 to 1674, and who died in or near Norwich, Connecticut, in 1679,[3] but that identification is disputed by other authorities, and must still be regarded as uncertain. In New Amsterdam one Henri Couturier is supposed to have painted between 1650 and 1660 the still extant portrait of Peter Stuyvesant. At least two other portraits [3] by him have survived, that of Oloff Stevense van Courtlandt being an admir-

---

[1] C. K. Bolton, *Portraits of the Founders*. See pp. 1019–1054 for list of portraits of persons born in the colonies before the year 1701.

[2] "There were more practitioners during the eighteenth century than is usually supposed, though they were but indifferent workmen, and it is well-nigh impossible to place any names on the canvases that survive from the period before 1750." — Isham, *History of American Painting*, 1905. But since Isham wrote, a good deal of information has come to light about these early "practitioners"!

[3] See *Portraits by Early American Artists*, collected by Thomas B. Clarke, and exhibited at the Philadelphia Museum of Art, 1928.

able work in the Dutch manner. At least two similar and no less admirable works, painted in 1654 and 1655 by the Dutch emigrant Jacobus Gerritson Strycker, also survive.[1]

Mr. Bolton reproduces the portrait of John Endecott,[2] who died in 1665, painted in Boston or Salem in the last year of his life, by an unknown artist. Mr. Bolton also notes the existence of a group of a dozen portraits representing New England settlers, which show such marked similarities that he assumes them to be the work of a single painter, and which he ascribes to the period between 1670 and 1682.[3] At present no information has come to light which enables us even to guess the painter's name.

Yet further evidence of the presence of a portrait painter in New England is found in Cotton Mather's *Magnalia*, where he describes the vain attempt to persuade the Rev. John Wilson, who died in 1667, to sit for his picture. The limner, whose name Cotton Mather unfortunately neglected to give, may have been the above-mentioned "W. R.," or the unknown painter who did the Endecott portrait, or the one who did the group of portraits just referred to. As the episode is sometimes related in garbled form to illustrate what is supposed to be the characteristic Puritan dislike of art it is worth while to give the passage in full. Mather is emphasizing the humble-mindedness of Wilson, who was of gentler birth and better education than most of the colonists. "From the same humility it was, that a good kinsman of his . . . Mr. Edward Rawson, the honored secretary of the Massachusetts Colony, could not with all his entreaties persuade him to let his picture be drawn; but still refusing it he would reply, 'What! such a poor vile creature as I am! Shall my picture be drawn? I say, no, it never shall!' And when that gentleman introduced the limner, with all things ready, vehemently importun-

[1] See *Portraits by Early American Artists*, collected by Thomas B. Clarke, and exhibited at the Philadelphia Museum of Art, 1928.
[2] *Portraits of the Founders*, p. 387.   [3] *Ibid.*, p. 2.

ing him to gratifie so far the desires of his friends, as to sit a while, for the taking of his effigies, no importunity could ever obtain it from him." [1] Wilson was merely using the language peculiar to his time to state a personal repugnance rather than an attitude typical of the Puritans as such, for it will be noted it was his fellow-Puritans who importuned him to allow his "effigies" to be drawn. Edward Rawson himself had his picture drawn in 1670 and Rev. Richard Mather's portrait was painted before his death in 1669.[2] The earliest wood engraving cut in New England was the portrait of Rev. Richard Mather,[3] made in 1669 by John Foster, a young parishioner of his in Dorchester. It is a small and crude print, but it is of interest as the precursor of the mezzotint reproductions of Smibert's portraits of ministers, engraved by Peter Pelham and others in the next century.

The Quakers of Newport and Philadelphia, like the Puritans of New England, while governed by strong religious scruples against anything savoring of extravagance or worldly display, had a keen eye for excellence both of material and workmanship in all the necessary articles of daily use. They wore the "plain dress," but with both men and women it was commonly of the best materials which they could buy. Their furniture was soberly patterned, but it was of solid mahogany when they could afford it. Their silver was plain, but heavy and durable. It was no accident that good craftsmanship in these lines developed simultaneously in New England and in Philadelphia. But the Quakers were less ready than the Puritans to patronize painting. In their otherworldliness they went even further, or were more consistent than the Puritans, while, on the other hand, they had less appreciation of the historical value of pictures of conspicuous individuals.

[1] Cotton Mather, *Magnalia Christi Americana*, I (1855), 320.
[2] Bolton, *Portraits of the Founders*, pp. 421, 457.
[3] Reproduced in George Francis Dow's *The Arts and Crafts in New England* (Topsfield, Mass.), p. xiv. See also, p. xv.

Hence there are not many portraits of eighteenth-century American Quakers. Even silhouettes or drawn representations of them, like the very crude drawing of John Woolman,[1] are infrequent. While they stimulated the lesser arts and crafts it was other elements in Philadelphia society which encouraged portraiture, and it is noteworthy that all the Philadelphia portraits by Feke, and most of those by Gustavus and John Hesselius, represent persons attached to other religious bodies.[2]

Undoubtedly a number of itinerant artists came to the colonies from Europe in the seventeenth and eighteenth centuries, some of whom settled here. Many portraits in the South, fondly ascribed to Lely or Kneller, are by Charles Bridges, an Englishman who painted there between 1730 and 1750, or by itinerant artists of mediocre ability who had picked up the mannerisms current in English portraiture. The fact is, of course, that there was no indigenous "American" art among the settlers. "American painting is . . . European painting transplanted to America."[3] Certainly most of the early painters in the colonies were born in Europe and had studied their profession there. Thus John Watson was a Scotchman who emigrated to America in 1715 and lived at Perth Amboy until 1768. John Smibert was another Scotchman who came to America with Berkeley in 1728, landing at Newport and migrating before 1730 to Boston, where he died in 1751.

---

[1] *The Journal of John Woolman*, ed. A. M. Gummere, frontispiece.

[2] An interesting illustration of the Quaker attitude is given in *Hannah Logan's Courtship*, ed. A. C. Myers, Philadelphia, 1904. Hannah was the younger daughter of James Logan, William Penn's secretary and commissioner, who had general charge of Penn's affairs in the colony, and who was a man of high standing, character, and position. Although he was a Quaker, he did have portraits painted of himself and of his daughters Sarah and Hannah, probably by Gustavus Hesselius. The pictures of James Logan and of Sarah are reproduced in the book, but that of Hannah has disappeared. After her marriage to John Smith her religious convictions led her to disapprove of such exhibitions of worldliness, and when, after James Logan's death, her brother proposed sending her portrait to her husband, she announced her intention of destroying it (pp. 8, 9, note, 55). As the picture is not now known to exist she probably carried out her threat.

[3] Isham, *History of American Painting*, p. 3.

Peter Pelham came from England to Boston in 1726, and painted some portraits, but he is best known for his engravings, and for the fact that he became the stepfather of Copley.   Gustavus Hesselius came about 1711 from Sweden to Delaware, but very soon removed to Philadelphia, where he lived and worked until 1755.[1] In Charleston, South Carolina, the only place in the South where artists found a permanent foothold, Henrietta Johnson, for about two decades beginning in 1708, painted pastel portraits which she signed and dated, some fifteen of which have been identified.[2] As Charleston was not founded until 1680 it would seem unlikely that she was native born. She was followed by Jeremiah Theus, who came to this country about 1735 with some Swiss or German immigrants, and who established himself in Charleston about 1740, painting in the next thirty-five years many portraits, of which about forty can be clearly attributed to him.[2]

The earliest American-born painter appears to have been Jeremiah Dummer of Boston (1643?–1718), who was a silver-smith by trade. His own self-portrait [3] and a companion portrait of his wife, signed and dated 1691, are still extant. A portrait of Thomas Fitch, now owned by the Sears Academy of Art at Elgin, Illinois, is also attributed to him, as are several other extant portraits, some of which are signed. They show considerable merit and are obviously modeled upon the style of Kneller, some of whose portraits were to be seen in Boston.

Following Dummer the next portrait painter of American birth appears to have been Gerret Duyckinck, baptized in New Amsterdam on April 11, 1660, the son of Evert Duyckinck I, who

[1] "The Earliest Painter in America," by Charles Henry Hart, in *Harper's Magazine* (March, 1898), pp. 566–570. (But Gustavus Hesselius was *not* the earliest painter in America!)

[2] See article on "Art and Artists in Colonial South Carolina," by Rev. Robert Wilson, D.D., in the *Year Book of the City of Charleston, S. C.*, 1899, summarized in John Hill Morgan's *Early American Painters*, pp. 7–11.

[3] Reproduced in Bolton's *Portraits of the Founders*, III, 597.

had emigrated from Holland to New Amsterdam in 1638, who probably survived as late as 1702, and who is described as a limner, painter, and burner of glass. The portrait of Lieutenant-Governor William Stoughton in the Boston Athenaeum, probably painted in 1685, is ascribed to Evert Duyckinck I. Gerret, his son, was also a glass maker and painter, as were Evert Duyckinck III (1677–1727) and Gerardus Duyckinck (1695–1752), grandsons of Evert Duyckinck I. The New York Historical Society owns four portraits attributed to Gerret Duyckinck, and certain pictures of the Beekman family are attributed to Evert Duyckinck III. There were thus four painters in three generations of this important family of Dutch colonial artists, all but the first being American born.[1] Mr. Thomas B. Clarke of New York owns specimen works attributed to each of these four related artists.[2] Contemporary with the younger Duyckinck was Pieter Vanderlyn (1687–1778) who worked in and about New York, and a little-known artist named Doornick. All these painters, like Couturier and Strycker, clearly exhibit the Dutch rather than the English tradition in their work.

Following the Duyckincks came Nathanael Emmons, born in Boston about 1704, whose death on May 19, 1740, at the age of thirty-six, is recorded in the *Boston News-Letter* for May 27 of that year. Emmons painted a portrait of Governor Jonathan Belcher, and four others which have been preserved.[3] The obituary of him in the *News-Letter* says:

He was universally own'd to be the greatest master of various Sorts of Painting that ever was born in this Country. [Note the implication that there had been other native-born artists.] And his excellent Works were the pure

[1] For information about the Duyckinck family, and for reproductions of pictures attributed to Gerret Duyckinck and to Evert Duyckinck III, see John Hill Morgan, *Early American Painters* (New York 1921), pp. 17–20.

[2] *Portraits by Early American Artists*, collected by Thomas B. Clarke, Philadelphia, 1928.

[3] *Ibid.*

Effect of his own Genius, without receiving any Instructions from others. Some of his Pieces are such admirable Imitations of Nature, both in faces, Rivers, Banks and Rural Scenes, that the pleased Eye cannot easily leave them; and some of his Imitations of the Works of Art are so exquisite, that though we know they are only Paints, yet they deceive the sharpest Sight whyle it is nearly looking on them, and will preserve his memory till age or some unhappy accident or other destroy them. He was sober and modest; minded accuracy more than Profit.[1]

Alas, "age or some unhappy accident" has long since obliterated most of this excellent man's work.

Dummer, the three younger Duyckincks, Vanderlyn, and Emmons are the only American-born portrait painters so far discovered who certainly ante-date Robert Feke, whose birth is tentatively dated 1705, and who was soon followed by Joseph Badger (1708–65) of Boston. Of all these early American-born painters Feke was far and away the best.

The work of all of these painters, whether European or native-born, was almost wholly confined to portraiture. Hesselius did indeed, paint a picture of the Last Supper for a parish church in Maryland, but even in the southern colonies there was small demand for religious paintings. Watson and Smibert are said to have brought with them some copies of pictures hanging in European galleries. Watson is believed to have kept his collection together till his death, but it was scattered or destroyed during the Revolution. Smibert's copies perhaps formed that "Collection of pictures in Oil Colors" which he advertised for sale, with a "collection of valuable prints," in the *Boston News-Letter* of May 15/22, 1735."[2] There was too little acquaintance with such pictures in the colonies for there to be much demand for them. Aside from the evidence, cited above, that Nathanael Emmons of Boston painted landscapes early in the eighteenth century, and the existence of one landscape attributed to Jeremiah Theus, we know of few attempts at that type of picture until a much later date.

[1] Quoted in Dow's *The Arts and Crafts in New England*, pp. xxi, 1–2.
[2] *Ibid.*

Even in England there was in the eighteenth century so little interest in landscapes that Gainsborough turned to portraiture chiefly because he could not find purchasers for his landscapes, and Richard Wilson had difficulty in disposing of his early landscapes.

The demand for portraits is, in fact, the first expression of an awakening interest in painting, and it was wholly natural and significant that the best painting done alike in England and America in the eighteenth century was portraiture for ever-widening circles of people. Portraits interest persons untrained in art because of their appeal to family affection or pride. As in England, so in the colonies, to have one's portrait painted was a mark of personal or social prestige. The same desire for social distinction was gratified in a less expensive way by minor artists who travelled through the colonies painting coats-of-arms for all who would pay a small price for them. Many an old New England family has inherited from the eighteenth century such a coat-of-arms, often quite delightfully executed, and as often worthless as proving descent from an English family entitled to bear arms, but which is good evidence of the status which the family had attained here at the time the fictitious coat-of-arms was drawn.

While a good many portraits, especially in Maryland and Virginia, were painted by itinerants who passed from one plantation to another, and presently either returned to England or settled down to a less uncertain life, those painters who desired a fixed habitation and a more assured support for their art, inevitably settled in the chief towns, — Charleston, Philadelphia, New York, Newport, and Boston, — though making occasional excursions elsewhere. These communities alone offered a subsistence, though even there painting must usually have been supplemented with work of other kinds. They also offered as agreeable a social and intellectual life as was to be found in the colonies. Newport for example, where Feke made his home, was a prosperous seaport of some six thousand people, rivaling Boston and New York in its trade. After the visit of Dean Berkeley, who lived there for a year and a half with Smibert in his train, Newport had something of a literary and artistic atmosphere, and one of the earliest libraries in the country was located there.

From the foregoing review it is evident that Feke, who is said to have been self-trained, nevertheless as a youth had opportunities to see portraits in this country. His own early self-portrait, painted about 1725, when he was hardly more than twenty years of age, so far as one can judge from the face, is the work of an artist who, if not yet a practiced hand, is, at least, no longer a mere beginner. It must have been done before Feke could possibly have seen any of Smibert's work in Newport, and it is unbelievable that Feke could have painted it without having had a good deal of previous practice in handling a brush and without having seen completed portraits by painters who knew something of the technique of their profession. The most probable explanation is to be found in the proximity of Oyster Bay to New York. Feke may well have gone there repeatedly as a youth, and, when his interest in painting was aroused, might easily have seen the work of John Watson or of the artists of Dutch descent who painted occasional portraits there. It is by no means an impossible supposition that he may have seen either Gerardus or Evert Duyckinck III or Vanderlyn actually at work upon a portrait. In any case before 1725 there was certainly a considerable number of fairly creditable portraits scattered through the colonies which an eager boy could have studied. The question of his education will be discussed in the following pages, but the foregoing survey makes it clear that, though in his lifetime art was still in "its difficult beginnings" in the colonies, opportunities for observing the work of the painter were not altogether lacking.

CHAPTER II

ANCESTRY AND BOYHOOD

ROBERT FEKE,[1] the subject of this study, — whom I shall call Robert "the Painter" whenever necessary to distinguish him from his father, Robert "the Preacher," or his great-grandfather, Robert "the Emigrant," — was born at Oyster Bay, Long Island, in the colony of New York. Family tradition, unsupported by evidence, gives the year as 1705. He was descended from a numerous and prosperous English family originating in Wighton, Norfolk, representatives of which were goldsmiths in London for at least three generations in the sixteenth and seventeenth centuries.[2] The wills of several of this family are printed in Waters' *Genealogical Gleanings in England.*[3] It is difficult to trace the family ramifications in the sixteenth and seventeenth centuries because in several instances the identical name is borne by two or more cousins in the same generation. It appears certain, however, that Robert "the Painter's" great-grandfather, Robert "the Emigrant," was descended from William Feake the elder, son of James Feake, born in Wighton, County Norfolk, before the

---

[1] The spelling of family names was, at best, none too certain in the early eighteenth century, and the painter's surname lent itself in unusual degree to the play of fancy. It is found in all the following variants: Feke, Feek, Feecke, Feac, Feak, Feake, Feks, Fekes, Fecks, Feeks, Feecx, Feaks, Feakes, Fewkes. Thus the painter's grandfather is recorded as John Feaks, or Feake; the name of the painter's widow appears in her father's will as Eleanor Feake; and the painter's nephews were known as Feeks, which was the form of the name generally adopted by later generations of the family. The painter spelled his name Feke on seven of the nine portraits where his signature is found with more than initials, and Feak in the other cases. The spelling *Feke* has, therefore, been adopted for this book so far as he is concerned, but in the case of other members of his family the variant forms are used which are found in the records referring to them.

[2] For his pedigree, see Appendix B.

[3] I, 788-791.

middle of the sixteenth century, later a prosperous citizen and goldsmith of London dwelling in "Lumbard" street, whose will was proved May 18, 1582. That will is a document of considerable length, with numerous bequests to charity, besides provision for his wife Mary and his children. The will of Mary, William's widow, was proved August 23, 1619, and in it, among the bequests to her numerous descendants, is one of a hundred pounds to her grandson Robert Feake, son of her son James and of Judith his wife. That this Robert is the "Emigrant" is indicated from an entry in Thomas Lechford's *Note-Book* [1] where it is recorded that "Lieuten^t Robert Feke of Waterton in New England and Sargeant William Palmer of Yarmouth in New England & Judith his wife, and Tobyas Feke aged 17 sonne and daughter of James Feke, late of London goldsmith Deceased makes a le^r of Attorney to Tobyas Dixon Citizen & mercer of London to sell one tenement or house & shopp in Lumbard street London held of the Company of Goldsmiths in London whereof he dyed poss^ed, late in the occupacion of one Brampton, dat '5 10^bris. 1639. Coram Jo Winthrop, Govr James Luxford & Meipse. 3 s"

The tenement in question had been held by William Feke, who bequeathed it to his widow for her life, and after her, to his son James, from whom it had passed to his sons James and Robert. Tobias Feke and Judith (Feke) Palmer were children of the younger James and therefore nephew and niece of Robert "the Emigrant," and had accompanied or followed him to America before 1634, as Judith was married in that year to William Palmer, who had been brought as a boy to Plymouth in 1621. Tobias Dixon was their maternal grandfather.

Robert "the Emigrant" probably came to Massachusetts Bay in one of the ships which accompanied or followed Governor John Winthrop in 1630. A year later, November 1631, came

[1] Pages 228–229.

Elizabeth Winthrop and her infant daughter. Elizabeth was the widow of young Henry Winthrop, the governor's son, to whom she had been married in 1629, who had preceded her to America and who had been drowned at Salem the day after his landing. She was daughter of Thomas Fones and a granddaughter of Adam Winthrop. She was thus a first cousin of her husband Henry Winthrop, and her sister Martha had married Henry's brother John Winthrop, Jr. It must have been very soon after her arrival that the young widow married Robert Feke, for Winthrop's *Journal*[1] has the following entry under date of January 27, 1632. Winthrop is writing of an expedition which he and several others made up the Charles River, presumably on the ice, to a point about eight miles above Watertown. Above Beaver Brook "they came to a high pointed rock, having a fair ascent on the west side, which they call Mt. Feake,[2] from one Robert Feake, who had married the governor's daughter-in-law." Feke thus became connected by marriage with the governor's family. He was admitted freeman in 1631. From 1632 to 1636 he was lieutenant to Captain Daniel Patrick. In September, 1634, he was appointed with Captain Underhill, Captain Patrick, and others to fix the site for the fort on Castle Island. He had his "homestall" at Watertown, and represented the town in the general court from 1634 to 1636.[3]

He was one of the organizers of the town of Dedham, Massachusetts, and his name appears first in the list of subscribers to the town covenant. He is the first named in the lists of those attending town meetings in 1636 and 1637, taking precedence over Philemon Dalton, John Dwight, John Coolidge, and other forebears of families now better known; and he alone among them is

---

[1] Ed. J. K. Hosmer (1908), p. 73.
[2] The name is still to be found on maps of that locality.
[3] For these details, see paper by John J. Latting in *New York Genealogical and Biographical Record*, XI (1880), 12–24. See also H. M. Cox, *The Cox Family in America* (New York, 1912), pp. 285–288.

distinguished by being called "Mr" Robert Feke and "Robte. Feks, gent." On August 11, 1637, he was assigned twelve acres in Dedham for a house lot, one hundred and fifty acres of woodland, and twelve acres of meadow. On September 21, 1638, however, he resigned to the town the land allotted to him and was to be paid twenty marks of English money for expenses incurred, a sum later changed to thirteen pounds, six shillings and eight pence. An entry in the Town Records as late as 1650 refers to the land as "Mr. Feeks's farm." [1]

Robert "the Emigrant" appears to have been a restless person, for soon after resigning his assignments of land at Dedham, he made arrangements to sell his "homestall" in Watertown [2] that he might take part in the westward migration which resulted in the settlement of Connecticut. On July 16, 1640, "Rob't Feaks" accompanied Captain Daniel Patrick in landing upon what is now Greenwich Point, Connecticut, where they bought land from the Indians. Part of Feke's share he named "Elizabeth Neck" and it was described in the deed to be the "peticaler purchase" of his wife. Both Patrick and he must soon after have moved their families thither. The Greenwich venture, however, did not turn out happily, for although the settlement had been made under the sanction of the New Haven Colony, the territory was in dispute between the Dutch and New Haven Colony, and the Dutch authorities, under date of October 15, 1640, warned the settlers to leave. The dispute lasted for two years or more, until Captain Patrick accepted Dutch jurisdiction in 1642 on behalf of himself and the Fekes, and Captain Underhill at Stamford entered the service of the Dutch against the Indians. No doubt it was an attempt to settle this dispute which took Captain Patrick and Robert Feke to New Amsterdam in 1642. Each was

[1] *Early Records of the Town of Dedham*, III, 3, 21, 22, 23, 25, 26, 35, 49, 50, 55, 57, 69, 167.
[2] Waters, *Genealogical Gleanings*, p. 169.

presumably accompanied by his family, for on July 17 of that year each had a child baptized in the Reformed Dutch Church there. Feke is recorded as "Robbert feecke" and his child as "Robbert."[1] That they were strangers in the town is indicated by the fact that there were no witnesses. In January, 1644, Captain Patrick was assassinated by a Dutch soldier in Feke's own house at Greenwich.[2] Feke was again in New Amsterdam in 1647, presumably for further negotiations with the Dutch, for on April 14, of that year, Sara, daughter of "Robbert Fecks" was baptized in the Reformed Dutch Church there,[3] again with no witnesses. In October, 1647, Feke appeared in Boston on his way to England, for he wrote to friends in Stamford referring to the management of his property, saying that he "reserved the whole propriety of his estate until he saw how God would deal with him in England." His affairs appear to have been entrusted to his wife and one William Hallett. The cause of his return to England is not known, but a resolution was passed in the House of Commons on March 4, 1649, granting a pardon to Robert Feake, and others, for some unnamed offence. There were other Roberts in the Feke family in England at that period, so that it is by no means certain that it was Robert "the Emigrant" who was the beneficiary of the pardon, but the fact that he did return to England at that time, and the phrase "how God would deal with him in England," makes the identification perhaps probable. It is, however, difficult to imagine what the offence could have been which, nearly nineteen years after his departure from England, required pardon by act of Parliament.

[1] See *Collections*, New York Genealogical and Biographical Society, II (New York, 1901), 14. In the case of baptism of children of the Dutch inhabitants of New Amsterdam there are always several witnesses recorded. Between 1640 and 1646 there are only six baptisms without witnesses and at least three of the six are of children with English names, i. e., strangers, temporarily resident.

[2] Winthrop says the murder occurred in Captain Underhill's house, *Journal*, II, 154.

[3] *Collections*, New York Genealogical and Biographical Society, II (New York, 1901), p. 22.

Robert "the Emigrant" returned to the colony before September, 1649, for in that month he reappeared at Greenwich. He had earlier given evidence of occasional unsoundness of mind, as is evident from a letter to the Dutch governor dated September 18, 1649, from some of the residents of Greenwich who had taken title to land from Mrs. Feke, in which they protest against a conspiracy of people in Stamford to deprive them of their claims. The writers say that "Mr. Feke being returned again from Old England, they make use of his weakness and silliness to wring the land out of Mr. Hallett's hands."[1] A further statement respecting "Mr. Robert Feke, sometime an inhabitant of Greenwich near Stanfort," testifies that he "was a man whose God-fearing heart was so absorbed with spiritual and heavenly things, that he thought little of the things of this life, and took neither heed nor care of what tended to his external property. We moreover considered and regarded him as a man so unsettled and troubled in his understanding and brain, that although he was, at times, better settled than others, nevertheless he was in his last years, and about the time he agreed with his wife, respecting the division of his temporal property, he was not a man of any wisdom, or capable of acting understandingly like any other man regarding his own benefit, profit and advantage."[2]

A yet further document from the same source makes it evident that, probably before he went to England, he had made over the bulk of his property, at least that at Greenwich, to his wife, on the ground that she had taken the children and needed it more than he did. It is quite clear that they had agreed to separate. Probably some sort of divorce was secured, since in 1648 she married William Hallett.[3] Before Robert "the Emigrant" returned

[1] *New York Genealogical and Biographical Record*, IX, 15.
[2] *Ibid.*, XI, 16.
[3] A writer in the *New England Historical Genealogical Register* (XLVIII, 1894) notes the scandal caused by the relations of Elizabeth Feake and William Hallett, and

from England they, and her children, abandoned Greenwich, apparently under pressure from the Dutch and the New Haven authorities, and sought refuge at New London, under the protection of her brother-in-law John Winthrop, Jr.

There is no evidence that Robert "the Emigrant" ever saw his wife and children again. The unhappy gentleman appears to have been permanently demented, and to have led a wandering existence until his death in Watertown on February 1, 1663. An inventory of his property dated February 18, of the same year, gives its value as only nine pounds, nine shillings and two pence. He is the tragic figure of one who, through whatever fault or misfortune, had lost his property, his family, and his reason in the new world in which he had made so auspicious a beginning.

His former wife, with the children and William Hallett, spent some months at New London in an impoverished condition, during which John Winthrop, Jr., carried on a correspondence with Governor Stuyvesant in the endeavor to salvage some of her property at Greenwich.[1] In 1649 Hallett, accompanied by the former Mrs. Feake and her children, removed to Long Island, probably to Flushing, and there settled. They maintained correspondence with John Winthrop, Jr., who at that time entertained some idea of following them.[2] Elizabeth (Fones, Win-

states that in July, 1648, there was question as to the validity of their marriage. The reader who has the curiosity to look further into this unhappy affair is referred to *Proceedings of the Colonial Society of Massachusetts*, Vol. XXVII, the article on "Verses by Adam Winthrop" by Professor G. L. Kittredge, where he will find detailed references to documents referring to Feake's insanity, and to his wife's relations with William Hallett. No doubt she gave cause for gossip, but it should be noted that Feake, before he left for England, when he presumably knew that he was separating permanently from her, turned over much of his property to her; that John Winthrop, Jr., later wrote that at that time Feake had spoken well of Hallett, and that he, Winthrop, had found his commendation justified; and that, as Professor Kittredge says, Winthrop, who, as her cousin and brother-in-law, "must have known all the facts, stood her friend and appears to have recognized the validity of the Hallett alliance." Furthermore, after Hallett and the former Mrs. Feake and her children removed to Long Island, they kept up communication with John Winthrop, Jr.

[1] *New York Genealogical and Biographical Record*, XI, 17–18.
[2] *Ibid.*, p. 19.

throp, Feake) Hallett died before 1673, in which year Hallett married again. She had had a strange, adventurous, turbulent career for an English gentlewoman.

She had, in addition to her daughter by Henry Winthrop, five children by Robert Feake. Of these Elizabeth, Hannah, and John were probably born at Watertown before 1640. The other two were the "Robbert" and Sarah baptized in New Amsterdam in 1642 and 1647 respectively. Elizabeth married Captain John Underhill, then of Setauket, Long Island, in 1659, as his second wife. Hannah in 1656 married John Bowne, who was then twenty-nine, and of whom Underhill wrote to John Winthrop, Jr., as follows: "Sir: I was latli at Flushing. Hanna Feke is to be married to a verri jentiele young man of good abilliti, of a livli fetture and gud behafior." [1] Robert married, and died in 1668 or 1669, since in the records of the Surrogate's office in New York is a letter of administration granted to Sarah, widow of Robert Feake of Flushing, June 18, 1669.

Of these five children Elizabeth, Hannah, and John became Quakers about 1660. The story of Hannah and her husband, John Bowne, as Quaker pioneers, is a moving and beautiful one, but it does not immediately concern us. [2] Their elder cousin Tobias, who had accompanied Robert "the Emigrant" to Greenwich, also removed to Long Island, and was at one time sheriff there under the Dutch. Probably he too became a Quaker. [3] In any case he was sympathetic in his attitude towards them because in 1658 he led the protest against Governor Stuyvesant's stringent enactments relating to them, and was punished by degradation from office and a fine of two hundred guilders and costs. At some date before 1650 he married the widow of his

[1] *Ibid.*, p. 20.   [2] *Ibid.*, pp. 20–24.

[3] Besse, *Sufferings of the Quakers*, II, 183, 197. "Tobias Feak, Englishman and officer in the town of Flushing in New Netherlands of Long Island was cast into prison."

uncle Robert's friend Captain Daniel Patrick, a woman of Dutch birth. Before 1660 he appears to have returned to London, to have married again and to have died about 1667.

Robert "the Emigrant's" son John was associated with his elderly brother-in-law Captain John Underhill in the settlement of Killingworth, later called Matinecock. The territory had been purchased from the Indians about 1653. The first attempts to settle Matinecock seem to have been made about 1661 by Thomas Terry and Samuel Deering, who did "Ingage themselves, and those they bring, and their successors to bring in no Quakers, nor any like opinionists to bee inhabitants among them." [1] In spite of this "engagement" Captain Underhill, after he had moved thither from Setauket (now part of Brookhaven), brought in John Feake, and Matthew Prior, a well-known English Quaker with an adventurous record, also moved there from Setauket before 1667. Underhill assigned to John Feake the southeast part of the tract received from the Indians. On September 15, 1670, John Feake married Elizabeth, daughter of Matthew Prior. A sister of Elizabeth Prior married Captain Underhill's son John. Probably about the time of his marriage John Feake built his house in what is now known as Locust Valley. It stood at the foot of what is still called Feke's Lane, one of the earliest roads in the district, in a lovely situation close to Beaver Pond dam, where the stream flows into Mill Neck Creek, some three miles from Oyster Bay. Presumably most, if not all, of his children were born there. It was rebuilt, at least in part, in 1840, and after serving various purposes, was burned down in 1911, but the cellar is still clearly traceable. John Feake and his wife Elizabeth had seven daughters and two sons,[2] and though John must have been

---

[1] *History and Genealogy of the Cock-Cocks-Cox Family*, p. 7. See also G. W. Cocks, *Old Matinecock*, 1910.

[2] Elizabeth, b. June 9, 1674; m. 1710   Benjamin Field.
Hannah, b. Oct. 6, 1675; m. 1698   James Cock.

too young to have any vivid recollection of his father, Robert "the Emigrant," he held his memory in sufficient regard to name his second son for him.

John Feake became an ardent Quaker and was one of the leaders in the Westerley Monthly Meeting, which included the local meetings at Matinecock, Mannahasset, and Westerley. His name and those of his daughters appear frequently on the opening pages of the records of the Westerley Monthly Meeting. Thus on "26 day 1 mo. 1697," at a meeting held in a house at Oyster Bay, he was one of a committee appointed to admonish a neighbor for neglecting attendance. The next year, "29th 5mo 1698," the monthly meeting was held at his house at "Matinnecong." Several years later he was one of those appointed to select a site for a meeting-house. The records between 1698 and 1716 contain the declaration of intention of marriage of five of his daughters, and a sixth daughter, Abigail, was married in the Friends' Meeting at Newport in 1726. His first son, John, died at the age of four, and his second son, Robert, became a Baptist in early manhood.

It must have been this Robert, rather than Robert "the Painter," whose conversion to Baptist principles so aroused his father's opposition that the father followed the youth to the water's edge with threats of disinheritance.[1] The oral tradition has confused the two Roberts, and very likely heightened the color of the episode, but in substance it may well be true, for one can readily believe that the sturdy Quaker convert was bitterly opposed to seeing his son turn to other paths, although that was

Mary, b. Apr. 30, 1678; m.	Henry Cock.
John, b. Jul. 10, 1679; d. 1683.	
Robert, b. June 22, 1683; m.	Clemence Ludlam.
Sarah, b. Feb. 7, 1685–6.	
Martha, b. Oct. 27, 1688; m.	John Carpenter.
Abigail, b. Aug. 7, 1691; m. 1726	Josiah Coggeshall.
Deborah, b. Jan. 5, 1695; m. 1716	Thomas Whitson.

[1] See Appendix A.

just what he himself had done in leaving the Puritanism of his own father, Robert "the Emigrant."

John Feake died in May, 1724, and he was probably buried on the beautiful hilltop overlooking the Sound, about half a mile from his home, which contains within a small space several generations of families of the neighborhood. Its most conspicuous monument is that to Captain John Underhill, but the Fekes lie close by. The oldest graves are marked by rough field-stones, from which the rude inscriptions, if there were any, have been effaced by time. It is not unlikely that John Feake and his wife lie under two of these, for the adjacent graves of some of his children are marked by stones with inscriptions still decipherable.

Although Oyster Bay was settled soon after 1660 it had no meeting-house until more than half a century later. About 1700 a Baptist named William Rhodes, who was a preacher but not an ordained minister, came thither from Rhode Island and organized a church. "Among Mr. Rhodes's converts was an individual by the name of Robert Feeks. He was the son of a Quaker preacher in this town; and having early 'manifested gifts for the ministry' became an assistant and afterwards the successor of Mr. Rhodes. He was ordained in 1724 by Elders from Rhode Island. He was what is called a 'free-will' Baptist and as no other qualification was considered necessary in a candidate for baptism, than a desire to be saved, his church was of course numerous. His descendants for four generations have been members of the church, one of whom is at present a Deacon. He labored for many years and died in the 89th year of his age."[1] It is further said of him that, "he dwelt but little in his public discourses upon doctrinal matters. His talents were not popular, but he was a steady, perserving, sensible and prudent man."[2] He is said to have served the Baptist church for full forty years, and when he died he was laid

[1] Prime, *History of Long Island*, p. 285.
[2] Charles S. Wightman, *History of the Baptist Church in Oyster Bay*, 1873.

to rest beside his wife in the hilltop burial ground at Matinecock, where their graves may still be seen.[1] A descendant, Mr. Robert Feeks Cox of Media, Pennsylvania, owns a small pewter cup, ornamented in the style of the late-seventeenth century, with a later inscription stating it to have been used by Robert Feke as a communion cup in 1724 in the Baptist Church at Oyster Bay. Perhaps it was given to him at the time of his ordination.

The Baptists, like the Quakers in this small, isolated farming community, met in one another's houses for worship, and it was not until after 1720 that their meeting-house was erected. It was a small frame building, which, when it was outgrown, was turned to commercial uses. It stood across the street from the modern building of the Baptist Church, down to a half-century ago.

Robert "the Preacher" was not dependent upon his preaching for a living. His wife Clemence Ludlam, from the neighboring Hog Island, brought him property. He owned much land at Mill Creek, as well as the mill there, and a large homestead at Oyster Bay, where he built a house called "Meadowside." It was this house which was destroyed by fire with its contents, including family portraits, about 1768. It was rebuilt, and there several generations of his descendants lived. There, presumably, his four sons and four daughters were born.

No record of the date of birth of any of his children appears to have survived. The written records of his church do not begin until many years later and the family Bible very likely was destroyed when his house was burned. In view of the fact that in 1705 he would have been only twenty-two years old one might surmise that his son, Robert "the Painter," if born in that year,

---

[1]
Here lieth
the body of
Robert Feke
who died April
The 1 1773 aged
89 years.

Hear lieth the
body of
Clemence Feke
Who died Augost
ye 8th 1760
aged 76 years.

was the eldest child. In the list of his children as given in *Long Island Genealogies*,[1] however, Robert "the Painter's" name is preceded by those of Clemence and Henry, and is followed by John, Charles, Deborah, Sarah, and Elizabeth. The order in which these children of Robert "the Preacher" are named raises doubts whether Robert "the Painter" could have been born as early as 1705. That date for his birth has been assumed from the correspondence in the Dawson's *Historical Journal*, in which he is said to have died in 1750 in his forty-fourth year. In Hoag, Wade, and Company's *History of Rhode Island*, published in 1878, the dates 1705–50 appear beneath the crude lithographic reproduction of Feke's late self-portrait. The picture was then owned by Mr. Bullock of Providence, who presumably supplied the publishers with the lithograph, dates, and the brief biographical sketch of Feke. Both dates and sketch, that is, rest solely upon family tradition, orally transmitted for more than a century and a quarter. If Robert "the Painter" really was born in 1705, as the third child of the family, his father must have been married when not more than nineteen or twenty years of age. That such may have been the case is indicated by the fact that Deborah, the sixth child in this family of eight, was born early enough to have been married and to have given birth to a child about 1730. It is, therefore, probable that Robert "the Preacher" married very young, begot children in quick succession, and that 1705 may be at least the approximate date of birth of Robert "the Painter." That Robert "the Preacher" named his third son John after the old Quaker grandfather would indicate that the family breach caused by his adoption of Baptist principles had been healed, and it may be noted that Robert "the Painter" in turn named two of his sons John and Charles after his own brothers.

[1] *Long Island Genealogies*, compiled by Mary Powell Bunker (Albany, 1895), pp. 202–203. No dates are given for any of the children, nor any authority for the list, and the genealogy is certainly erroneous at several points.

We have no information whatever about Robert "the Paint-er's" upbringing, though we can surmise the piety of the Baptist preacher's household, with the Quaker grandparents living only three miles away, and the certainty of at least the rudiments of an education, though the Baptists of that period were not by any means as conspicuous as the Congregational ministers of New England for their intellectual attainments. However limited his early advantages may perhaps have been they were at least suffi-cient to start him on a course of self-education which carried him a good way, for we know that in the seventeen-forties he was acquainted with Richardson's novel *Pamela Andrews* and with the writings of Lord Shaftesbury.

The plain, simple life of farm and seashore in this community composed chiefly of Baptist and Quaker settlers seems to offer an unpromising beginning for an artist, but his home had a setting of great natural loveliness, and New York, where painters found occasional opportunity for work, was not far away. And it is evi-dent that Robert "the Painter" came of sound and intelligent stock, which took religion seriously but which was independent in spirit. That independence was shown in the pioneering restless-ness of Robert "the Emigrant," in Tobias Feake's protest to Governor Stuyvesant, in John Feake's adoption of Quakerism, in Robert "the Preacher's" conversion to Baptist principles. In Robert "the Painter" it was shown by his adoption of an art which had so little prestige and offered so poor a living that one must believe that he began painting chiefly from love of it, and by his roving career which took him often and for considerable periods away from home. And perhaps his love of painting was a reawakening of the creative instinct which had found expression in the goldsmith's art practised by his English ancestors more than a century earlier.

CHAPTER III

EARLY MANHOOD, 1725–1740—VISITS TO NEW YORK AND PHILADELPHIA

THE family tradition that Robert "the Painter" went to sea at an early age is probable enough. Seafaring was the natural outlet for an enterprising youth of that day, brought up in sight of salt water, and the tradition is reinforced by the description of him as a "mariner" on the marriage certificates of his daughters, years after his death. It is, indeed, difficult to picture him as a seafaring man, for neither of his two self-portraits nor Dr. Hamilton's description of him in 1744 gives the smallest impression of the sailor; they all suggest the scholar and the artist. But the evidence seems too strong to be set aside that for a considerable part of his life he followed the sea for a livelihood, if not from natural inclination. One might surmise that with the degree of education which he acquired he went as supercargo, or as a mate if not as captain of a small vessel, if the term "mariner" can be stretched to cover these positions.

We have no knowledge where his voyages carried him. They might have been coastwise, or to the West Indies, or to Europe, especially if he made Newport his headquarters. The story that on one of his voyages "he was taken prisoner and carried to Spain where, in the solitude of his prison he succeeded in procuring paints and brushes and employed himself in rude painting which on his release he sold and thus availed himself of the means of returning to his own country" is discussed by Poland. He points out that Feke was certainly too young to be made prisoner during the war of the Spanish Succession, which lasted from 1702 to 1713, or in the conflicts of 1717. But England and Spain were in conflict between 1726 and 1731, and fighting went on between the English in Georgia and the Spaniards in Florida from 1738 to 1743, leading to the "War of Jenkins' Ear" between England and Spain, 1739 to 1741. Poland also cites by name two sailors from Tiverton and Portsmouth, Rhode Island, who were taken prisoners in 1739 and held at Barcelona. While, therefore, the episode has a legendary sound, it is not impossible that a similar misadventure happened to Feke, but, if so, it probably occurred between 1726 and 1731.[1] It cannot be said, however, that Feke's portraits show any trace of the influence of Spanish art; they are rather of the English school.

The earliest document which has survived giving authentic evidence of the painter's existence is his own self-portrait, which, assuming the year of his birth to be 1705, cannot be much later than 1725. It represents a youth of about twenty, with abundant black, curling hair, falling to his shoulders, with a rather pale, thin face, corresponding perfectly to the "phiz" described as Feke's by Dr. Alexander Hamilton in his *Itinerarium* twenty years later. Perhaps it was painted before he went to sea at all, to be left with his parents.[2] At any rate it is the work of one who has already had some experience in handling an artist's brush. While the figure is thin and stiff, the head is well placed on the shoulders, and there is a good deal of character in the face. It is certainly no first attempt, but rather the work of a painter who

[1] See Appendix A; also Poland, *Robert Feke . . . and the Beginning of Colonial Painting*, pp. 18–19. Poland gives the name of one of these sailors as Peleg Thurston. The *Thurston Genealogies*, Portland, Maine, 1880, includes several persons of that name in the Rhode Island branch of the family, but no one of them can be clearly identified as the man to whom Poland refers. It is, however, worth noting that Feke's daughter, Sarah, married John Thurston, son of a Peleg Thurston who was born at Freetown, Mass., about 1700. Possibly the legend of a captivity in Spain has been transferred in the family tradition from Peleg Thurston to Robert Feke.

[2] If this was the case the portrait did not remain in their hands, for it has been transmitted with the portraits of Gershom Flagg IV and his wife to four generations of their descendants. In any case there is no doubt as to the authenticity of the self-portrait as the earliest extant work by Feke.

has seen other portraits and who knows how a figure is posed on a
canvas. For all its juvenile naïveté it is quite as natural and lifelike as most of the portraits painted in the colonies in the opening
years of the eighteenth century. It is difficult to explain this
youthful self-portrait otherwise than on the supposition that
Feke had already seen portraits, and perhaps painters, like the
Duyckincks, at work in New York, or had had the greater opportunities for such observation which an early trans-Atlantic voyage might have brought him.

There is no certain evidence as to when Feke first went to
Newport, but that place undoubtedly would have had certain
attractions for him. With its flourishing trade it offered a seafaring man good opportunities for employment. Furthermore it
was the natural center for Baptists and Quakers, much more so
than New York. The family at Oyster Bay already had connections at Newport. Robert "the Preacher" was ordained to the
Baptist ministry by representatives of the Newport Church. And
on January 5, 1726–27, Abigail, the aunt of Robert "the Painter,"
was married in the Friends' Meeting in Newport to Josiah Coggeshall.[1] The young painter-mariner would, therefore, have
found friends and kinsfolk in Newport.

Thirty years ago Professor Poland caused the records of the

[1] The entry in the manuscript *Book of Records of Marriage Certificates Belonging to
the Monthly Meeting of Rhode Island*, now at the Newport Historical Society, begins as
follows:

" { day mo.
  { 5: 11: 1726. Whereas Josiah Coggeshall of Newport on Rhode Island Son of
Joshua Coggeshall and Sarah his wife and Abigail Feaks Daughter of John Feaks and
Elizabeth his wife Having declared their Intentions of taking each other in Marriage
before Several Public Meetings of the People of God called Quakers in Rhode Island
according to the good Order used Amongst them . . . and Having Consent of Parents
. . ." etc.

This was Josiah Coggeshall's second marriage. Abigail Feaks bore him three children, but all died in childhood. It will be noted that in the foregoing record the custom-
ary statement as to residence is omitted in the case of John Feaks. Furthermore
neither he nor his wife signed Abigail's marriage certificate as witnesses. Presumably
they did not make the voyage from Matinecock for the marriage.

Baptist churches of Newport to be searched in the hope of finding some evidence that Feke was a member of one of them. The fact that Feke was married by Rev. John Callender of the First Baptist Church, whose portrait he afterwards painted, seemed to warrant the conclusion that he might at least have been a worshipper at that church. The search was disappointing in that nothing was found to indicate that he ever had any active connection with any Baptist church in Newport; nor do we know that he was a member of his father's church at Oyster Bay. The clerk of the Second Baptist Church at Newport did, however, report to Poland that among some papers belonging to the church which were said to antedate the year 1729 was a list of subscriptions taken to build a Baptist Church in New York. In the list of contributors appeared the name of Robert Feke, who gave the sum of two pounds sterling. Poland, without himself inspecting the document, drew from it the conclusion that Feke "probably had some connection with the church, perhaps being an attendant of worship there. It seems also to prove that he had begun to reside, at least occasionally, in Newport before 1729." [1] Poland goes on to suggest that the unnamed church for which the subscription was taken might possibly have been that in Oyster Bay.

Unfortunately the conclusions which Professor Poland reached are not borne out by a closer examination of this document, which is still among the papers of the Second Baptist Church. It consists of a single sheet with the heading, "The Baptist Meeting House in New York," dated "A° 1727." The debit column includes a long series of items for building materials and labor, with a total expenditure of £210.9.4½. The credit column shows subscriptions received, to the amount of £94.16.2. "The Church at Rhode Island" is credited with £29.13.9. On the back of the sheet is a memorandum of (other?) assessments on seven Baptist churches

[1] *Robert Feke . . . and the Beginning of Colonial Painting*, pp. 14–15.

"to Ballance within." "Rhode Island" and Providence are each assessed £30, the others lesser amounts, the total being nearly enough to meet the deficit. The remaining subscriptions are from individuals, and Robert Feke's name appears near the bottom of the list, in the hand of the clerk who made out the whole account. The names of none of these individual subscribers appear in the membership lists of the Second Baptist Church of Newport, but one of them, Nicholas Eyres, who subscribed £14, four years later became minister of the church. The church records run, "The Rev. Nicholas Eyres called to the Ministry here from New York as a Coleague with Mr. Wi[g]htman in year 1731."

It seems quite clear, therefore, that this document is the building account sent from New York to the Second Baptist Church at Newport, which was giving financial backing to the new enterprise; that the individual subscribers are not, as Professor Poland thought, residents of Newport and worshippers at the Second Church there, but interested persons in or near New York; and that the Robert Feke who gave the £2 was Robert "the Preacher," of Oyster Bay.

This interpretation of the document deprives it of any value as evidence that Robert "the Painter" was in Newport at this time. In fact, prior to his marriage there in September, 1742, when he is described as "of Newport" we have no evidence of his being there, save for the portrait of Rev. Nathaniel Clap which may be his work. The phrase "of Newport" does, indeed, imply that he was not a stranger. He must at least have been there long enough to have courted his wife, and, for reasons already stated, it is highly probable that he may have been there frequently over a considerable period of years, but no written record of these visits has as yet come to light.

Feke's panel-portrait, believed to represent his little niece "Phiany" Cock, is the next document in his career. "Phiany"

LEVINAH ("PHIANY") COCK

was a nickname for Levinah, obviously arising from a child's mis-pronunciation. She was the daughter of Feke's sister Deborah, who married James Cock, of the same family into which two of Deborah's aunts had married. "Phiany" was born in 1730 and the picture shows her at about two years of age, so that it must have been painted at Oyster Bay or Matinecock about 1732 or 1733. If Feke was still following the sea, it is evidence that he returned home for visits, and it adds to the credibility of the tradition that the house at Meadowside when it was burned contained other portraits of his family by him.

The portrait of "Phiany" is not a very successful piece of work, though in its present poor condition it is easy to under-value it. It shows a little girl with auburn hair, and looks like a good likeness. On the back is an inscription reading:

> To Robert Feke
> at Mr. Judea Hayes
> in Newyork.

This would seem to offer clear evidence that Feke was in New York for a time, after 1732.[1] The panel may have been sent to him for finishing touches, but the more probable interpretation of the inscription is that he was seeking commissions there and wished to show it as a specimen of his handiwork to possible patrons. Other portrait painters were in New York at that time, and it would have been only natural for him to go there in search of work.

Aside from the evidence offered by the portrait of "Phiany" that Feke was doing some painting, and was at least temporarily resident in New York at some time during the decade between 1730 and 1740, only one picture has come to light which may pos-

---

[1] To Mr. John Hill Morgan of New York I am indebted for the information that Judah Hays was one of several members of a Jewish family which migrated from The Hague to New York about 1720. He was apparently a man of considerable standing, and died in 1764. Perhaps Feke took lodgings with him, or found him useful as an agent.

sibly be his work during his New York visit, that of "Rev. Heysham," which is attributed to him on very slender evidence.
While the head is fairly good, it is not one which is at all characteristic of Feke's work. If it be indeed his, it is certainly one of
his earlier attempts and must be dated from the early seventeen-
thirties. But he signed so few of his pictures, and those generally
the later and more important ones, that it is quite possible that
he painted a considerable number in his earlier years which have
been ascribed to other artists or which have survived nameless in
obscure corners.

The only portrait discovered in Newport which may perhaps
be his work of the period prior to 1740 is a small one showing the
bust and head of Rev. Nathaniel Clap, now the property of the
United Congregational Church of Newport. Clap was born in
Dorchester in 1667, came to Newport in 1695, and died there in
1745. The portrait shows him with bent shoulders, silvery hair,
and leathery skin, a man approaching seventy years of age. It
must date from the late seventeen-thirties, and may be tentatively assigned to Feke. It is indeed, a much cruder work than
his portraits of Rev. John Callender and Rev. Thomas Hiscox,
painted in 1745, with which it may naturally be compared, but
the face shows a good deal of character, despite the dilapidated
condition of the picture.

Until recently the only visits which Feke was known to have
made to Philadelphia were that of 1746, evidenced by signed and
dated pictures of Philadelphia people of importance, and that of
1750, known from the entry in John Smith's Diary,[1] at which
time he painted at least two and probably several other portraits.
The portraits listed in the descriptive catalogue as those of Tench
Francis, No. 1, and Mrs. Tench Francis, No. 1, seem to show,
however, that he must have painted some pictures in Philadelphia

[1] Quoted in *Hannah Logan's Courtship*, see Chap. IX.

TENCH FRANCIS (No. 1)

TENCH FRANCIS (No. 2)

as early as 1740. The present owner of those portraits strongly believes them to be the work of Copley, but Tench Francis was born in 1690 and is shown as a man in middle life, so that the portrait cannot have been painted much later than 1740, when Copley was still a small child. Furthermore Feke indubitably painted the same couple in 1746 (the portraits listed as Mr. and Mrs. Tench Francis, No. 2), for he signed and dated his portrait of Tench Francis of that year. The earlier portraits closely resemble the later ones in manner and pose, and as certainly depict the same individuals at an age at least six to eight years younger. Finally, Mr. J. Francis Fisher, who inherited the portrait known as Tench Francis, No. 2, stated that Feke painted "several" portraits of his family,[1] a statement fulfilled if the four portraits of Tench Francis and his wife, the two portraits of their daughter Ann (Mrs. James Tilghman, Nos. 1 and 2) and the portrait of their son-in-law Edward Shippen are all attributed to Feke. It is difficult, therefore, to avoid the conclusion that the early portraits of Tench Francis and his wife are the work of Feke during an early visit to Philadelphia, not later than 1740, and very likely earlier.

One other portrait is known to have existed which may well have been painted by Feke during this first visit to Philadelphia. It represented Anne Yeates, wife of George McCall, who emigrated from Scotland to Philadelphia, where he prospered as a merchant and died in 1740. His wife, whom he married there, died in 1746. This picture was destroyed by fire about forty years ago, but a small photogravure of it shows a portrait with marked characteristics of Feke's work. Mrs. McCall was the mother of Mary McCall, who married William Plumstead in 1753, and who was the subject of the portrait described on pages 90–92. The portrait of Mrs. McCall certainly bears a strong resemblance to

[1] See Appendix A.

that which represents her daughter and to two other portraits, the subjects of which have not been definitely identified, though it seems likely that they may represent other members of the McCall family.

A portrait of George McCall is still in the hands of a descendant, but was painted by a different hand from that which did Mrs. McCall. Probably it is by Hesselius, and was painted in the seventeen-thirties. That of his wife, however, seems clearly to be the work of Feke. The probable date would make it contemporaneous with the earlier pair of Francis portraits, giving additional ground for the conviction that Feke was pursuing his profession as a portrait painter in Philadelphia in the late seventeen-thirties.

MRS. GEORGE McCALL

CHAPTER IV

THE FIRST BOSTON VISIT, SUMMER OF 1741

THE strongest ground for believing that during the decade 1730–40 Feke was practising his art, at least intermittently as he found occupation between voyages, is that he definitely appears in 1741 as a professional portrait painter executing an important commission, the picture of Isaac Royall and his family.

This notable painting, while by no means the best of Feke's work, is of the first importance in the story of his career as an artist. It is the largest but one of all his extant paintings, and the only one of the "conversation" type, no other of his known portraits showing more than a single individual. It is, indeed, one of the earliest attempts made in this country to portray a group of individuals. Poland cites the altar-piece showing "Our Blessed Saviour and ye Twelve Apostles at ye Last Supper," which Gustavus Hesselius painted in 1722 for St. Barnabas' Church in Queen Anne Parish, Maryland;[1] and Smibert's portrait group of the household of Dean (later Bishop) Berkeley, painted in 1729 at Berkeley's home "Whitehall" at Middletown, three miles from Newport, as the first two pictures including more than a single figure to be painted in the Colonies.[2] Feke presumably had not seen the altar-piece by Hesselius, though he may have heard

---

[1] Reproduced, with a descriptive note in *Early American Paintings, Catalogue of Exhibition*, Brooklyn, N. Y., 1917.

[2] *Robert Feke . . . and the Beginning of Colonial Painting*, p. 6. Possibly correct as regards pictures showing a group of *several* persons, but there were certainly earlier pictures showing at least *two* persons: for example the portrait of Captain and Mrs. Johannes Schuyler, dating from about 1710–15, reproduced in Morgan's *Early American Painters*, and the portrait of two children, dated 1717 and attributed to John Watson, now in the Sears Academy of Art at Elgin, Ill.

about it and have seen portraits by Hesselius when he visited Philadelphia for the first time, or on his later visits of 1746 and 1750. Indeed, he may well have met the painter there, for Hesselius did not die until May 25, 1755, and his son John, also a painter, lived in Philadelphia till 1778. But Feke indubitably had seen Smibert's group of the Berkeley household before he painted the Royall group. He might have seen it in Newport if he was there before 1729, since Smibert did not migrate to Boston until the end of that year. If, however, he had no opportunity to see it in Newport he would have had a chance to do so in Boston when he went thither in 1741 to execute the Royall commission, for Smibert lived in Boston from the time of his marriage on July 30, 1730, until his death in 1751, and is reputed to have kept the Berkeley portrait group in his house.

In any case a comparison of the two pictures makes it quite evident that Feke's grouping is a simplified and rather naïve imitation of Smibert's. Each group is placed about a table covered with a decorated cloth; the chief personage in each stands at the end of the table at the spectator's right, holding a book in his right hand; in each the wife sits next, behind the table, holding an infant, who in Smibert's picture grasps an apple, in Feke's a toy in its right hand; in each another woman sits next the wife, pointing with her left hand towards the further side of the picture, while behind her there is a vista of landscape and sky; in each another figure is posed at the left end of the table. The attire of the women in Feke's picture closely resembles that in Smibert's, as does the drawing of the child. Feke's picture is simpler and smaller, without the additional figures which crowd Smibert's background, but the general resemblance is so striking as to indicate not only that Feke was familiar with Smibert's picture but that Isaac Royall had commissioned him to produce a painting of a similar type.

ISAAC ROYALL AND FAMILY

More important, however, than the size of the picture, its not altogether successful attempt to portray a group, and its dependence upon Smibert's earlier work, is the fact that the Royall portrait, alone among all of Feke's paintings, is fully documented. On the back are painted in black letters the names and ages of the subjects, concluding with the words "Finisht Sept. 15th, 1741, by Robert Feke." The whole inscription, which, though faded and stained is still clearly legible save for two or three doubtful words, is freely painted in a flowing, eighteenth-century script, as though done quickly by a practiced hand. There is not the smallest reason to doubt that it is contemporary with the portrait, and who but the painter himself would put down the exact date upon which he finished the work? The Royall portrait is the only picture to which he signed his full name.[1]

If the date assumed for his early self-portrait is correct, we are left with an interval of some sixteen years between it and the Royall group, punctuated only by the picture of "Phiany," the Francis and McCall portraits, and, possibly, by the portraits of "Rev. Heysham" and of Rev. Nathaniel Clap. A clue to other

---

[1] The only other portraits which he is known to have signed are the following:

Rev. John Callender	R. Feak, Pinx, A.D. 1745
Rev. Thomas Hiscox	R. Feak, 1745
Miss Williamina Moore	R. Feke, Pinx, 1746
Tench Francis	R. Feke, 1746
Mrs. Charles Willing	R. Feke, 1746
Miss Ruth Cunningham	R. Feke, 1748
Charles Apthorp	R. F.,1748
Mrs. Charles Apthorp	R. F., 1748
Robert Auchmuty	R. F., Pinx, 1748
James Bowdoin	R. F., Pinx, 1748
Mrs. James Bowdoin	R. F., Pinx, 1748
William Bowdoin	R. F., Pinx, 1748
Mrs. William Bowdoin	R. Feke, Pinx.
Isaac Stelle	R. Feke, Pinx.
Stephen Sewall	R. F., Pinx, 1748
Oxenbridge Thacher	R. F., 1748
Mrs. Oxenbridge Thacher	R. F., Pinx, 1749

Feke's signature is always inconspicuously painted and is often difficult to discover. It is not improbable that a closer examination of others of his portraits than has hitherto been made would reveal some additional instances.

work done by him during this period is given by the statement in the letter of "J. G. S."[1] to the effect that when the house of Feke's father at Oyster Bay was burned in 1768, it contained family portraits which he had painted. The portrait of "Phiany" escaped because it doubtless was in the house of Feke's sister Mrs. Cock, or of her children. It is, of course, possible that the pictures thus destroyed were juvenile sketches made before Feke left home for the first time. But we have no reason to suppose that he may not frequently have been at home exercising his art by painting other members of his family. While he might have stopped at Oyster Bay to do them on his way to or from Philadelphia, on any one of his three visits, it seems more reasonable to suppose that he did the family pictures in his earlier period, more or less as practice pieces, rather than after he had become a professional portrait painter who could charge fairly good fees for his commissions.

In any case it is obvious that Feke must have done enough painting between 1725 and 1741 to keep his hand in. For certainly the youth who painted the naïve self-portrait of 1725 could not possibly have produced the much more pretentious Royall group a decade and a half later if his only use of the paint brush in the meantime had been to keep the vessels upon which he sailed looking clean and shipshape! It is true that the Royall group shows nothing like so great an advance in skill over the early self-portrait as is indicated in Feke's Philadelphia portraits of 1746 or his Boston portraits of 1748. The Royall picture still has something of the flatness, the naïveté, the unsophisticated character of the self-portrait. The faces of two of the young women are not modeled well, nor colored effectively. Their hair is plainly done up, without the curl falling over one or the other shoulder which is always shown in his later picture, after the convention followed by the artists of the day. Their costumes are

[1] See Appendix A.

simple, unadorned by jewels, and are rendered with little feeling
for the fabrics. Comparison with the portraits of the wives of
James and William Bowdoin, or of Mrs. Charles Apthorp and Mrs.
Barlow Trecothick, reveals the great strides made by the artist
between 1741 and 1748. But we cannot avoid the conclusion that
Feke had done considerable painting during the decade and a
half preceding 1741, at least at such times as he was ashore either
at Newport or New York, or revisiting his father's home at Oyster
Bay between voyages.

But it is hardly probable that his opportunities for painting
can really have been limited to portrayals of his own family, and
to such objects as possible tavern signs and figureheads, for the
simple reason that one can explain Feke's commission to paint
the Royall group only by supposing him to have already acquired some reputation as a portrait painter. Isaac Royall, the
younger, in 1739, at the age of twenty, had inherited the mansion
which his father had a year or two before completed in Medford,
then a part of Charlestown. The elder Isaac Royall, though of
New England descent, had made a large fortune as a sugar planter
in Antigua, one of the then highly prosperous British colonies in
the West Indies. He had removed thence to New England in
1732, bringing with him twenty-seven negro slaves, "for his own
use and not any of them for merchandise," as he himself stated.
The Royall House at Medford, with its slave quarters, still stands.
Soon after Isaac Royall, Jr., inherited this establishment it was
described by a traveler as "one of the grandest in N. America."
It was presumably to adorn this house that the young master had
the painting executed showing himself, his wife and child, his
sister and sister-in-law. Obviously he would not have asked an
unknown "mariner" to come from Newport to Medford on a
commission of this importance, especially when well-known painters like Smibert and Peter Pelham were living and working in

Boston only a few miles away. Feke must have already acquired something of a reputation as a portrait painter for Royall to have sent for him at all. Very likely he had not done many pictures, perhaps painting was still an avocation for his occasional leisure, for certainly he had not done enough of it fully to develop his technique, but there must have been some handiwork of his which he could show, pictures which Royall and his friends must have seen and approved.

But one other picture has come to light which can plausibly be attributed to Feke's Boston visit in the summer of 1741, and it strongly corroborates the argument just presented for believing that Feke was already an artist of considerable accomplishments and growing reputation. It is the charming portrait of James Bowdoin II as a boy of about fourteen, now owned by Bowdoin College. The boy's father was a wealthy merchant of high standing, whose own portrait was twice painted by Badger a few years later, and who employed Feke, at the time of the latter's second visit to Boston in 1748, to paint the four well-known Bowdoin portraits now at Bowdoin College. As in the case of Isaac Royall, Jr., he is not likely to have asked a wholly unknown artist to depict his youthful son in the summer of 1741. The painter abundantly justified the father's choice. The picture represents the boy as a young archer, dressed in green, set against what is the loveliest and most imaginative of all Feke's landscapes. It is, in truth, one of the most delightful pictures of youth painted in America before Copley. The portrait has, indeed, long been attributed to Smibert, but it is not in his manner, being a lovelier thing than he was wont to produce. On the other hand it bears many marks of Feke's brush, and the apparent age of the subject fits into the period of Feke's visit. The chief difficulty in attributing it to Feke is that it discloses a more accomplished artist than Feke is commonly supposed to have been at so early a date. The

JAMES BOWDOIN II (No. 1)

figure itself, however, is no finer than that of Isaac Royall, Jr., and, in view of the presumptions in his favor, it will not do to say that such painting was beyond Feke's powers in 1741. After all, Feke was then about thirty-six, and had been painting portraits, at least occasionally, for not less than fifteen years. This portrait of young James Bowdoin, even more than the Royall group, compels us to recognize that Feke by 1741 was an accomplished artist, capable, within somewhat narrow limits, of doing as good work as was then to be found in the colonies.

CHAPTER V

MARRIAGE AND SETTLEMENT IN
NEWPORT, 1742–1745

IF FEKE'S career as a painter had hitherto been casual and uncertain, — the occupation of a more or less enforced leisure between voyages, — it seems wholly probable that this first Boston
visit marks the point at which he turned to painting as his chief
business in life. Presumably when the Royall group was done
Feke returned to Newport, for the next information we have regarding him is that on September 23, 1742, when he was about
thirty-seven years old, he was married there by Rev. John Callender of the First Baptist Church to Eleanor Cozzens.[1] The
entry in the Town Records describes them as "both of Newport."
That Rev. John Callender should have married them was natural
enough from the point of view of Feke, with his Baptist connections, but it gives rise to some inquiry in view of the fact that the
bride and her family belonged to the Society of Friends. In many
places, not only then but for a century and a half later, a Quaker
marrying "out of meeting," and with a service performed by a
"hireling minister," would have been promptly "disowned" by
the Meeting, if not by her family. Evidently the marriage of

---

[1] Eleanor Cozzens, born November 15, 1718, was the fourth of thirteen children of
Leonard and Margaret Cozzens. Her father was born in 1690 in the parish of All
Cannon, Wiltshire, England, and had married in July, 1712, whether before or after
coming to Newport is uncertain. He was evidently a man of substance, for his will,
made in 1765 and recorded October 2, 1769, made several considerable bequests, including "Item. I Give and Bequeath unto my Daughter Eleanor Feake of Newp. Fifty
Spanish Milled Dollars or an Equivalent in Paper Money [to be paid?] within Six
Months after My Decease by my Executrix." Mrs. Feke outlived her husband by more
than half a century. The *Newport Mercury* of Saturday, August 11, 1804, records her
death in a belated item, "Died — In this town, on the 6th ult, after a lingering ilnes, Mrs.
Eleanor Feke, relict of the late Robert Feke, aged 86 years."

Eleanor Cozzens had no such unhappy consequences. Tradition says that she remained a Quaker and habitually attended Meeting, while her husband continued to worship with the Baptists. Perhaps the "Discipline" disowning members of the Society who married "out of meeting" was not enforced in Newport because of the unusually tolerant atmosphere of that city. Rhode Island had a tradition of religious liberty, founded on the principles of Roger Williams, which is the noblest heritage of the State. There the Society of Friends was strong and at ease, as were the Baptists. They had a good deal in common, and Robert Feke had his own Quaker antecedents, and the Quaker aunt who married in Newport in 1726 and lived there subsequently. These facts may have caused the Meeting to look leniently upon the marriage of Eleanor Cozzens. Furthermore Rev. John Callender was an honored and beloved minister. We can only surmise what were Feke's own religious views. He does not appear ever to have been a church member and probably he did not much concern himself with the petty items of denominational differences. Feke's earlier voyages, as well as his later journeys as a painter must have brought him into contact with many kinds of people, in itself a broadening process, and he was acquainted with Shaftesbury's moral philosophy, which was accounted skeptical in outlook.

After his marriage Feke presumably went no more to sea, but is said to have "settled at Newport, where he lived in a large old house on Touro Street, facing School Street, next door to the Historical Society, which was standing till last spring [i. e., March, 1920] when to the sorrow of many of us, it was ruthlessly torn down. It was probably in this house that the portrait of the sprightly Mrs. Wanton, sometimes referred to as Lady Wanton, was painted." [1] Mrs. Elliott gives no authority for the location of

---

[1] Mrs. Maud Howe Elliott, *Some Recollections of Newport Artists*, Newport Historical Society, No. 35, January, 1921.

Feke's residence, but her statement embodies the tradition which is referred to by Mr. J. Francis Fisher when he speaks of being told that Feke's descendants "about the end of the [18th] century occupied a house on Touro Street near the synagogue." [1] In this case the tradition has a solid foundation, since the property in question had been in possession of Feke's father-in-law for more than a quarter of a century before Feke married Eleanor Cozzens. On September 17, 1716, Leonard "Cozens," "taylor," and Margaret, his wife, bought of Charles Whitefield and Sarah, his wife, a lot of land fifty feet front on Griffin [now Touro] Street by one hundred feet deep.[2] The exact boundaries are now difficult to locate from the description in the deed, but they were probably identical with those of the lot of land immediately adjoining and now owned by the Historical Society, the dimensions of which are approximately fifty by one hundred feet. Upon this site Leonard Cozzens built a house, presumably soon after his purchase. Photographs of it at the Newport Historical Society, taken shortly before its destruction, show a roomy, substantial structure of the eighteenth-century New England type, with a simple but finely modeled door, attractive even in its dilapidated state, the kind of a house in which one likes to think that a colonial portrait painter lived and worked. If Cozzens built without much delay, his daughter Eleanor must have been born there, and it seems to have remained her residence throughout her long life.[3] There is

---

[1] Appendix A.

[2] *Land Evidence*, Newport Historical Society, IV, 63.

[3] In a list of occupants of houses in Newport during the Revolution, apparently compiled by order of the commander of British troops there, Horace Feeke is put down as owner of an eight-room house on Griffin Street, which he occupied himself with five other persons. The house had a stable for one horse (*Newport Historical Magazine*, II [1881–82], 43). This house is, of course, that which had been built by Leonard Cozzens, and Horace — properly Horatio — Feke was the second son of Robert "the Painter," and was in his thirties at the time. The title to the property had evidently passed to him. He was married but had no children, so that we may surmise that his mother and, perhaps, his younger, unmarried brother Charles were two of the other persons who made up the household at this time.

MRS. ROBERT FEKE

no evidence that Robert Feke ever became a freeman, which would mean that he was not a voter, and was not qualified to hold real estate in his own name. He might, therefore, very naturally have taken up his domicile in his wife's home after their marriage. Possibly Feke shared the house with his father-in-law's family, but it would seem more likely that Leonard Cozzens moved elsewhere, as he had several unmarried children in his large family, and three sons and two daughters were born to Robert Feke and his wife between their marriage in 1742 and his death in 1750 or soon after.

The eldest son, John "was a very promising young master of a ship in the English trade, which by the mistake of the pilot, was lost with all on board, in the English Channel." [1] The second son was the above-mentioned Horace, born in 1744, whose death is recorded, without date, in the *Newport Mercury* of March 22, 1803.[2] He was married to Catherine Nichols by Rev. Gardiner Thurston, pastor of the Second Baptist Church of Newport, on September 14, 1768, and died leaving no children. The third son, who must also have been the youngest child, was Charles, born in 1750, who never married. Charles Feke became a prosperous and benevolent apothecary and doctor, described as small and insignificant in person, and thought by some to be eccentric, but singularly noble and generous in disposition.[3] Charles was, if not

---

[1] *History of the State of Rhode Island*, Hoag, Wade & Co., p. 354. This is the only reference which has come to light regarding Feke's son John. It occurs in the brief and unsigned biographical sketch of Feke, which, for the rest, is clearly based on the letters in Dawson's *Historical Magazine*. Presumably the information was furnished and probably the sketch was written by Mr. W. P. Bullock, of Providence, whose wife was a descendant of Feke, and who then owned Feke's late self-portrait and his portrait of his wife. The former portrait is reproduced in the *History*, opp. p. 200, in a crude lithograph.

[2] *Newport Mercury*, March 22, 1803, "Died, — In this town, Mr. Horatio Feke, in the 59th year of his age."

[3] A very creditable anecdote illustrating his fineness of character and the esteem in which he was held is told in *The Jonny-Cake Papers*. As a young man he became "apothecary" to Dr. William Hunter, who came from England to Newport about 1752, and married there. Dr. Hunter was a Loyalist, who died in 1777, leaving his estate

a Quaker, at least sympathetic with the Society of Friends. Among the death notices in the *Newport Mercury* of April 27, 1822, is included "Dr. Charles Feke, in the 72nd year of his age," who had died two days before. The brief obituary speaks in glowing terms of "this distinguished Philanthropist" and announces his funeral for the following day. Two streets in Newport, Charles Street and Feke Street, are said to have been named for him.

Robert Feke's two daughters, Phila[1] and Sarah, were Quakers and were married in Friends' Meeting on the same day, October 15, 1767. In the manuscript *Book of Records of Marriage Certificates Belonging to the Monthly Meeting of Rhode Island*, the entry for the marriage of Phila Feke to John Townsend appears on p. 279, and that of Sarah Feke to John Thurston on p. 280. Both bridegrooms were "of Newport," and each bride is described as "daughter of Robert Feke, late of said Newport in said County and Colony, Mariner, deceased, and of Eleanor his wife, now widow." Sarah Thurston must have died before 1772, as her

---

much embarrassed on account of the Revolution. His widow went to England in 1786 to endeavor to secure settlement of his claims, leaving her two younger children in charge of Charles Feke. She died in England in 1813, and an extensive correspondence through the intervening years between her and Charles Feke is still extant in the hands of a descendant, Miss Anna F. Hunter of Newport. This correspondence testifies to Charles Feke's devotion to the Hunter family, and contains many references to "his excellent mother," but gives no information about his father.

[1] Poland assumes her name to have been Philadelphia, but on the marriage certificate it appears only as Phila, and, as Friends were very particular to be detailed and exact in the wording of their marriage certificates, it seems unlikely that Phila is an abbreviation. Furthermore she thus signed her name on her sister's certificate as a witness. I have come across only one other instance of this unusual name. It will be recalled that Feke, in the early seventeen-thirties, had some connection with Judah Hays, who was one of the little circle of Jews in New York. Among the leaders of that Jewish group was the family of Jacob Franks, who had a daughter named Phila, born in 1722. Phila Franks was painted several times in early life (see Hannah B. London, *Portraits of Jews by Gilbert Stuart and other early American Artists*). None of these pictures seem to be Feke's work. If, however, Feke became well acquainted with Judah Hays while in New York, he would probably have known the Franks family also. The striking similarity between the names Phila Franks and Phila Feke at least suggests the possibility of such acquaintance.

husband was married a second time on April 23rd of that year. Phila Townsend died March 15, 1802, at her husband's house at Easton's Point, Newport. Her son Christopher Townsend was also a wise and generous benefactor of Newport. He and his wife inherited the house on Broad Street, owned by his uncle Charles Feke, with whom they appear to have lived during the latter part of his life. Inasmuch as all three of Feke's sons died childless his only descendants are through his two daughters.

From the time of his marriage Feke presumably turned to painting as his means of livelihood, but in view of the small number of known portraits which he executed before his Philadelphia visit of 1746 the question inevitably arises as to how he supported himself and his family. On any scale of fees which he could have charged for his pictures he would have had to paint an average of something like twenty portraits a year to do this, which is several times the number of his extant pictures which can possibly be ascribed to the decade between 1740 and 1750. Badger is known in 1757 to have received six pounds apiece for his large portraits of Timothy Orne and his wife.[1] In 1767, at the height of his popularity in Boston, Copley made three hundred guineas a year and counted it a good living.[2] Copley's bill for his large portraits of Ezekiel Goldthwait and his wife, receipted for him by Henry Pelham on July 1, 1771, shows that he received £19.12.0. apiece for the pictures, and he charged £18.0.0. for the two beautifully carved frames which still enclose them. It would seem unlikely that Feke would have been paid more than three or four pounds for his smaller works or more than six pounds for any except his largest pictures. With the possible exception of Hesselius in Philadelphia it does not seem likely that any portrait painter in the colonies before 1750 made enough money by painting alone to

[1] Lawrence Park, *Joseph Badger* (Boston, 1918), p. 5.
[2] Isham, *History of American Painting*, p. 2.

support himself. Jeremiah Dummer, although he painted some portraits in Boston before 1700, was a silversmith; Smibert kept a shop at which he sold paints, oils, and picture frames, and in 1734 he found it necessary to sell his collections of prints and of the oil copies which he had made in European galleries before coming to America, although later he perhaps made a fairly good living from painting.[1] Peter Pelham, Copley's stepfather, made and sold engravings, taught school, and even opened a dancing-school. Badger was a house-painter by trade. The Duyckincks in New York were glaziers as well as painters. The evidence is clear that none of these men, with the possible exceptions of Hesselius and of Smibert in his later years, found portrait painting alone a sufficient means of support.

In Feke's case we have no evidence that he resorted to any of the means employed by these other painters to supplement his income. When he came to Boston he did not advertise in the *Boston News-Letter*, either because he thought it beneath his dignity or because he had already secured a satisfactory number of commissions. There is no evidence that at Newport he was engaged in any other remunerative occupation save that of "mariner." It is, of course, possible that he continued to earn money by going on short voyages after his marriage, but that seems improbable. Possibly he had saved and invested enough money in the years preceding his late marriage to assure him of a modest income. Or he may have had a share in the family property at Oyster Bay, though it could not have been much, for both his parents, though well-to-do, long outlived him and had several other children to provide for. His wife's father, although described as "taylor" in 1716, became a prosperous man, and Feke was not obliged to provide a home for his family because he went to live in the Cozzens house on Touro Street. We are, there-

[1] G. F. Dow, *Arts and Crafts in New England*, pp. xx, 3.

fore, led to surmise that in the seventeen-forties Feke was not wholly dependent upon his painting for means of support, and that he lived in modest comfort.

That his seafaring life was well known in Newport is clear from the description of him as "mariner" instead of "limner" in the marriage certificates of his daughters some seventeen years after his death. That identification of him is, however, a little puzzling. Why was it that this man, who for very nearly a decade before his death, and probably longer, was a professional portrait painter in Newport, and whose work was in demand in Boston and Philadelphia, was still remembered as a "mariner"? Neither of his self-portraits depicts him as such; indeed the later one shows him with palette and brush in hand. Perhaps the simplest explanation is that the good Quaker who was clerk of the Meeting was inclined to look with disapproval upon Feke's activities as a painter. He very likely thought that portrait painting was a profession savoring of worldliness, and, for the sake of the daughters, recorded their father as following the more seemly occupation of mariner, as he could truthfully do. The stricter members of the Society of Friends were wont to look on portraits as manifestations of worldly pride, ostentation and extravagance, and it may be noted that not a single picture of the numerous and prosperous Quakers of Newport or Philadelphia has come down to us from Feke's brush, except his portrait of his own wife, unless we may surmise that a young Quakeress sat as his model for his charming picture known as "Pamela Andrews."

That portrait, now in the Providence School of Design, must date from about 1741 or a little later. It represents the heroine of Richardson's novel of that title, which was published in London in 1740, and which leapt into popularity. It is not necessary to allow for more than a very few weeks for it to cross the ocean so that by 1741 it may have been known in Newport and by 1742 have been widely popular there. The picture seems to prove both its popularity and Feke's acquaintance with it. It may, indeed, be argued that the picture was not originally intended to represent Pamela Andrews at all, but that the name was afterwards attached to it. That is possible, but the costume would seem to indicate that it was intended as an ideal representation of Richardson's heroine. Perhaps Feke painted it at a time when he had no commissions to work upon, in the hope that it might find a purchaser. That was not the case, however, for it was in the possession of his widow in 1755, when she gave it to her brother Benjamin Cozzens, whose descendant, Miss Sarah Durfee, bequeathed it to the School of Design. That it was given to Benjamin Cozzens suggests at least the possibility that some member of his family sat for the picture. None of his daughters would have been old enough. Conceivably it may represent the young woman who became his wife, or his next younger sister Deborah, born in 1724, who did not marry and to whom her father in his will recorded in 1769, bequeathed "[illegible] . . . hundred pounds old tenor." It is at least a pleasant fancy that Feke in this charming picture may have portrayed a sister-in-law.

His lovely portrait of Mrs. Joseph Wanton, now hanging in the Redwood Library at Newport, Rhode Island, must also date from the early seventeen-forties. Mrs. Wanton was Mary Winthrop, daughter of John Winthrop of New London, and therefore great-great-granddaughter of Governor John Winthrop of Massachusetts, and, on her mother's side granddaughter of Governor Joseph Dudley, and great-granddaughter of Governor Thomas Dudley—a daughter of the Puritans indeed. Robert Feke was her cousin in the fourth degree, through his descent from Elizabeth Fones, wife of Robert "the Emigrant" and sister of Martha Fones who married John Winthrop, Jr., of Connecticut. Elizabeth Fones was herself a granddaughter of Adam Winthrop. It is improbable

that Feke's relationship to the Winthrops was unknown and un-
recognized by either Feke or Mrs. Wanton, and it may be noted
here that when Feke's daughters were married in Friends' Meeting in 1767, a few months after Mrs. Wanton's death, three of her
children signed the marriage certificates as witnesses. The family
of Joseph Wanton had originally settled in Boston, but, becoming
Quakers, had migrated first to Scituate, Rhode Island, to find a
more congenial atmosphere, and then to Newport, Rhode Island,
where they had prospered. There her husband's father transferred his allegiance to the Church of England. Four of his family
became governors before the Revolution.

It is always difficult to estimate the age of the women whom
Feke painted, for they are usually painted with less individuality
than his men, especially in his earlier portraits. Thus the women
in the Royall group, all of whom were in fact under twenty, might
be anywhere between eighteen and twenty-eight. Mrs. Wanton
seems, in her portrait, to be in her early thirties. As she was born
in 1708 this would indicate that the picture might have been done
about 1740, but the painting is distinctly superior to that of the
Royall women, alike in its modeling of the beautiful face, neck,
and bosom, in its contrasted lights and shadows, and in its rendering of the fabrics. One is, therefore, inclined to date it as somewhere between 1742 and 1746.

The portrait is now disfigured by a bunch of gay flowers inserted in the bosom of the gown. They were reluctantly painted
by Miss Jane Stuart in the middle of the nineteenth century
after the portrait had been bequeathed to the Redwood Library,
by order of the board of directors who considered the gown so
low-cut as to be immodest, and who sought thus to protect Mrs.
Wanton's lovely bosom from the public gaze! As a matter of
fact the gown was cut only after the fashion of the seventeen-
forties, and is no lower than those worn by most of Feke's women

sitters. There is something decidedly humorous in the thought that mid-Victorian Newport found the dress of this Puritan lady immodest, but the story is well attested, and a poor copy of the picture, now hanging in the Massachusetts Historical Society, shows Mrs. Wanton without the bouquet. The copy was either made before it was added, or the copyist knew it ought not to be there.

In the Redwood Library a portrait of Joseph Wanton hangs beside that of his wife. Mrs. Wanton's picture has apparently always been attributed to Feke, although it is neither signed nor dated, and it is entirely characteristic of him. But in the catalogue her husband's portrait is ascribed to an "unknown English painter." Yet the portraits of husband and wife were evidently intended as companion pieces, for they are of the same dimensions and the figures are so placed in similar painted ovals as to face one another. But they can hardly be by the same artist, for that of Joseph Wanton seems quite inferior in style and certainly does not look like Feke's work. Joseph Wanton in his portrait looks considerably older than his wife, though he was born but three years earlier. He appears a man in his forties, dressed in red, with a rather unattractive face. It seems probable, therefore, that his picture was painted later than his wife's by another hand, perhaps after Feke's death.[1]

About the same time that he did Mrs. Wanton's portrait Feke painted his picture of John Gidley, Jr., now in the Newport Historical Society. As Gidley was killed on September 30, 1744, at

[1] It should be noted that in the Rhode Island Historical Society at Providence there is another pair of portraits reputed to represent Joseph and Mary Wanton, said to have been brought from England in 1891. The face of the man is so different from that in the portrait in the Redwood Library that it seems hardly possible that it can represent the same individual. That of the woman might possibly be the same Mrs. Wanton that Feke pictured, and, curiously enough, she wears the same costume. Both pictures are poorly painted, and neither can be by Feke. Both are reproduced in Updike, *History of the Episcopal Church in Naragansette* (2d ed., 1907), where they are attributed to Thomas Hudson. Lawrence Park, in his pamphlet on *Joseph Blackburn* (p. 9), refers, however, to this portrait of Mrs. Wanton as by Smibert.

JOHN GIDLEY, JR.

the age of forty-four, the portrait must have been done before that date, but probably after 1740. Although now in poor condition it is a fine picture, showing a pensive face and a well-poised and handsomely dressed figure.

The portrait of the "Unknown Man with the Spaniel" possibly belongs to this period also, although there is no clue to the identity of the subject or to the date or place of painting. The picture turned up in New York in 1926, in the hands of a dealer who either knew or would tell nothing of its origin, and was sold in January, 1927, by the Ehrich Galleries to the Sears Academy of Art at Elgin, Illinois, as the work of Feke. The attribution seems reasonable enough, for the picture is in Feke's earlier manner, and the costume of the subject is that of the seventeen-forties. It is a work of minor importance, which might have been painted any time between 1740 and 1746, at Newport or elsewhere.

That Feke by 1744 had an established place and reputation in Newport as a portrait painter is proved by a priceless bit of documentary evidence regarding him which dates from that year, the first of the two contemporary references to him as yet unearthed. On July 16, 1744, there arrived in Newport a Scotch traveller, Dr. Alexander Hamilton, whose narrative of a journey from Maryland to New Hampshire and return in the summer of 1744 was published some twenty years ago.[1] The entry in his journal reads:

I dined at a tavern kept by one Nicolls at the sign of the White Horse, where I had put up my horses, and in the afternoon Dr. Moffatt, an old acquaintance and schoolfellow of mine, led me a course through the town. He carried me to one Feake, a painter, the most extraordinary genius ever I knew, for he does pictures tolerably well by the force of genius, having never had any teaching. I saw a large table of the Judgment of Hercules, copied by him from a frontispiece of the Earl of Shaftesbury's, which I thought very well done. This man had exactly the phiz of a painter, having a long pale face, sharp nose, large eyes, — with which he looked upon you steadfastly, — long curled black hair, a delicate white hand, and long fingers.

[1] *Itinerarium* (St. Louis, 1907), pp. 123–124.

This entry is invaluable for several reasons. In the first place it gives our only pen picture of Feke, and its description of him exactly fits the individual portrayed in Feke's two self-portraits. It certainly does not read like the description of a seafaring man.

In the second place it proves that Feke had a studio in Newport, presumably in his own home, where he was working as a professional portrait painter. And he was regarded by Dr. Moffatt as a person of sufficient interest to be worth introducing to a European visitor. Furthermore he evidently made a striking impression on that visitor, who noted that he was "the most extraordinary genius I ever knew," though he gives inadequate grounds for what seems like an extravagant statement. But we may perhaps legitimately surmise from it that Feke was an attractive person conveying an impression of some distinction, an inference corroborated by the type of people among whom he found acceptance and whose portraits he painted between 1740 and 1750, many of whom were leaders in Boston, Newport, and Philadelphia and who appear to have recommended him to their friends. It may be noted, however, that Hamilton refers to him as "Feake," whereas, when he reached Boston and visited Smibert, he twice refers to the latter as "Mr." Smibert. Yet Feke was of better birth and breeding than Smibert, though the latter was older and had more local prestige.

In the third place Hamilton notes his surprise that, though "having never had any teaching," Feke should "do pictures tolerably well by the force of genius." The information that Feke had had no instruction in painting may have come from Dr. Moffatt and may represent merely the current gossip in Newport, but inasmuch as Hamilton had just come from an interview with the artist it is more probable that he had received the information from Feke's own lips. In either case it confirms the family tradition that he was self-taught. Perhaps the statement may be interpreted to mean that he had had no *formal* instruction. As stated above, he can hardly have failed of acquaintance with Smibert and his work and he may have received valuable hints from him or from some of the New York painters without actually being the pupil of any of them. And if Feke really ever was in Spain, or if his voyages had taken him to London, he may have seen not only pictures in those countries, but also artists at work there. But, with all allowance for these possibilities, the statement that Feke was self-taught must be accepted as substantially correct. The limitations of Feke's technique also support the tradition. While much of his work is admirable, at its best surpassing anything done in America before Copley developed his greater skill, Feke has little variety or originality in pose or accessories. With the caution and the limited resources of a self-taught man he repeats again and again the formulas which he had learned to execute successfully.

Hamilton's reference to the specimen of his work which particularly excited his admiration — "a large table of the Judgment of Hercules, copied by him from a frontispiece of the Earl of Shaftesbury's" — calls for a somewhat detailed explanation since it throws light upon Feke's methods of self-education. The Lord Shaftesbury in question was the third Earl, a man of letters and connoisseur of art. He published in 1711 his book of moral philosophy entitled *Characteristicks*. In July, 1711, he left England in poor health, and proceeded to Naples, where he arrived on November 15 and remained for the year and a quarter intervening before his death on February 15, 1713. During this sojourn he attempted the composition of a book which was to contain four treatises on art, of which the second was to be "A Notion of the Historical Draught or Tablature of the Judgment of Hercules." This essay, commonly called "The Judgment of Hercules," was completed and printed first in French, in the *Journal des Scavans*, November 1, 1712. An "original translation" appeared in English separately in 1713, and was included in the second edition of "*Characteristicks*," which was handsomely printed in 1714 in three volumes, illustrated throughout with beautiful engravings by Simon Gribelin.[1] These essays of Shaftesbury's were very widely read, running to six editions before 1740. Shaftesbury uses the story of the choice of Hercules between Virtue and Pleasure, as recorded by Xenophon in the second book of his *Memorabilia*, to illustrate his theory of aesthetics and to formulate the rules for portraying an historical scene. To accompany his text Shaftesbury caused a now-forgotten painter, Paulo de Matthaeis,[2] presumably a Neapolitan, to paint a picture of the episode. This work was ordered early in 1712, for Shaftesbury, in a letter of February 23, writes, "the history piece bespoke and now actually working." Inasmuch as Gribelin's small engraving of it — a vignette rather than a true frontispiece — is fitted into the lower half of the sub-title to Shaftesbury's essay at the end of the 1714 edition of *Characteristicks*, the painting itself must have been sent to London either before or soon after Shaftesbury's death.

It is this small engraving which Feke had attempted to reproduce in a fairly large painting,[3] with results which excited Hamilton's admiration. The important thing is not the measure of his success, but the revelation of Feke as a student. Shaftesbury's writings were, indeed, widely known and were very influential on

[1] Gribelin was a French engraver born in or near Paris about 1661, who had migrated to London in 1680, where he lived until his death in 1733. His earliest known engravings date from 1700. In 1707 he published a series of engravings from Raphael's cartoons at Hampton Court, and afterwards he engraved portraits of King William and Queen Mary and of various other notabilities, and made engravings from famous paintings. He was, doubtless, the best engraver of the day in London. See Benezit *Dictionnaire Critique et Documentaire des Peintres, Sculpteurs, Dessinateurs et Graveurs, etc.*, Paris, 1913.

[2] Paulo de Matthaeis is not included in Benezit.

[3] It is interesting to note that in 1754 the youthful Copley, then seventeen, "produced an allegorical picture thirty inches long by twenty-five wide, of Mars, Venus, and Vulcan." — Isham, *American Painting*, p. 23.

ENGRAVING OF REV. THOMAS HISCOX

(REDUCED IN SIZE)

ENGRAVING: "THE JUDGMENT OF HERCULES"

European thought, but that Feke should have studied "The Judgment of Hercules," and presumably have read the rest of *Characteristicks*, throws a good deal of light upon his intellectual standards and his desire to make use of the best thought of the day along the lines of his professional interests. Feke may "have never had any teaching" in the sense of never having been a pupil in a studio, but obviously he was highly intelligent in educating himself.

We would gladly know what other pictures Hamilton saw in Feke's studio, for though the entry mentions none, one copy of "The Judgment of Hercules" would hardly lead a European traveller to describe Feke as "the most extraordinary genius I ever knew." The picture of "Pamela" may well have been one; perhaps the portraits of Mrs. Wanton, of John Gidley, Jr., or of the "Man with the Spaniel," were others. Very likely there were other portraits which have since been lost to sight.

We know that Feke was in Newport the year following Hamilton's visit because of a pair of important portraits of two Rhode Island worthies each of which bears the unusual signature "R. Feak, A. D. 1745." They represent John Callender of Newport and Thomas Hiscox of Westerley, the two leading Baptist divines of that locality and period, and were painted on the order of Henry Collins, the rich Newport merchant and philanthropist. They are Feke's only surviving pictures of ministers, with the doubtful exception of "Rev. Heysham," who in any case was probably not ordained when his picture was painted whether by Feke or another, and of Rev. Nathaniel Clap, which is more likely to be Feke's. The portraits of Callender and of Hiscox are of the same size and style and were evidently intended as companion pieces. That of Callender was purchased from Collins's heirs by Henry Bull and given in 1848 to the Rhode Island Historical Society. That of Hiscox is now owned by Mrs. Vanderbilt, who received it, with other portraits, by inheritance through Henry Collins's niece, Mrs. Ebenezer Flagg, in whose house Collins died.

Although companion pieces the two pictures strikingly contrast the characters of the two sitters, who are portrayed with as fine effect as Feke ever achieved. Rev. John Callender, who had performed the marriage ceremony uniting Feke with Eleanor Cozzens three years before, was a well-educated, gentle, refined man, whose highly intelligent face fully justifies his reputation and the high esteem in which he was held. Callender was the author of an *Historical Address on Rhode Island*, delivered in March, 1738, on the one-hundredth anniversary of the settlement of the colony, which is of prime importance for historians as a source of information. This address was printed in the last century in Volume IV of the *Collections of the Rhode Island Historical Society*, and in his introduction the editor says that Callender is described as having been,

about the middle size, graceful and well-proportioned. His complexion was fair, his features were regular, his forehead was high and prominent, and in his countenance there was an admirable mixture of gravity and sweetness. His eyes were dark blue, and said to be remarkable for their intelligence and brilliancy.[1]

[1] Pages 21–22. On page 44 the editor, Romeo Elton, quotes a letter written to him by Dr. Benjamin Waterhouse, as follows: "Henry Collins, a wealthy merchant and a man of taste, the Lorenzo de Medicis of Rhode Island, caused a painting to be made of parson Callender, as well as some other divines, as Hitchcock, Clap, and Dean Berkeley. I conjecture that the portrait you mention is the very one that I often admired in the Collins collection." The editor adds in a footnote, "This fine original portrait, supposed to have been executed by Smibert, is now in the possession of Henry Bull, Esq., of Newport." The portrait referred to is, of course, Feke's picture of Callender, and it is significant of the inattention paid to such matters that it should have been attributed to Smibert although Feke's signature is easily discernible upon close examination. Of the other portraits of divines referred to by Waterhouse, that of "Hitchcock" is, of course, Feke's pictures of Hiscox, which of recent years has been mistakenly supposed to represent Callender. That of Clap is, no doubt, the one already discussed as not improbably an earlier work by Feke. I do not know to what portrait of Dean Berkeley Waterhouse referred, unless it be Smibert's group picture of Berkeley and his entourage, now owned by Yale University. Waterhouse was mistaken in thinking that this was painted on commission from Henry Collins.

REV. JOHN CALLENDER

Although the portrait is now in bad condition it sufficiently reveals a person of whom this is an admirable description.

Rev. Thomas Hiscox was a rugged, vigorous personality, about sixty years of age when he was painted, largely self-educated, who disdained a wig in favor of his own flowing white hair. He too has an intelligent face, but with the eyes, the thin, firm lips, the determined uplifted chin of a man who would dominate by bulk of body and strength of will. His portrait has the additional interest of being the first of Feke's portraits to be reproduced. Hiscox was a noted figure locally, and five months after his death on May 20, 1773, at the age of eighty-seven, Samuel Okey engraved and Reak and Okey, print sellers in Newport, published a small and now rare mezzotint from the "Original Picture Painted by Mr. Feke."[1] Although the mezzotint has this historical interest, it is crudely done and by no means does justice to the vigor and fine characterization of the portrait.

This completes the list of known portraits by Feke which can well be attributed to his Newport sojourn between his return from Boston in the fall of 1741 and his second journey to Philadelphia in 1746. The number is so few that they could have taken but a small part of his time. It is difficult to believe that during that period he did not paint a good many more pictures that have disappeared. Indeed, when one considers his total known product from 1740 to his death in 1750, or soon after, it is evident that, unless he went to sea, or occupied considerable periods with other work when no commissions came to him, he may easily have painted twice as many pictures as have yet come to light.

[1] This engraving was again reproduced in lithograph in *The Seventh-Day Baptist Memorial* in 1882. No other picture by Feke is known to have been reproduced until 1878, when the very crude lithograph of his late self-portrait appeared in the *History of Rhode Island*.

CHAPTER VI

THE SECOND PHILADELPHIA VISIT, 1746

FEKE's visit to Philadelphia in 1746 is the next event in his life of which we have any knowledge. The evidence for it is the existence of two portraits of Philadelphia people, Tench Francis, No. 2, and Mrs. Charles Willing, No. 1, which are signed and dated "R. Feke, 1746," and that of Williamina Moore, signed "R. F. 1746." There are also more than a dozen other unsigned and undated portraits of Philadelphians which are attributed to Feke, some of which must have been painted during this second visit, though at least two, and probably several others, must be assigned to his third visit in the spring of 1750.

As a matter of convenience the portraits of Josiah Martin and his wife may also be included among the fruits of this journey, though they were no doubt painted at the Martins' home at Hempstead, Long Island, only a short distance from Oyster Bay. The age at which the sitters are represented, and the technique of the painting, would indicate that they date from the late seventeen-forties and it seems a reasonable surmise that Feke stopped at Oyster Bay to visit his parents on his way from Newport to Philadelphia in 1746 or 1750, and during that visit painted these handsome pictures, each of which shows in the background a glimpse of the Long Island shore. Feke would no doubt be known to the Martins through their residence near his old home, but it may be noted that Josiah Martin had made his money in Antigua, as had Isaac Royall, Senior, with whom he must have been acquainted, and Martin may easily have known that Feke had painted the portrait of young Isaac Royall.

Of the portraits almost certainly painted in Philadelphia in 1746 the most interesting from an historical point of view is that of Benjamin Franklin, now owned by Harvard University. This picture long bore a label with the words "London, 1726," and, although the portrait was frequently reproduced by Franklin's biographers, this absurd label was apparently not seriously questioned by any one until Mr. Charles Henry Hart pointed out how gross an error was the notion that it could have been painted during Franklin's youthful visit to England. In 1726 Franklin was a poor youth of twenty, struggling to make a living in London and in no condition to pay for a large portrait of himself. Furthermore he is shown in the picture as a man approaching forty years of age, soberly but handsomely attired, and wearing one of the curled wigs which were expensive articles of adornment. On these grounds Mr. Hart denied that the portrait could represent Benjamin Franklin. Lawrence Park later made a critical examination of the picture, clearly establishing the identity of the sitter, and attributing the portrait to Feke.[1] It is the earliest known representation of Franklin,[2] and shows him much as we may suppose him to have looked after he had attained prosperity and a position of influence. Park points out that the picture, "if not directly at least very soon after it was painted, came into the possession of Franklin's older brother, John Franklin (1690–1756). Indeed the picture may have been painted to his order." Park further notes that John Franklin left it to his widow, to go after her death to his nephew James Franklin of Newport, who, however, predeceased her, so that it was, instead, inherited by her children by her first husband.

[1] *Art in America and Elsewhere*, Vol. XIII, No. 1, December, 1923.

[2] Antedating by ten years the portrait by Matthew Pratt which, in Dunlap (p. 110, footnote), is stated to be "the earliest authentic portrait of Benjamin Franklin, made about 1756."

Park did not, however, follow up the clues which suggest how it came about that Feke was commissioned to paint Benjamin Franklin's portrait for his older brother John. John Franklin had left Boston for Newport in 1718, and established himself there as a soap and candle maker, though he returned to Boston later in life. Benjamin, as a youth of eighteen, on his second voyage to Philadelphia in 1724, stopped at Newport to visit him. James Franklin, the printer-brother to whom Benjamin had been apprenticed as a youth and with whom he had quarrelled, also went to Newport about 1726, after he got into difficulties with the Boston authorities for his articles in the suppressed *New England Courant*. There he started the first newspaper in Rhode Island, the *Rhode Island Gazette*, and, after its speedy demise, made another try and established the longlived *Newport Mercury*, using the same press with which he had printed the *Courant* in Boston. In 1733 Benjamin Franklin, at the age of twenty-seven, again visited Newport on his third voyage to Philadelphia, after revisiting Boston; was reconciled to his brother James, with whom he spent several days; and took his nephew, the younger James, to Philadelphia with him for schooling and to be trained as a printer.

Benjamin Franklin, therefore, visited Newport at least twice, in 1724 and in 1733. He came to Boston again in 1743 and 1746, and might conceivably have stopped at Newport on either trip, but neither the biographies of Franklin nor his correspondence give any evidence that he was ever in Newport after 1733. It seems probable, therefore, that John Franklin, feeling affection for his younger brother, and proud of the distinction which he had already attained, commissioned Feke to paint his portrait when the artist visited Philadelphia in 1746, for it is entirely reasonable to suppose that both John and James Franklin were acquainted with Feke in Newport, and knew of his abilities as a painter.

Although Feke's early portraits of Mr. and Mrs. Tench Francis, referred to on pp. 38–39 are evidence that he had already some acquaintance in Philadelphia, this commission to paint Franklin's portrait may well have given Feke a valuable introduction to other Philadelphians of importance, and it may have led to Feke's portrait of Thomas Hopkinson. The latter, a judge of the Admiralty Court, was a friend and associate of Benjamin Franklin, being the first president of the Philosophical Society, which was established in Philadelphia early in 1744, of which Franklin was the originator and the first secretary. Hopkinson's portrait, now in the National Gallery at Washington, is unsigned and undated, but it is entirely typical of Feke's best manner. It is, however, an open question whether it was painted in 1746 or in 1750. Hopkinson was only thirty-seven in the earlier year, but his face in the portrait suggests a somewhat older man. Perhaps, therefore, 1750 is the more probable date.

The fine second portrait of Tench Francis showing him about fifty years of age, being both signed and dated, indubitably belongs to this second Philadelphia visit. Feke has depicted him in almost the same pose as in his smaller and earlier picture. Inasmuch as the early portraits of Mr. and Mrs. Tench Francis have descended in the Tilghman family, while the later ones have come down in other lines, it would seem that they must have been given at an early date to Ann Francis, who married James Tilghman in 1743. Such a gift would explain Feke's commission to paint a second pair of portraits in 1746. It is this second picture of Tench Francis which is referred to by J. Francis Fisher in his letter which opens the correspondence in Dawson's *Historical Magazine*. Mr. Fisher there writes of it as a "kit-kat," though in reality it is too large to be so described, being three-quarters length. The later portrait of Mrs. Francis, which descended to her daughter, Mrs. Shippen, is by no means as fine as that of her husband, but as it is almost identical in size and is so posed as to be a companion piece to his, it must be assigned to Feke's visit of 1746.

The second of Feke's portraits which is signed and dated 1746 is that of Mrs. Charles Willing, No. 1, a beautiful picture of a handsomely dressed matron. This is the portrait of the existence of which J. Francis Fisher informed Dunlap, causing him to give three lines to Feke in his *History of the Arts of Design in America,* though Dunlap misprinted her name as Welling. It descended in the Willing family and is now owned by Mr. Vincent Astor. It seems certain that Feke also painted a replica of this portrait, in which the figure is identical with the original, although the background is different and more pleasing. This replica has not been definitely located, though it is said to be in storage in New York, but the portrait of Mrs. Charles Willing has been reproduced in both of the variant forms, and the original gives no evidence that the background has been extensively repainted. If the theory of a repainted background is dismissed the only other explanation of the variant forms shown in the reproductions is that No. 2 is a replica of the original, presumably done by Feke in 1746 or 1750. There are also in existence two portraits which have been supposed to represent Mrs. Willing's daughters, Anne and Margaret. That identification is almost certainly mistaken. They perhaps represent two members of the McCall family and will be discussed in Chapter IX.

The third portrait which Feke signed and dated 1746 is that of Williamina Moore, a young woman of excellent family and of obvious intelligence, but plain of face and meager in person. Recognizing the pictorial insufficiency of the subject Feke evidently laid himself out on the accessories, and none of his portraits is a more carefully studied or more beautiful work of art.

Of the remaining unsigned and undated Philadelphia por-

MISS WILLIAMINA MOORE

traits, — those of Edward and Joseph Shippen, of Mr. and Mrs. William Peters, of Dr. Phineas Bond, of William Plumstead and of the woman who is called Mrs. Clement Plumstead (though it seems probable that it represents Miss Mary McCall who became Mrs. William Plumstead), of Miss Richea Meyers, and of Mrs. James Tilghman — the first two were certainly painted during Feke's third visit to Philadelphia in 1750, and the others, and perhaps that of Thomas Hopkinson as well, may as reasonably be assigned to 1750 as to 1746. They will, therefore, be discussed in Chapter IX.

From the character of the persons whom Feke painted in Philadelphia it is evident that by 1746 he had an established reputation there.

CHAPTER VII

THE SECOND BOSTON VISIT, 1748–1749

THERE is no evidence as to when Feke returned from Philadelphia to Newport, or how he was engaged during the year 1747. Either in that year or in 1749, after his second Boston visit, he probably painted the eleven extant portraits of Newport people which represent his latest work in the city of his home, save for the portraits of his wife and of himself which he left unfinished. As there seems no way of dating these eleven pictures it will be simpler to consider them as a group after the second Boston visit.

That visit must have been a prolonged one, occupying probably the greater part of the year 1748 and running into the early part of 1749, for in the course of it he painted more than twenty pictures, including several of his largest and most elaborate. They form by all odds the most important group of his works and, aside from any other of his pictures, are quite sufficient to establish his reputation as the foremost colonial artist before Copley. They include the four later Bowdoin portraits, all of them signed and three of them dated 1748; the three Apthorp portraits, of which two are signed and dated; the two Thacher portraits, signed, and dated, one 1748 and the other 1749; the Sewall portrait, dated 1748; and the unsigned and undated portraits of General Samuel Waldo; of Mrs. Benjamin Lynde, Jr.; of Mr. and Mrs. Ralph Inman (the latter twice); of Mr. and Mrs. John Rowe; of Gershom Flagg IV, and his wife, whose brother, Ebenezer Flagg, and cousin, Gershom Flagg III, Feke painted in Newport either shortly before or after his Boston visit; of Richard Saltonstall; of Robert Auchmuty; and of Thomas Goldthwait.

Of this group the four later Bowdoin portraits are much the best known. They are among his finest and most carefully studied pictures, though the flesh tints have either faded to a marked degree or been reduced by injudicious cleaning at some time in the past. They represent the two sons of James Bowdoin of Boston; William, aged 35, and his brother, who became much the more distinguished, James Bowdoin II, aged 21; Mrs. William Bowdoin, and Miss Elizabeth Erving, who married James Bowdoin about the time the pictures were painted. All four are full-dress portraits, the figures well posed, the fabrics painted with much skill, the backgrounds charming landscapes painted with more detail and light than in almost any other of Feke's pictures. They show the artist at the height of his technical skill, but convey the impression that these young people of wealth and elegance interested him less than the opportunity to show what he could do in the way of producing handsome pictures. Certainly their faces show far less of character than do a good many others of his portraits.

The portrait of General Samuel Waldo seems clearly to belong with this group of Bowdoin portraits, though it has long been attributed to Smibert. The late Lawrence Park was convinced that it was by Feke, and the picture bears every indication of his handiwork, save that it lacks any signature. For example, the technique with which the gold braid is painted is precisely that shown on the Bowdoin portraits. In addition it may be added that Waldo's second wife was a sister of Elizabeth Erving, to whom James Bowdoin was betrothed, and that the town in the background, though no doubt intended to represent Louisburg, "looks much like New York as we know it from the earliest engravings," [1] a view with which Feke was familiar. It is the largest of all Feke's extant works, besides being one of his finest. It is of

[1] *Art in America and Elsewhere*, VII, 217.

historical interest also as representing one of the popular heroes of the Louisburg expedition, a number of whom were painted in Boston after their triumphant return.

The three Apthorp portraits are hardly less admirable specimens. That of Charles Apthorp is perhaps most characteristic of the artist in its subdued coloring, and closely resembles the Wilkinson portrait in its use of table, inkstand, and quill as accessories, and the portrait of Isaac Stelle in costume, and the background of sea and hill. Apthorp was one of the leading figures in the Boston of his day. He came to America as commissioner for the king's military and naval forces, engaged extensively in trade, and became a very rich man. In its obituary notice of him the Portsmouth, New Hampshire, *Gazette* called him " the Greatest Merchant on this Continent." He and his wife, with their eighteen children, worshipped at King's Chapel, where they completely filled two of the largest pews, and there is a monument to his memory in the church, executed by Henry Cheere of London in the characteristic style of the eighteenth century. He and his wife were also painted by Blackburn. Feke's portrait of Mrs. Apthorp, with an open copy of *Paradise Lost* in her lap, is a capital example of his workmanship, and his picture of their daughter Grizzell, wife of Barlow Trecothick, painted on a nearly square canvas, is perhaps the loveliest of all his portraits of young women. She holds a book of music in her lap, and is the embodiment of dignity and grace as she looks out at the spectator. The flesh tints in these Apthorp portraits, as in those of the Bowdoins, have faded rather badly, suggesting that, at the time he was painting them, Feke was using paint which has not stood the test of time as well as that used in most of his other pictures.

Hardly less beautiful is the picture of Ruth Cunningham, who later became the wife of the patriot James Otis. She too holds an open book, with the artist's signature and the date painted across

MRS. BARLOW TRECOTHICK

the top of the left-hand page. The face is that of a handsome woman whose character and individuality are emphasized by her unusual dress and manner of doing her abundant brown hair. Smaller, and less striking, but with the face beautifully modeled and colored, is the portrait of Mrs. Benjamin Lynde, long attributed to Smibert. Smibert did paint the companion portrait of her husband, which is decidedly inferior, but that of Mrs. Lynde seems clearly to be Feke's. One may surmise either that Smibert's declining health prevented him from painting the wife, or that Feke's growing reputation in Boston caused the sitter to choose him instead. Mrs. Lynde lived in Salem, and it is, of course, possible that Feke journeyed thither to paint the picture, but no other portraits by him of Salem people are known except that of Judge Sewall, and it is much more probable that it was done in Boston, inasmuch as her father lived in adjacent Roxbury, and her husband, who was a distinguished lawyer and was later chief justice, would, like Judge Sewall, no doubt have occasion to visit Boston frequently. In coloring and manner the portrait is much like that of Mrs. Gershom Flagg IV, whose picture, with that of her husband, though unsigned, has always been known to be by Feke.

These last are among Feke's least pretentious pictures, but are among his best in characterization. Gershom Flagg IV was a man of means and position, but, among all Feke's sitters, he represents most definitely the sturdy Puritan type, as distinguished from the more official and Church of England set whom Feke chiefly painted in Boston. It was with the Flaggs that Feke left his early self-portrait, which has been inherited by their descendants. How Feke formed a connection with the Flaggs is not known, but they were close friends of the Apthorps, naming a daughter Grizzell Apthorp Flagg, and the brother of Gershom Flagg IV, Ebenezer, and a cousin, Gershom Flagg III, were both residents of Newport and were both painted by Feke.

The portrait of Thomas Goldthwait is a charming picture, painted in low tones, with much of the "pearliness" which is often a characteristic of Feke's work. It was long believed to be by Copley, and was included in Bayley's *Life and Works of Copley*. From the apparent age of the subject, however, the picture fits into Feke's Boston visit of 1748, and Mr. Bayley now attributes it to Feke. Very similar is the situation with regard to the fine portrait of Richard Saltonstall, which though unsigned, bears every other mark of Feke's workmanship. Saltonstall died while Copley was still under twenty, and the tradition that he painted it appears to have no foundation.

The Inman pair of portraits were identified as Feke's a number of years ago by Lawrence Park. That of Ralph Inman is pleasing; that of his wife is a more perfunctory portrait, which bears so close a resemblance to that of her (twin?) sister, Mrs. John Rowe, that the two are easily confused. There is a second portrait of Mrs. Inman (listed as Mrs. Inman, No. 2) which differs more from the first, not only in pose and costume, but in countenance, than one might expect, yet it seems clearly to be a good specimen of Feke's work, and the family tradition as to the identity of the subject is quite definite. It seems not unlikely that it may have been painted on order from Mrs. Inman's sister. While Mrs. Rowe's portrait has been mistakenly attributed to Copley, that of her husband, which has descended in another line, has carried the attribution to Feke in the family tradition. Though an unpretentious picture, of simple composition and modest dimensions, it is less conventional in pose and stronger in characterization than some of Feke's more elaborate works.

The Sewall and Thacher portraits are signed and dated. They are among his larger and more notable canvases. That of Judge Sewall shows a vigorous personality, standing, at three-quarters length. The Thacher pair are also fine, vigorous por-

MRS. RALPH INMAN (No. 2)

trayals, and the date of Mrs. Thacher's (1749) proves that Feke's visit of 1748 lasted into the beginning of the following year.

The signed and dated portrait of young Robert Auchmuty, though quiet and unpretentious, is like the portraits of the youthful James Bowdoin, Isaac Royall, and Edward and Joseph Shippen, in that it beautifully displays the artist's sympathetic skill in portraying intelligent and high-minded youth.

We would gladly know more of Feke's second Boston visit, but this apparently silent and unobtrusive man came and went without leaving a trace behind him, save the portraits which he painted. No notice of him has been found in the *Boston News-letter* nor in any letters or diaries which have come to light. The length of his stay, the number of pictures which he painted, and the character of his patrons, are sufficient testimony to the sucess of his visit. It seems certain that his personality must have commended itself. Clearly he made a striking impression on Dr. Alexander Hamilton when the latter saw him in Newport. And both in Philadelphia and in Boston he was patronized by the people of cultivation and distinction who recommended him to their kinsfolk and friends, so that he seems never to have resorted to advertising to secure sitters. Though his own dress, in both his self-portraits, is plain, and he wears no wig, which his abundant, dark waving hair made unnecessary, and though his family ties were with Quakers and Baptists who were given to simple ways of living even when well-to-do, he came of good stock, and must have acquired a considerable measure of cultivation. In all respects he was much superior to his contemporary Badger, the Boston portrait painter of humble station and limited outlook, and, no doubt, to the English itinerant Joseph Blackburn as well. Smibert had a wider reputation, but perhaps less personal presentability. It seems a legitimate surmise that Feke's patrons recognized him as a man whose personal qualities they respected and admired, and that he moved among them as a friend.

That Feke found Boston a pleasant place is also a legitimate surmise. It is altogether likely that he met Smibert during his visit of 1741, and presumably Peter Pelham also, for Boston was then a small place and he had interests in common with them. In 1748 Smibert was just closing his career as a painter; he died three years later after a period of poor health. He lived for a good many years (from at least as early as 1734 until his death) on the corner of Brattle and Court Streets, in the house which his wife had received from her father, as Feke lived in his wife's house at Newport. The house is said to have been previously used by Nathanael Emmons, and it was later occupied by John Trumbull and other artists, so that it was intimately associated with New England art throughout the eighteenth century.[1]

Peter Pelham, who had previously lived on Summer Street, married the widow Mary Copley in the summer of 1748, thereby becoming the stepfather of the eleven-year-old John Singleton Copley, and they moved into a house on the corner of what is now Congress Street, and Exchange Place,[2] not five minutes' walk from Smibert's home. Peter Pelham was less successful as a painter than Smibert, but he made a good many engravings, and

---

[1] Smibert's "painting room" was upstairs, perhaps above his shop, either in the house or in an adjoining building on Brattle St. Mr. Bayley, in *Five Colonial Artists of New England* (p. 340), writes, "Smibert's studio with connected shop was undoubtedly what today would be called an art centre in Boston. In his life it served for public distribution of prints and other imported works of art. After his death it was occupied by at least three artists, John Trumbull, John Johnston, and Washington Allston. The painting-room was mentioned by Charles Wilson Peale, when he wrote concerning his 1765 visit to Boston, as follows: 'Becoming a little acquainted with the owner of the shop, he told me that a relation of his had been a painter, and he said he would give me a feast: leading me upstairs introduced me into a painter's room, where were a number of pictures unfinished and some groups of figures: he had begun a piece, several of the heads painted, of the ancient philosophers: these were the last works of Smibert. He had been to Italy and spent a fortune in travelling to gain knowledge of the art. It was at this shop I heard of Mr. Copley.'"

[2] "Mrs. Mary Pelham (formerly the Widow Copley on the Long Wharff, Tabacconist) is removed into Lindel's Row, against the Quaker Meeting-House, near the upper end of King Street, Boston, where she continues to sell the best Virginia Tobacco, Cut, Pigtail and spun, of all sorts, by wholesale or Retail, at the cheapest rates." — Adv. in the *Boston Gazette*, July 12, 1748, quoted in *The Arts and Crafts of New England*, p. 286.

taught his precocious stepson the rudiments of his art. It is very difficult to believe that Feke spent many months at work in Boston without forming acquaintance with Pelham, and without young Copley's having seen him and heard his work discussed. Furthermore Copley began drawing when very young, and at an early age developed his marked powers of portraying the handsome fabrics which he loved. Feke had left behind him in Boston more than twenty portraits in his best manner, showing good draughtsmanship and much technical skill, which were owned by families of the same social group that presently began to employ Copley. These portraits were among the finest and most recently executed works of art in the city. They offered him the best models to study, and it is not without significance that in so many cases portraits now believed to be by Feke have been traditionally ascribed to Copley. Copley, in a word, began about where Feke left off, and it seems impossible that the youth eager to succeed in his profession should not have scanned very carefully the work of this painter whom he probably remembered personally and whose portraits represented the best and latest local achievements.

Many years after Copley's death his son, Lord Lyndhurst, wrote of him that he "was entirely self-taught, and never saw a decent picture, with the exception of his own, until he was nearly thirty years of age,"[1] when he first went to Europe in 1774. So far as his being self-taught is concerned this statement may be substantially correct. Even if Smibert or Feke, as his stepfather's friends, took an interest in the lad, he was doubtless too young for them to have given him any formal lessons. Badger and Blackburn were also painting in Boston and its vicinity in the seventeen-fifties. The former would have had little to teach Copley, and the latter did not reach Boston until about 1754, when Copley had begun painting portraits on his own account. One would

[1] Martha Babcock Amory, *The Domestic and Artistic Life of John Singleton Copley* (1882), p. 9.

suppose, however, that Peter Pelham, who died in 1751, when Copley was fourteen, might have given some instruction to his stepson who showed promise in the line of his own activities. But the statement that Copley "never saw a decent picture, with the exception of his own, until he was nearly thirty years old," is a sweeping generalization which is palpably false. Lyndhurst had a natural pride in his father's genius, which he sought to bring into relief by exaggerating the narrow provincialism of Copley's youth, and, though as a young man Lyndhurst had revisited the city of his birth, he evidently knew little of the conditions under which his father was brought up. Instead of never having seen a "decent picture" Copley would have had opportunity to see a fair number of very respectable portraits in Boston, including the one of Sir Richard Saltonstall attributed to Rembrandt, and that of Judge Paul Dudley by Kneller, and others in New York by the local artists of Dutch nativity or descent.[1] It is true that the paintings which he saw were almost entirely portraits, and that not until he went to Europe could he have seen more than a very few pictures, and those mediocre at best, representing landscapes or historical, religious or allegorical subjects.[2] It is only in refer-

[1] For corroboration see Isham, *American Painting*, p. 23, where the author discusses the artists who may have influenced Copley's youth. But he omits Feke altogether, and, I think, overemphasizes the possible influence of Blackburn. See also, in the same book, p. xv, where the author quotes "a recent critic" as saying that "the best of the American Colonial painters were but second-rate English painters." He continues, "but they were second-rate only if Reynolds and Gainsborough be placed in a class by themselves as alone first-rate. With the best of the others Copley and Stuart are substantially on an equality, and West, though now antiquated, was an important influence on the art of his time. That they were *English* painters, however, cannot be denied."

It may be added that Feke slightly antedates both Reynolds and Gainsborough and that his work compares not unfavorably with that of their English-born predecessors, Thomas Hudson and Joseph Highmore, both of whom were several years older than Feke, though they long outlived him. It should also be noted that the earliest portrait painters of New York, Couturier, Strycker, the Duyckincks, and the elder Vanderlyn, were not English but clearly Dutch in their artistic traditions.

[2] That he was familiar with an *engraving* of at least one famous picture is clear from his letter from Rome dated October 26, 1774, in which he speaks of "the sweet picture of the Virgin with Jesus by Raphael, . . . I mean the one that hung over our chimney." — Amory, *The Domestic and Artistic Life of Copley*, p. 38.

ence to paintings of this type that Lyndhurst's statement can be accepted as even partially true. Copley, in later life, himself believed that his best portraits were those which he painted in America before leaving for Europe.[1] In London, like West, he turned more to painting large historical or allegorical canvases, then highly praised but now held in less esteem. So far as Feke is concerned it is probably not too much to say that, next to the atmosphere of Peter Pelham's household in which young Copley lived for five impressionable years, his was the strongest artistic influence upon Copley's early work.

One would like much to know where Feke stayed during his Boston visit. Not a scrap of evidence has survived, but there is one possible clue upon which the imagination likes to dwell. When Feke returned to Newport he either left his own early self-portrait behind him, or sent it back to Gershom Flagg IV and his wife, to whose descendants it has been transmitted. No family tradition survives as to how or why they acquired it. Possibly Feke brought it with him to Boston as the only specimen of his work at hand to show to possible patrons, though it was but a juvenile production. But why did he leave it with the Flaggs, or send it to them later? Was it left as security for a loan which was never paid? That seems unlikely in view of the large amount of work which he did that year in Boston and of the fact that we have no other evidence of his ever being short of money. Did the Flaggs become so attached to him that he gave them, or they bought from him, this youthful picture? That might have happened if he had lodged with them during his visit. Gershom Flagg IV lived on Hanover Street, next door to "The Orange Tree" which stood on the corner of Hanover and Sudbury Streets, adjacent to Smibert's house. It was a location which would have suited Feke well, and the Flaggs were the sort of

[1] *Ibid.*, p. 20.

people who would have been congenial, Puritans, who, though prosperous, dressed plainly and lived more simply than their near kinsmen in Newport or than most of his Boston patrons. It is, at least, not impossible that it was with them that Feke made his home while in Boston.

GERSHOM FLAGG IV

CHAPTER VIII

LATEST WORK IN NEWPORT
1749–1750

It is to be supposed that Feke went home to Newport early in 1749 after his long stay in Boston, which must certainly have covered several months, and that he remained there until he went to Philadelphia in the spring of 1750. The eleven portraits of Newport people referred to on page 72 were presumably painted either during this interval, or in 1747 between his second Philadelphia and his second Boston visits. Only one of these pictures, that of Isaac Stelle, is signed, and none are dated, but the period during which they were painted can be guessed to within two or three years from their style and from the known age of the sitters.

That of Philip Wilkinson, now hanging in the Redwood Library at Newport, has been attributed to Smibert, but is clearly by Feke. Wilkinson was forty years old in 1750, when Smibert had ceased painting, and in the picture he appears to be about that age. The table with its hanging cloth, pewter inkstand and white quill pen, and the ship putting out to sea in the background, so closely resemble the accessories in the portrait of Charles Apthorp of Boston that one feels that the painter, having very recently used them successfully in the portrait of one prosperous merchant, repeated the same motifs in the portrait of another in a different town. Similarly the pose and the bad foreshortening of the left leg upon which the hand rests are repeated in the portrait of Gershom Flagg III of Newport. The head of Wilkinson, indeed, is not strongly characteristic of Feke's work. It represents a different type of sitter from his usual subjects, and one suspects that the artist may not have been altogether sympathetic with this red-headed, choleric Irishman, whose flushed face looks as though he had dined and wined rather too well.

The portrait of Isaac Stelle also resembles that of Charles Apthorp in pose, and in the way in which the costume is painted, the mannerisms being closely similar in both pictures. The face is that of a vain, shrewd, hard man, and his ledgers, now in the possession of the Newport Historical Society, disclose his trafficking with Antigua for molasses and rum, with at least one venture in negro slaves. Isaac Stelle visited Antigua in 1750, and the portrait must have been painted before he went thither. It was originally a fine portrait, in Feke's latest manner. Unfortunately it is now in poor condition. It was signed "R. Feke, Pinx.," but several of the letters have been rubbed off by abrasions. It has also been repainted in spots, the culprit being disclosed by the words in the back, "Touch up by W. O. Hathaway." Its condition, however, is not nearly so bad as that of the companion piece, his wife's portrait, which is in a ruinous state. At some time in the past this has been put into a smaller frame, the canvas being folded back with disastrous results to the paint. Several holes have been crudely patched. But worst of all, the whole face and figure have been thickly daubed over with muddy paint by the same Hathaway, a Newport house painter who took the opportunity to advertise his misdemeanor by painting on the back another notice of his "touch up" done in 1882. Only the vista behind the figure has escaped. It is entirely characteristic of Feke, as is the pose, and the costume is of the same period as that of the sitter's husband. It may, therefore, be assumed that beneath the superimposed daubs there lies the handiwork of Feke himself.

Seven of the eight other portraits of Newport citizens are well preserved. They represent Ebenezer Flagg and his wife, and Gershom Flagg III, respectively a brother and a sister-in-law,

ISAAC STELLE

and an older cousin of Gershom Flagg IV; a woman called Mrs. Tweedy; and Mr. and Mrs. John Channing, whom Feke painted twice. The smaller and later portrait of John Channing was lost many years ago, and it is not known whether it is now extant. Mrs. Ebenezer Flagg was the daughter of Governor Richard Ward of Rhode Island, who was half-brother of the distinguished merchant and philanthropist Henry Collins, for whom Feke painted the portraits of Rev. John Callender and Rev. Thomas Hiscox in 1745. Collins died, unmarried, in the house of his niece, Mrs. Flagg, and these Flagg portraits, and that of Hiscox, passed to her descendants.

As already stated, Feke painted two pairs of portraits of Mr. and Mrs. John Channing. It is difficult to determine which pair was painted first, as the only basis for an opinion is a comparison of the apparent age of Mrs. Channing in the two pictures of her. As she appears slightly more mature in the smaller of the two portraits representing her, the pictures showing the couple at three-quarters length may be tentatively assigned to 1747, soon after their marriage. These portraits are dignified and adequate, though not so pleasing as some of his other works. In the smaller portraits only the head and bust of the sitters was shown. Many years ago the portrait of John Channing was lost or stolen during the removal of household goods from one state to another, and it has never been traced. The portrait of his wife is in the hands of a direct descendant in a different line from that which now owns the large pictures. While it is an unpretentious picture, it is lifelike, well colored, and pleasing. Probably it dates from about 1750.

The portrait of Mrs. Flagg, like that of her husband, has been attributed to Copley, but she is clearly too young to have been painted by him, being shown as a woman in her middle thirties, which she would have been between 1745 and 1750, whereas Copley would have been only thirteen years old at the latter date.

In addition the picture is distinctly in Feke's manner, though not a conspicuously successful picture. It may also be noted that she is the only one of his women sitters shown with fair hair and complexion, though she has brown eyes. The portrait of her husband is one of the finest of all Feke's works. The pose is conventional, but the costume is beautifully painted — a white wig, black waistcoat, and a light gray coat lined with red silk. The head is no less admirable, well modeled, freshly colored, showing the pleasing countenance of a vigorous and high-minded man. None of Feke's portraits of men surpass this one.

The portrait of his cousin, Gershom Flagg III, shows in equal degree Feke's skill in painting fabrics, but the head, though fine, is somewhat less pleasing, and the seated figure is marred by the same foreshortening of the crossed legs which characterizes the Wilkinson portrait, which, as already noted, closely resembles it in this respect and in the pose.

The last of the portraits to be assigned to Feke's late period in Newport is that known as "Mrs. Tweedy," one of the most beautiful of all his pictures. It is now owned by the Rhode Island School of Design, but was bought in 1907 by a previous owner, who passed on no information about it. The identity of the subject is uncertain, but she was probably a member of the Tweedy family which was prominent in Newport before the Revolution but which later removed to Providence. The portrait has been attributed to Smibert, but it is too fine to be his work, and is strongly marked by Feke's characteristic touches. It represents a woman of noble aspect, with an enigmatic half-smile suggestive of Mona Lisa's. She is handsomely gowned in fabrics rendered with much skill. There seems little reason to doubt that the picture is one of the latest of Feke's works at Newport.

MRS. JOHN CHANNING (No. 1)

CHAPTER IX

THE THIRD PHILADELPHIA VISIT,
SPRING OF 1750

THAT Feke paid a third visit to Philadelphia, in the spring of 1750, is proved not only by the existence of at least two portraits, — those of the youthful brothers, Edward and Joseph Shippen, — which could have been painted only in that year, but by the entry in the diary of John Smith of Philadelphia noting that on April 7th of that year, he and his brother-in-law, William Logan, "went to Fewke's the painter's and viewed several pieces and faces of his painting." [1] This is the second of the two references to Feke by his contemporaries which have come to light, and, like that in the *Itinerarium* of Dr. Alexander Hamilton, it was not printed until this century. Unfortunately it does not tell us much, not even whether Feke himself was actually in Philadelphia at the time. It seems reasonable, however, to interpret the entry as implying that Feke had journeyed thither in the winter or early spring, either to execute commissions already promised or in the hope of further patronage as a consequence of his successful visit four years earlier. Even if he was not actually present at the moment when Smith and Logan visited his studio, he must have been there earlier, to paint the portraits which date from this year, to arrange his little exhibition, and because it would have hardly been practicable or profitable for him to have maintained quarters there where his pictures could be shown in his absence.

[1] *Hannah Logan's Courtship* (ed. Albert Cook Myers, Philadelphia, 1904), p. 290. In the footnote giving the dates of Feke's birth and death the Editor has confused the painter with his father; so also in the list of illustrations.

One would gladly know what the pictures were which John Smith saw. When he says "several pieces and faces," does he mean that there were a number of paintings other than portraits, "pieces" like "The Judgment of Hercules," for example? If so, they were doubtless pictures which Feke had carried with him for exhibition and sale, whereas the "faces" were presumably the portraits which he had recently finished and which he was showing before sending them to their owners, though it is possible that he borrowed a few of his portraits of 1746 for exhibition.

The portrait of Edward Shippen, which must certainly date from 1750, is one of Feke's most beautiful works. It shows a handsome, debonair youth with a dimpled chin, elegantly dressed in a dark blue velvet coat, lined with pink silk, and a pearl gray satin waistcoat. Young Shippen in 1750 was just turned twenty-one and had recently returned from London where he had studied law for two years at the Middle Temple. No doubt his clothes represent the latest London style. Family tradition says that the picture was painted in England, and while a youth of his station might have had his portrait done by an English painter on an order from his parents, the tradition is supported by no documentary evidence and is probably nothing more than the guess of later generations who had forgotten the name of Feke. On the other hand all the evidence points to Feke as the painter. Shippen returned shortly before Feke's visit. Feke was already known to the Shippen connection, having in 1746 painted the portrait of his aunt, Mrs. Charles Willing, besides the portraits in the family of Mr. and Mrs. Tench Francis, whose daughter Margaret, Edward Shippen married three years later. And even were these links lacking the portrait bears every mark of Feke's brush. It strongly resembles that of young Isaac Royall, painted nine years earlier, though far more accomplished in technique. The look of the eyes, the painting of the fabrics, the subdued back-

EDWARD SHIPPEN

ground, all are preëminently characteristic of Feke. It is clearly one of his latest, most accomplished, and most lovable pictures. Edward Shippen was doubly fortunate in being thus portrayed in his youth by Feke and no less finely in his old age by Gilbert Stuart.

At the same time Feke must have painted, as a companion piece to the portrait of Edward Shippen, that of his younger brother Joseph, then about eighteen years of age and a student at Princeton. He is shown facing in the other direction, holding a book. His dark hair is brushed back from his fine forehead and he is less handsomely dressed than his older brother, but he carries himself with a very similar air. This portrait was unfortunately destroyed by fire a few years ago.

Mrs. James Tilghman was Ann, daughter of Mr. and Mrs. Tench Francis, and an older sister of Margaret, who married Edward Shippen. She was born in 1727, married at sixteen, and was mother of two children before she was twenty. Her portrait has come down to us in two forms, so nearly identical as to suggest that the second is a contemporary replica by the original artist. She is shown as a robust young matron, handsomely gowned and holding a flower in her hand. In face and figure she strongly resembles her mother. It seems hardly possible that even her early marriage would have given her so matronly an appearance in 1746, when she was only nineteen, but by 1750 she might well have looked as she is portrayed in these pictures.

The portrait of Thomas Hopkinson, the friend of Franklin and first president of the Philosophical Society is also a fine picture, though lacking Shippen's youthful charm. The only reason for assigning it to Feke's third rather than to his second Philadelphia visit is the apparent age of the subject, who appears too old for the thirty-seven years which he would have attained in 1746.

The same reason is the ground for provisionally assigning to the visit of 1750 the portraits of William Peters and his wife. These are smaller and rather mediocre paintings in which the artist seems to have been little interested. At the Historical Society of Pennsylvania, where they hang, they are attributed to Hesselius, but that of Mrs. Peters strongly resembles Feke's two portraits of Mrs. Tench Francis in pose and manner. It is hardly open to doubt that both are inferior works by Feke. In the same year is probably to be assigned the portrait of Dr. Phineas Bond, a leading Philadelphia physician, who, in 1750 would have been thirty-three, his apparent age in the picture. The pose of the figure and painting of the head closely resembles that of Tench Francis, No. 2, while his right hand, holding a cane, is almost identical with that shown in the portrait of William Bowdoin. In 1748 Dr. Bond married Williamina Moore, whom Feke had painted two years earlier, so that it would have been natural for him to have employed Feke when the latter returned to Philadelphia in 1750.

The portrait of William Plumstead is a good example of Feke's art, the face being very well modeled and expressive. Plumstead was elected mayor of Philadelphia for the first time in 1750, and perhaps this portrait also dates from that year. It now hangs in the Historical Society, on loan from the Academy of Fine Arts, to which it was bequeathed by a descendant of William Plumstead.

Near it hangs the portrait of a woman, evidently the work of Feke, done either in 1746 or 1750. The figure is stiffly and awkwardly posed against a pilaster, like that of Mrs. Tench Francis (No. 2), but the head is finely painted, representing a handsome, robust woman in her twenties. All the mannerisms are those of Feke, and, in spite of the stiffness of its figure, it ranks among his finer and more strongly characterized works. The identity of the subject is uncertain. On the relined back in recent times has been painted the preposterous inscription, "Mrs. Clement Plumstead by Sir Peter Lely." The portrait cannot represent any Mrs. Clement Plumstead, nor can it be by Lely. Clement Plumstead was a Quaker, who married three times and died in 1745. Lely died about two years after Clement Plumstead's first wife was born; and the dress of the sitter is that of a woman of fashion of the seventeen-forties. Clement Plumstead's third wife, who survived him, would have been little likely to have her portrait painted in any case, and certainly not handsomely gowned in gay colors soon after his death. Perhaps the best guess is that the portrait represents Mary McCall, who was born in Philadelphia on March 31, 1725, and who married William Plumstead as his second wife on September 27, 1753. She was the seventh of fourteen children of the Mr. and Mrs. George McCall whose portraits are discussed on pages 39–40. If Feke painted the mother on his earliest visit to Philadelphia, he might well have painted the yet unmarried daughter on either the second or third visit. The probability that this is the correct identification is increased by tracing the line of descendants of William and Mary (McCall) Plumstead. Of several children the youngest, George, alone left issue, by his wife Helena Ross. Of their children only one, Anna Margaretta, who married John H. Scheetz, left issue. Of their four children none left issue, and the last survivor, Helena Ross Scheetz left these portraits to the Pennsylvania Academy of Fine Arts.[1] It would

---

[1] The portraits of William Plumstead and of the so-called Mrs. Clement Plumstead were exhibited by Miss Scheetz at the Loan Exhibition of Historical Portraits at the Pennsylvania Academy of Fine Arts, December 1887–January 1888. With them she also exhibited another portrait listed in the *Catalogue* as "No. 344, Plumstead, Mrs. William; J. Hesselius; Bust, facing right, 25 × 30, 1753." This portrait has not been located. One is tempted to surmise that this picture may really have represented William Plumstead's mother or stepmother, the second or third Mrs. Clement Plumstead, painted by either Gustavus or John Hesselius, but that later generations have confused her with Plumstead's wife, so that an exchange of labels has occurred. In such case the missing portrait might well have represented a Mrs. Clement Plumstead, and the portrait by Feke would be correctly described, as suggested above, as representing Mary McCall who became Mrs. William Plumstead in 1753.

have been quite natural for a portrait of Mary McCall to have come down in that line of descent. In the collections of the Historical Society of Pennsylvania there is also a small oval reproduction (apparently from a miniature), representing Mrs. William McCall. While by a different hand the person shown may well represent the same individual as Feke's portrait.

The portrait thus tentatively identified as representing Mary McCall bears a very striking resemblance to another Philadelphia picture, one of a pair supposed to represent Anne and Margaret Willing, daughters of Mrs. Charles Willing. Margaret Willing married Robert Hare, and the two pictures are now owned by the Hare family, which came into possession of them by inheritance some forty years ago. The portraits show two young women who look enough alike to be sisters, but that of the young woman now called Margaret Willing resembles even more closely the portrait of Anne McCall. The beautiful costume is identical in the two pictures, and the facial resemblance is such as to suggest that if the same young woman was not the subject of both, at least the subjects were closely related. Furthermore the identification of these portraits as representing the Willing sisters must be set aside as untenable because Anne and Margaret Willing were not born until the early seventeen-fifties, and would not have reached the age of the persons shown in these pictures until twenty years later. The present owners have accepted a late family tradition as to their identity and have tentatively attributed them to Copley, dating them from the early seventeen-seventies. They bear no marks of Copley's workmanship of that period, however, whereas they are strongly characteristic of Feke, and the costume is that of the seventeen-forties. Finally, the identification of the subjects as Anne and Margaret Willing rests on nothing more certain than a modern surmise. The pictures were shown at the Loan Exhibition of Historical Portraits at the Pennsylvania Academy of Fine

MISS MARY McCALL (?)

(Mrs. Clement Plumstead, so-called)

Arts, 1887–88, by the Mrs. Charles Willing of the nineteenth century who then owned them, and in the *Catalogue* each is listed as "Miss Willing?" It is evident that there was then uncertainty as to the identity of the subjects. Mr. Charles Henry Hart, in his notes in the *Catalogue*, called attention to their similarities to the portrait of Anne McCall (listed there as Mrs. Clement Plumstead) saying, "There is a striking resemblance in the subjects, as in the work." On all these grounds the identification of these pictures as representing the Willing sisters must be set aside. Perhaps the best guess is that they depict two daughters of the McCall family, and passed into the Willing family when a granddaughter of Mrs. George McCall married a son of Mrs. Charles Willing. They are fine pictures, that called Margaret Willing being particularly pleasing.

It was presumably in the spring of 1750 that Feke also painted the portraits of William Nelson and his wife, of Virginia. William Nelson was a conspicuous person in that colony, and his picture is an excellent example of Feke's work. No other portraits of Virginians painted by Feke have yet come to light, nor any evidence that the artist travelled south of Philadelphia in the colonies, so that the most reasonable explanation of the pictures is that the Nelsons made a journey to Philadelphia and seized the opportunity of having these portraits done.

The last picture assignable to this third visit of Feke's to Philadelphia is his striking portrait of Miss Richea Meyers (or Mears), a young Jewess who later married Bernard Gratz. The portrait shows a handsome young woman with dark hair and complexion, dressed in red, and the pose and costume strongly resemble the portrait of Hannah Flagg.

This closes the list of the Philadelphia portraits which at the present time can be attributed to Feke. The number is so small —the list making only twenty-five in all, including the replica of the portrait of Mrs. James Tilghman, for his three visits of about 1740, of 1746, and of 1750 — that it is difficult to believe that he did not paint a number of others. He painted as many pictures, including several of his largest, on his second visit to Boston in 1748. Probably, therefore, others are yet to be discovered which were done in Philadelphia.

CHAPTER X

DISAPPEARANCE AND DEATH

WE HAVE no knowledge of what happened to Robert Feke after his visit to Philadelphia in the spring of 1750. No portraits by him are known which can plausibly be assigned to a later date, with the possible exceptions of the pictures of his wife and himself and one or two of the late Newport portraits, already discussed, which might have been painted later in 1750 or even early in 1751. With the entry in John Smith's diary he disappears from the sight of man and we are left with no certain record of whither he went, of how or when he died. We are dependent on a rather unstable family tradition, orally transmitted for more than a century, upon which to erect a reasonable surmise as to the probable close of his career.

It seems certain that Feke died at the height of his powers, not long after John Smith and William Logan visited his studio, but the intervening period may have been but a few months, or may possibly have extended to November, 1752. It is not unreasonable to assume that Feke returned from Philadelphia to Newport, because his youngest child, Charles, named for Feke's second brother, was born after the date of John Smith's visit to Feke's studio in Philadelphia. The precise date of Charles Feke's birth has not, indeed, been ascertained, but the *Newport Mercury*, recording his death on April 25, 1822, states that he was in his seventy-second year, which seems clearly to imply that his birth took place later than April, 1750. It would have been natural for the father to have come home for the expected event, and to have lingered in Newport through the summer and fall of 1750, and perhaps into the early part of 1751.

If this assumption be correct, it is to the last weeks of his residence in Newport that the unfinished portrait of his wife and its companion piece, his unfinished late self-portrait, can most reasonably be assigned. He completed the heads and the upper part of each figure and outlined the rest. The pictures descended in the family of one of his daughters until that branch died out, when they were purchased, some seventy years ago, by Mr. Bullock of Providence, whose wife was a descendant of Feke's in another line. Disliking their incomplete appearance Mr. Bullock caused another painter to finish the pictures. It is unfortunate that this should have occurred, as they would have been much more interesting as Feke had left them.

The portrait of Mrs. Feke shows a very erect and capable-looking Quakeress dressed in gray silk with white kerchief and cap, who appears older than the thirty-two years she would have attained in 1750, — but she had had heavy family responsibilities since her marriage, bearing five children in eight years, and with her husband absent often and for long periods. Her face is plain, and somewhat austere, but fine in expression, full of character and not unkindly. The head and shoulders are clearly Feke's own untouched work. The late self-portrait is even more interesting. It is painted from almost exactly the same viewpoint as the early self-portrait of twenty-five years before, and unmistakably depicts the same individual in middle life, the abundant, dark hair somewhat thinner on top of the head, the face more full and sophisticated, the dark beard showing through the skin. He is plainly dressed in dark clothes and in his left hand holds his palette and brushes. It would seem, as Poland suggests, that he wished to be remembered as a painter.

Feke's failure to complete these pictures raises many questions. Was he at work upon them when an invitation reached him to revisit Philadelphia at once to accept fresh commissions, and

ROBERT FEKE (THE LATE SELF-PORTRAIT)

did he never return to Newport from Philadelphia? Or did he paint them after the Philadelphia visit, as suggested above, before sailing from Newport for Bermuda or Barbados, leaving them to be finished on his return because his ship left before he had time to complete them? Were they painted as a parting gift to his family because he was seeking a warmer climate on account of ill health and, as Poland suggests, had a presentiment that he would never return? We have, at present, no answer to these questions.

"S. F." in Dawson's *Historical Magazine*[1] says, "His health declining he sought the milder climate of Bermuda where he died at about the age of forty four," but "S. F." is certainly inaccurate in some of his other statements about Feke. Drake and Tuckerman both give the place of his death as Barbados, though without indicating any authority for the statement, and in other respects clearly drawing their information from the correspondence in Dawson's *Historical Magazine*. The similarity of names might easily lead an inaccurate writer to substitute Barbados for Bermuda, or, as easily, might have led "S. F." to write Bermuda, and he may have given ill health as the reason for Feke's going thither because it seemed the only obvious one.

That Bermuda was really his destination and the place of his death is open to grave question. So far as Feke's alleged ill health is concerned it can only be said that the late self-portrait, certainly painted shortly before his departure, portrays a healthy rather than a sickly person. Furthermore the church registers at Bermuda have been carefully searched without revealing any trace of Feke's burial there. Nor have any portraits been found in Bermuda which can possibly be from his hand, though there are a dozen or more by Joseph Blackburn. In addition it may be stated that there was comparatively little trade between Bermuda

[1] See Appendix A.

and the continental ports at that period, and that there is no
other record of persons going to Bermuda for reasons of health
before the very end of the eighteenth century.

On the other hand there was constant traffic between Barbados and New England. Ships from Newport, engaged in the
now notorious but then complacently accepted triangular slave
trade, must have frequented Barbados as they did Antigua, landing slaves there and carrying sugar and molasses back to Newport. Though we have no knowledge where Feke's voyages as a
"mariner" may have taken him, one or more trips to Barbados
would have been entirely possible. Furthermore, there was a
prosperous English family named Feake resident in Barbados
from at least as early as 1668 until as late as 1726, and perhaps
until after 1750, some of whom were Quakers.[1] No blood relationship between them and Robert Feke has yet been established,
but the name is unusual, and they probably had a remote common origin in England. Barbados at that time was still a rich and
prosperous colony, where Feke might well hope to find commissions for portraits. And finally, if ill health were a motive for
seeking a milder climate, Barbados would have offered one even
warmer than Bermuda. On several grounds, therefore, it would
seem much more probable that Barbados was his destination,
and only positive evidence would lead one to accept Bermuda
instead.

Unfortunately no evidence of Feke's presence in Barbados has
yet been discovered. If he went thither in search of work, no portraits by him are now known on the island. That, however, is no
proof that he may not have painted a number of pictures there,
for, after the commercial decline of Barbados, the wealthier merchants returned to England or migrated elsewhere, and would
naturally have taken their family portraits with them.

[1] See Appendix B.

Of the various Feakes whose names occur in the local records at Barbados only one, a *Richard* Feak who was buried at the parish of St. Michael on November 13, 1752, can possibly be identified with Robert Feke. The same name occurs more than eighty years earlier in the baptismal records of 1668 and 1670, in which a Richard Feake appears as the father of Margaret and Mary, children baptized in those years. As this earlier Richard Feake must have been born at least as early as 1650, and probably as early as 1645, it is most improbable that he survived until 1752. No other Richard Feake is recorded, and it is just possible that in this burial entry *Richard* is a scribal error for *Robert*. A careless clerk, noting the burial of a person little known to him, might jot the name down as R. Feak, and, entering the record a few days afterward with a vague recollection of the former Richard in his mind, might write *Richard* by mistake for *Robert*.

In addition to the assumption that such an error took place there is the further difficulty about the date, 1752, since the date of Robert Feke's death has been assumed to be 1750, when he "was about the age of 44." The date of 1750, however, appears to rest wholly upon family tradition. It is found nowhere in print or in any known written record until more than a century after the event. Now where an exact date is not written down it is easily forgotten, and, in oral transmission, November 13, 1752, might soon become "about 1750." Too much weight, therefore, should not be placed upon this discrepancy. If Feke lingered in Newport until early in the year 1751 and then sailed for Barbados in search either of health or work, he might quite conceivably have stayed there for either reason until death overtook him eighteen months later. Until further and less dubious evidence appears, one can only say that the presumption seems to favor Barbados as Feke's destination, and that it is at least possible that he died there as late as November, 1752. No will by him was recorded at Newport, nor any other evidence of his death earlier than the marriage certificates of his daughters in 1767, in which he is described as "Robert Feke, Mariner, deceased."

It is obvious that the foregoing surmise that Feke went to Barbados and died there lacks any positive evidence whatever, and is based only upon conjectures. The best that can be said for it is that it is the most plausible guess to be made on the basis of the surviving traditions. If it is rejected, we are left completely in the dark as to his fate. We have only the family tradition that he went somewhere on a voyage, from which he did not return. Perhaps he died at sea without reaching his destination. At present all that we know is that after 1750 he disappears from sight into an unknown grave far from home, leaving behind him only his painted canvases to be the mute witnesses of his silent, unobtrusive but fruitful career.[1]

It is evident that, as was said at the beginning of this study, the written records upon which to build the story of his career are very few and meagre. Though his extant portraits suggest many clues as to his activities, it remains true that for the most part we are dependent upon surmise and conjecture. Yet from the known facts it is possible to get some idea of the man. We know his ancestry — his English forebears who were goldsmiths, his great-grandfather the restless Puritan pioneer, his Quaker grandparents, his father the Baptist minister. His career testifies to his own independent and restless spirit. We may safely assume that he was brought up to be thoroughly familiar with the Bible, and we know from his acquaintance with *Pamela Andrews* and with Shaftestury's *Characteristicks* that he read something of the best contemporary literature. If he read those books he probably read a good many others.

[1] Mr. John Hill Morgan, of New York, in the spring of 1929 made an independent investigation of the records at Barbados without discovering any trace of him nor did he find any portraits which could be assigned to him. He is inclined to believe that Feke never went to Barbados at all.

We know how he looked from his two self-portraits, one painted at the beginning, the other at the end of his professional career, and from the written testimony of Dr. Alexander Hamilton. Not a little of his character is also suggested by his marriage at the age of thirty-seven to a Quakeress aged twenty-four. That action suggests sobriety of life, good principles, and romance well controlled by common sense. Eleanor Cozzens was not the kind to have married a loose-living ne'er-do-weel. His adherence to the church of his father, even if he was not a church member, indicates a man of character, though his views may have been liberal for his day. Finally, one may guess much from the portraits which he painted. His long, steady gaze read well the characters of his sitters, especially in the case of the men. He portrayed the leading men and women of Boston, Newport, and Philadelphia with serene dignity and often with charm, and he seems to have taken greatest pains in picturing the people who were most worth while; at least his finest characterizations are those of the more outstanding personalities among his sitters. He becomes, therefore, something more for us than the mere shadow of a name, and stands out, if not in clear perspective, at least as a very creditable representative of the artistic life in the colonial America of the first half of the eighteenth century.

CHAPTER XI

FEKE'S PLACE AS AN ARTIST

FEKE's portraits, from the early self-portrait of about 1725 down to his latest ones of about 1750, all show certain marked characteristics, although his technique developed notably in his last seven or eight years. Lawrence Park says of him, "He was a good draughtsman, and succeeded in producing lifelike expressions. In his poses he followed the conventions of his and earlier periods, but his subjects are dignified and well placed upon the canvas, and the painting of the elaborate costumes of satin and velvet is convincing. It is evident that some of the flesh tones have faded,[1] producing a pallor which did not exist in the pictures as originally painted, but the ensemble is attractive, and many of his works are suffused with a pearly tonality which renders them distinctive and appealing. The paint is usually thinly applied, and the method shows confidence and training."

His pictures are painted in quiet colors on finely woven canvas. The backgrounds are often a neutral brown, shaded so as to bring into relief the lighted and the shadowed sides of the subject's face, or, if a curtain or a distant vista is shown, it is so subdued in tone as to be wholly subordinate to the figure set against it. The distant views, where the sea and a ship are shown, — as in the Apthorp, Stelle, and Wilkinson portraits, — have a good deal of charm in spite of their rather gray, unlighted tone, but his trees and vegetation are often, though not always, painted in a somewhat rudimentary fashion. The accessories are frequently

---

[1] Park had particularly in mind the Apthorp and the Bowdoin portraits, of which this is true, but in many of Feke's pictures the flesh tones are still fresh and vital.

repeated, especially the use of a table covered with a cloth which
varies in color from portrait to portrait. The bust portraits are
usually set in painted spandrels, after the fashion of the day. The
three-quarters or full-length portraits usually show some sort of
vista behind the figure.

It has been said of Smibert that "it is characteristic of his
times that his sitters were chiefly the New England divines, those
leaders of a stern theocracy that exercised political as well as
spiritual authority." [1] Smibert did paint a number of the New
England clergy, because they were among the leading people of
the day. Even as regards Smibert, however, the generalization is
far too sweeping, for he painted many more pictures of men who
were not ministers, as well as of women. Whatever may have
been the case with Smibert, Feke is definitely known to have portrayed only two ministers, Callender and Hiscox, both of whom
were Rhode Island Baptists, though the portrait of the Newport
Congregationalist, Rev. Nathaniel Clap, may be tentatively assigned to him. The rest of his subjects were officials like Benjamin Franklin, Thomas Hopkinson, the Judge of the Admiralty
Court of Pennsylvania, and Charles Apthorp, the Commissioner
of the British Naval and Military forces of Boston; or persons of
wealth like the Royalls and the Bowdoins; or well-to-do merchants like the Flaggs, Philip Wilkinson, and Isaac Stelle. It was
persons of this type, and their wives and daughters, that Feke was
called upon to paint. Many of them, especially those who held
official positions, were members of the Church of England. As
has been pointed out, in neither Newport nor Philadelphia did he
paint any Quakers except his own wife. His portrait of Gershom
Flagg IV is his best, though not his only representation of the
plainer Puritan type, but most of his Boston subjects were of
Puritan descent.

---

[1] Caffin, *Story of American Painting*, p. 5. Caffin is grossly inaccurate and ill informed about the colonial period.

Feke was more successful in drawing his men than he was his women sitters. His men are often strongly individualized, and the painter shows a genuine insight into their several characters. His women are much more conventional and display less individuality, at least in the earlier portraits. Feke's only known pictures of children — those of his little niece "Phiany" and the infant daughter of Isaac Royall — show how slight was his familiarity with the anatomy and expression of the very young, at least in the years preceding his late marriage. Probably, in view of his seafaring life and his late marriage, Feke had been much more with men than with women and children, and understood them better.

The costumes of his men vary very greatly with the sitter. Feke, in both his self-portraits, and the Puritan Gershom Flagg IV are very simply attired in plain dark clothes with a plain white neckcloth. The ministers are shown in gowns and bands. On the other hand his merchants and officials are represented in full dress, sometimes soberly but handsomely dressed, as in the case of Philip Wilkinson and Benjamin Franklin, sometimes brilliantly attired like the youthful Royall and the Bowdoins and Waldo, wearing costly wigs, velvet or broadcloth coats lined with bright silk and with wide back-turned cuffs, satin waistcoats embroidered with broad gold braid, elaborately ruffled shirts, showing through the waistcoat left half unbuttoned with a calculated appearance of negligence. In those portraits the painter, like Sargent in our own day, sometimes gives the impression of being more interested in painting fabrics than in portraying their wearer.

His men are for the most part posed in the conventional attitudes which were no doubt familiar to Feke from the work of Smibert. The standing figures commonly have one hand resting upon the hip, holding back the coat to display the waistcoat, often with the index and the middle finger straight while the

others are turned under. The other hand is thrust into the waistcoat, or rests upon a table, or is half open as in gesture. Like the
accessories, the positions taken by the subjects are frequently repeated, although they show quite as much variety and originality
as other eighteenth-century portraits before Copley.

His women sitters are even more conventional in costume and
pose. With a few notable exceptions one might almost say that
they all wear the same dress — the very long, tightly laced waist,
moderately low-cut bodice bordered with a white muslin or lace
edge, and very full skirts. The sleeves come a little below the
elbow, showing a white undersleeve below. The cut and style are
practically the same in all, although the color varies, — red
green, and blue,—and, in the case of those who were most distinc-
tively ladies of fashion, as with Mrs. Wanton or Mrs. Charles
Willing, the gown is of brocade or of watered silk with lace edging.
Even Feke's Quaker wife wears substantially the same type of
gown in gray silk, with the addition of the Quaker under-cap and
a white scarf about the neck. In a few cases, however, like Miss
Ruth Cunningham, Mrs. Tweedy, and Miss Williamina Moore,
the dress is much more distinctive, probably because of the more
marked individual taste of those ladies themselves. In the case
of the bust portraits the lower arms and hands are not shown, but
in the large pictures the sitter holds a flower or fruit, a book or a
fan. Most of his women, after the Royall portrait, have a dark
curl falling over either the right or the left shoulder. Perhaps the
fashion came in during the early seventeen-forties. In many
cases he represents them with a tilt of the head which seems characteristic of him, as is his treatment of the eyes in both his men
and women. This last is perhaps Feke's most marked manner-
ism, the eyes being large and oval. Another characteristic of his
portraits is his way of placing the head rather too high on the
canvas. Most of these conventionalities of dress and pose Feke

shares with Smibert, who clearly influenced his earlier work, but in his later work Feke far surpassed Smibert in his mastery of technique, in the dignity which he gave his subjects, and in his power of characterization.

In the history of colonial painting in New England, Feke is the connecting link between Smibert and Copley, as in lesser degree he may be regarded as a link between Gustavus Hesselius and Benjamin West in Philadelphia. His connections with these latter painters may, it is true, have been slight. It is not unreasonable, however, to suppose that Feke, during some one of his visits to Philadelphia, would have sought out Hesselius and become acquainted with his work, which is roughly comparable to that of Smibert. It is less likely that Benjamin West ever saw Feke, since, at the time of the latter's last visit to Philadelphia, West was under twelve years of age and was presumably still living at Springfield, Pennsylvania. But West later worked at his profession in Philadelphia before going to Europe in 1760 at the age of twenty-two, and might quite well have seen some of Feke's portraits, which were assuredly the best paintings in Philadelphia in the seventeen-fifties. An aspiring young painter would presumably have been eager to study them.

It may seem strange that a painter who had done such excellent work should so speedily fall into the nearly complete oblivion which overtook Robert Feke. But several factors contributed thereto. He left no traces behind him, save his pictures, and in the scanty official records at Newport. Any documents which were in his father's house at Oyster Bay no doubt were destroyed when the house was burned in 1768. Not a scrap of his handwriting has come to light. Probably he was a silent and uncommunicative person. Yet it is somewhat surprising that no papers of any sort about him should have survived. It would seem that he must have written letters to his wife in Newport during his long absences, but apparently they were not preserved by his children. He married so late and died so soon thereafter that even his oldest children, who might have cherished his fame, could have had only very shadowy personal recollections of him. Perhaps his daughters shared the Quaker prejudice and did not look back upon their father's career as an artist with any pride. His elder and longer-lived contemporary, Smibert, was more prolific, and had the advantage in prestige. Badger and Blackburn, who came just after him, though inferior as artists, were perhaps as well or better known about Boston. The authorship of most of his unsigned pictures was presently forgotten, so that they were ascribed to the better-known artists. In New England he was overshadowed in the next generation by Copley, and in the generation following by Gilbert Stuart, while in Philadelphia he was similarly eclipsed by Benjamin West. Furthermore, after the Revolution, his pictures had begun to look old-fashioned when compared with Copley's more accomplished and Stuart's suaver works. It has been a common saying that Copley's portraits represent persons who had attained wealth and social prestige before the Revolution, while those of Stuart represent persons who came to the front after that event. Feke's pictures, like those of Smibert, Badger, and Blackburn, represent the influential people of the generation before Copley, and in some instances, like the Royalls, they belonged to families which remained loyal to George III in the Revolution, and which, therefore, suffered a marked decline in fortune and prestige. Few of those families maintained their former position into the nineteenth century; generally they left the country, or died out, or were in some degree displaced by new men. Furthermore in the opening decades of the nineteenth century there was little interest in pre-Revolutionary relics. Even the portraits by Copley suffered neglect and abuse to a degree which amazes us. All these factors contributed to forgetfulness of Robert Feke and his work.

No doubt he would have been better remembered had he lived twenty years longer and painted another hundred portraits as masterly as his later works, instead of dying in obscurity at sea or in a distant island, at the height of his powers. It would have been at least far easier to establish his place among our colonial painters, for he would clearly have stood with Copley, West, and Stuart among the early American artists. With the growing knowledge of the outlines of his career, and of colonial art in general, there is now an increasing appreciation of his accomplishments. The late Lawrence Park, than whom no one was better qualified to express an opinion, has said of him, "As a painter Feke has no superior in this country, prior to 1760"; and, again, in discussing Blackburn, "I consider that his best work is inferior both in drawing, color, and character analysis to the best work of Robert Feke, who in my opinion was easily our foremost painter up to the middle of the eighteenth century."[1] And Mr. John Hill Morgan calls Feke "the most important Colonial artist born within the borders of the province of New York," and adds, "He was the best of the native-born Colonial portrait-painters, ranking only below Copley."[2] There is little reason to doubt that when his career is known in greater detail than is now possible, and the full tale of his extant works can be made up as his forgotten and neglected portraits are rescued from the oblivion which has overtaken them, he will secure a long-deferred recognition and an honored place among the men who laid the foundations of art in America.

[1] *Joseph Blackburn, A Colonial Portrait Painter*, p. 11.
[2] *Early American Painters* (New York, 1921), pp. 5 and 46.

APPENDICES

APPENDIX A

CORRESPONDENCE IN DAWSON'S HISTORICAL MAGAZINE

[The following correspondence contains the earliest printed information about Robert Feke, and is therefore a valuable source. It is here reprinted because Dawson's *Historical Magazine* is not now easily accessible. It should be used with caution, however, as many of the statements included therein are incorrect, as will appear upon consultation of the preceding pages.]

Volume III (November, 1859), page 348.

R. Feke, the Artist. In the year 1746, an artist of no inconsiderable merit visited Philadelphia, and painted a number of portraits, several of which are still preserved in my family. They are, probably, the best family portraits which have come down to us, in Pennsylvania, from colonial times, except West's, whose only good pictures, indeed, were painted in England.

The portraits referred to are rather remarkable for drawing and expression; and the coloring, which is still fresh and natural, gives reason to think the painter must have been well taught. It is hardly possible that a native, self-educated artist could, at that time, have done so well.

The name inscribed is R. Feke. The same name, *I think*, is inscribed on a portrait of Rev. John Callender, of Newport, R. I., author of the "Centenary Discourse," formerly in the possession of Col. Bull, of Newport, and attributed to Smibert. This is supposed to be the same now in the collection of the Historical Society of Rhode Island. The object of the present inquiry is to ascertain who R. Feke was, where he was born and learned his art, and where he lived and painted.

I gave the artist's name to Mr. Dunlap, when he was preparing his "History of the Fine Arts in America," but he knew nothing of him, and only recorded in his book the name and (with a slight mistake) that of the lady painted — Mrs. Willing.

I was once told that the painter, R. Feke, lived at Newport, R. I., and that some of his descendants were still there about the end of the century, and occupied a house on Touro Street, near the synagogue. I forget my informant; but if correct, more could be easily learned.

In the "History of American Art" it is a matter of some curiosity, if not importance, to redeem from oblivion one of its earliest masters; and if his questions can be answered, the inquirer will be much obliged by the additional interest it will add to the portrait in his possession, which is a kit-kat (size of life) of a gentleman in the handsome full dress of the time, 1746?

J. F. F.
[JOSHUA FRANCIS FISHER]

PHILADELPHIA

Volume IV (January, 1860), page 20.

Robert Feke, Portrait Painter (Volume III, page 348). He was supposed to be a descendant of a Dutch family that settled at the head of Oyster Bay. His father is represented as a follower of George Fox, the Quaker, while the son embraced the principles of the Baptists, which was very offensive to the former, who went so far in his resentment as to follow him to the water, and there forbid him to enter it on pain of disinheritance. He then left the house of his youth, and was several years absent on voyages abroad, in one of which he was taken prisoner and carried into Spain, where, in the solitude of his prison, he succeeded in procuring paints and brushes, and employed himself in rude paintings which, on his release, he sold, and thus availed himself of the means of returning to his own country. He soon after settled and married in Newport, cultivated his talents, and painted portraits. That of the beautiful wife of Governor Wanton, in the Redwood Library, is ascribed to him, where is also a copy, by Miss Stuart, of the portrait of Callender, supposed to be from his hand, and presented by Henry Bull, Esq., to the Historical Society. He followed his profession for twenty years, and is said to have several times visited Philadelphia, where it is supposed other of his paintings may be found. His health declining, he sought the milder climate of Bermuda, where he died at about the age of 44. He left three sons and two daughters. One of his sons was Charles Feke, a worthy man, and many years a respectable apothecary in Newport, R. I., but no male descendants are now living.

A Robert Feke is mentioned by Bond as one of the earliest and largest proprietors of Watertown, Mass., and as having married a daughter-in-law of Governor Winthrop. He was admitted Freeman in 1631, and was a deputy to the General Court, and magistrate, and lieutenant in the train band. In the Massachusetts records the name is variously spelled — Feke, Feake, and Feakes.

Since writing the above I am informed that upon the portrait of Callender may be discerned the words "R. Feke, painter."

S. F.

Volume IV (September, 1860), pages 280–281.

Robert Feke. The family of Feeks, in the town of Oyster Bay, Long Island, to which Robert Feke, the painter, belonged, seem to be descended from Henry Feke, who settled at Lynn, in 1630, was admitted as a freeman, May 14, 1634, and about 1637 removed to Sandwich, from which he was a representative to the General Court, in 1643 and 1644. He had a daughter, Elizabeth, who on the 24th of March, 1654, married John Dellingham. Henry Feake, about two years after this, removed, apparently from matters connected with religion, to Newtown, Long Island, settling at Mespat [Savage, "Genealogical Dictionary," vol. ii, p. 150. Riker's "Annals of Newtown," p. 26, "Historical and Genealogical Register," 1849, p. 93; 1850, p. 257. Henry Fekes is mentioned as one of the first settlers of Dorchester. "Hist. Dorchester," pp. 38, 52.]

The Robert Feke alluded to in the *Hist. Mag.*, vol. iv, came probably with Winthrop, and in October, 1630, asked to be admitted a freeman, which he was, May 18, 1631. Between that and January, 1632, he married Elizabeth, the widow of Henry Winthrop, a daughter of Thomas Fones of London. He was a representative at the first General Court, and also in 1635 and 1636, and lieutenant in 1635. He lost his reason some years prior to his death, at Watertown, February 1, 1663. [Savage, *ubi supra*.]

The Feake that was one of the purchasers of Greenwich, in 1640, though called Robert [Trumbull's "Connecticut," p. 118] was, more probably, Henry, unless we may suppose that Robert intended to take part but was prevented by his health.

Henry Feake did not find much religious freedom, on Long Island, in those days. Stuyvesant issued stringent enactments against the Quakers; and in 1658, Tobias Feake, son of Henry, and sheriff, presented a protest against the governor's measures. He was the mainspring of the opposition, and on him fell the weight of Stuyvesant's indignation; he was degraded from office and fined 200 guilders, with the costs of the proceeding, the only alternative being exile. The family of Tobias is now extinct; but from another son, John, a somewhat numerous progeny have descended.

John Feake was a very earnest member of the Society of Friends, and, so far as any one can be said to be so, a preacher among them. He was buried in the Quaker cemetery at Westbury; and according to their custom, without a tombstone or aught to tell his age or the time of his death, although the records may give these particulars. His son Robert became a Baptist and a preacher, and the anecdote mentioned in the *Hist. Mag.*, vol. iv, p. 20, if founded, must refer to John Feake, the Quaker, and his son Robert, the latter of whom died at the old homestead, now called Meadowside, April 1, 1773, aged 89, and is interred beside Captain John Underhill, on a beautiful hill, overlooking the Sound. According to Thompson, he continued in the exercise of the ministry till 1740. He had three sons: Charles, from whom are descended Mr. Daniel Feeks, and his sons John D. and William, the present occupants of the old homestead; Robert Feke, the painter; and Henry, whose descendants settled in Westchester county.

The house at Meadowside formerly contained a number of family portraits executed by Robert Feke; but they all perished when the house was destroyed by fire, about ninety-two years since, prior to the Revolution. The only piece of this early New York artist, now preserved in the family, is the portrait of a little girl painted on a panel. It does not bear his name, but has written on the back, apparently an old direction, "To Robert Feke, at Mr. Judea Hayes, in New York." It would seem likely from this that he resided in New York also, and that portraits by his hand may exist in some old family there.

For information not derived from printed works, I am indebted to Mr. J. D. Feeks, who asks a line from J. F. F. and S. F.

J. G. S.

APPENDIX B

PEDIGREE OF ROBERT FEKE, WITH NOTES ON HENRY FEAKE AND ON THE FEAKE FAMILY OF BARBADOS

Pedigree

IN VIEW of the statements in Dawson's *Historical Magazine* [1] that Robert Feke "the Painter" was of Dutch descent, an error frequently repeated by later writers, or that he was descended from the Henry Feake who appeared at Lynn in 1630 and later migrated to Long Island, it has seemed worth while to trace his pedigree in greater detail than did Poland, who clearly established Robert "the Painter's" descent from Robert Feake "the Emigrant," who appeared at Watertown in 1630.

The pedigree on the opposite page has been compiled from a manuscript pedigree of the descendants of James Feake of Wighton, Norfolk, England, through his son William, in the New England Historical and Genealogical Society, Boston (taken from *Harleian Mss.* 1430 fo. 50. and printed with additions in *Surrey Archeological Collections*, vol. vi, p. 310), and from a pedigree of other descendants of James Feake of Wighton, printed in the *New York Genealogical and Biographical Record*, 1880 (compiled from *Harleian Mss.* 1096, p. 119), supplemented from data in the Feake wills collected by Waters in *Genealogical Gleanings in England*, vol. i, pp. 788–791.

In the pedigree as here sketched it has been possible to give but few dates, and the order in which the children were born in the earlier generations is often conjectural, but the main lines of descent are believed to be correct.

It should be noted that in the sixteenth and seventeenth centuries the Feake family appears to have been rather numerous and widely scattered in the eastern counties of England. Thus the name appears two or three times as that of persons who intermarried with families recorded in the *Visitations of Essex*, but in no case has their connection with James Feake of Wighton been established. The same is true of a William Feake, son and heir of a John Feake of London, who is found at Stafford, Staffordshire, between 1617 and 1621, and who bore arms sable, a fess dancette or, in chief three fleurs-de-lis argent—to whom, however, the Feake family in Jamaica appears to have been nearly related. A John Feake was also a goldsmith in London in the sixteen-forties. Probably all these persons were descended from a common family stock.

[1] Appendix A.

Note on Henry Feake

A Henry Feake settled at Lynn, Massachusetts, in 1630, and was admitted freeman on May 14, 1634. About 1637 he removed to Sandwich, Massachusetts, which community he represented in the General Court in 1643 and 1644. His daughter Elizabeth (his only recorded child) there married John Dillingham. About 1656 Henry Feake, perhaps on account of religious difficulties, removed to Mespat, now Maspeth, Newtown, Long Island. A Henry Fekes, perhaps the same individual, is also mentioned as one of the first settlers of Dorchester, Massachusetts.[1] Henry and Robert Feake, "the Emigrant," may have come over together in the fleet which brought Governor Winthrop and his colonists, since the former appears at Lynn and the latter at Watertown in 1630, and they may have been cousins, though the relationship has not been traced, nor is there any evidence of communication between them after reaching America.

It is barely possible that Henry Feake may have been the individual of the same name who died in Barbados in 1694, and who was ancestor of some of the Feakes resident in that island until the middle of the next century. (See the following note.) That identification, however, requires that he had other children, that he removed from Long Island to Barbados, and that he lived to a great age, since the Henry who came to Lynn in 1630 must have been born at least as early as 1610. There is no evidence for any of these suppositions. It is more probable that there were two men of the same name, both more or less distant cousins of Robert "the Emigrant," one of whom came to New England, the other of whom at a somewhat later date emigrated from England to Barbados.

Note on the Feake Family of Barbados

Mr. E. Maxwell Shilstone of Bridgetown, Barbados, has searched the local records for me from their beginning in the seventeenth century down to 1800 and reports twelve burials, seven marriages, eighteen baptisms, and one will of persons whose surname is variously spelled Feak, Feake, Feakes, Freke, Freake, Fowke, ffookes.

The Freake-Freke group of names appears to belong to a distinct family, which came to Barbados about 1725 and stayed there until after 1775. The name Freke also appears in New England, and in the record of a marriage in Bermuda in 1773, and I do not believe it to be a variant of Feke. The name Fowke-ffookes (three entries), I also take to be a distinct name, and not a variant of Feke.

The Feak-Feake-Feakes group appear to form one family, and account for more than half the entries under each heading. The earliest entry for this

---

[1] See the letter signed "J. G. S." in Appendix A.

family is that of the baptism of a daughter of Richard "ffeake" on November 10, 1668; the latest is that of the burial of (another?) Richard Feak at St. Michael's Parish, November 13, 1752. The name Robert appears only as that of an infant born March 18, 1713, and baptized a week later. The latest entry for this family, — aside from the burial of the suppositious second Richard Feake in 1752, — is that of the burial of the second wife of Major Frederick Feake on October 16, 1726. Probably, therefore, the family left Barbados either before or soon after 1750.

The will [1] is that of Henry Feake, of St. Michael, Merchant, dated August 23, 1713 (with later codicils) and proved February 25, 1716. It is a long and interesting document. From the combined evidence of the will and the above-mentioned records it appears that the first Richard and Mary Feake were in Barbados as early as 1668; that a Henry Feake (perhaps father of the Henry the testator) died there in 1694; that the second Henry survived his wife Elizabeth, and was old enough to be a grandfather before 1700; that he was entitled to a coat-of-arms, and had a widowed sister and a cousin living in Stafford, England, so that he no doubt belonged to the armigerous Feake family settled there; [2] that he had a son Frederick and at least three daughters, with several grandchildren.

This Henry Feake and Elizabeth his wife were evidently Quakers, because he leaves instructions that he is to be buried "according to the method of his friends the people of God called Quakers in the burying-ground next to John Harbin's as near as conveniently may be to my late wife Elizabeth." Two of his daughters, however, were baptized on the day upon which they were married (presumably according to the rite of the Church of England) and his son Frederick Feake was certainly not a Quaker, as he is called "Major"; killed one Benjamin Firebrace, perhaps in a duel, in 1725; and was a vestryman of the Parish of St. Michael in 1727. His will is also on record in Bridgetown.

Henry Feake must have been possessed of a considerable estate. Among the numerous items of his will were bequests to the poor both of St. Michael's Parish and "of the people called Quakers," and two shillings six pence "to each of my negroes." He divided sixteen slaves among his daughters, and freed four, including "Tom," to whom he gave his bass viol and bow and music books. To another slave "Baratus" he gave a violin and bow "together with the music booke he now uses." To a grandson he left "all my greeke latine and french books . . . and all my law books of all sorts." To his son Frederick he left his "large escutcheon of arms" and his two seals of arms, and to his grandson Henry, son of Frederick, some silver with his arms engraved on it. He also

[1] There is also a will of one Christopher Feake recorded in Jamaica under date of 1743.

[2] A William Feake, son of a John Feake of London, is recorded as living at Stafford, Staffordshire, between 1617 and 1621, whose arms are described as Sable, a fess dancette or, in chief three fleurs de lis arg.

ordered that £250 be used to build a "good strong bridge" in the town, "so that all persons, horses, coaches and carts may have free passage thereon." Further evidence of the wealth of this family at an earlier date is found in the Census Papers of Barbados. In 1679 Henry Feake (probably the father of the testator, whose death is recorded in 1694) owned two hundred and forty-five acres of land and one hundred and twenty negroes in St. James Parish; and in the same year Richard Feake had twenty acres and twelve negroes in St. Thomas' Parish.

There is nothing in these entries to indicate any near relationship of the Feake family of Barbados to the family of Robert Feake "the Emigrant" to New England in 1630, though presumably they were descended from a common stock. Nor is there anything indicating the presence of Robert Feke "the Painter" in Barbados soon after 1750, unless we assume, as suggested on p. 99 that in the entry of the burial of (the second?) Richard Feake at St. Michael's on November 13, 1752, the name *Richard* has, by a clerical error, been substituted for *Robert*. The possibility that the Richard Feake whose daughter was baptized in 1668 can have been the same man who was buried in 1752 is so remote that it may be dismissed. The earlier Richard must have been born before 1650, probably at least as early as 1645, in order to have been a father in 1668, so that in 1752 he would have been well over a century in age. But no other Richard appears anywhere in the records, and the latest preceding entry is that of the burial of Frederick Feake's second wife in 1726, more than twenty-six years before. The fact that no Feake entry is to be found between 1726 and 1752, although Frederick Feake had several children, suggests the possibility that the family may have removed from Barbados soon after 1726. If the entry recording the burial of Richard Feake in 1752 is correct as it stands we must suppose that a second Richard came to Barbados, and remained there a good many years after the rest of the family had probably departed thence. That is perfectly possible, but it does not entirely exclude the other possibility that this latest burial record is in reality that of Robert Feke "the Painter."

CATALOGUE OF PORTRAITS

CATALOGUE OF PORTRAITS

"PAMELA ANDREWS"

Subject.

The portrait is supposed to be an ideal representation of "Pamela Andrews," the heroine of Samuel Richardson's novel with that title, which was published in 1740 and which quickly attained widespread popularity. If the picture was painted in Newport with the intention of portraying "Pamela" it cannot be dated earlier than 1741 or 1742, and is probably a little later, as the maturity of manner with which it is painted would seem to indicate. It is, of course, possible that the name became attached to the picture after it was painted and when the novel came into vogue, but the style of cap and dress fit the romantic young heroine of the novel.

Description.

The subject is painted in the lower half of an oval. She is sitting with her figure in profile, the right shoulder to the spectator, her face turned three-quarters front. She has dark hair, partly covered by a white cap coming to two little upright points above the forehead. She is dressed in brown, with white trim of heavier cloth, and with white ruffles about the neck. Her arms and hands are gloved. The cheeks and lips are well colored, and the whole picture is unusually charming. It is in fairly good condition, though somewhat overlaid with varnish.

Date.

Unsigned and undated. The picture has been relined.

Size.

Height 31 inches; width 24 inches.

Ownership.

Rhode Island School of Design, Providence; bequeathed by Miss Sarah C. Durfee. She was the great-granddaughter of Benjamin Cozzens, brother of Eleanor Cozzens, Feke's wife, to whom the portrait is said to have been given in 1755 by Mrs. Feke.

Exhibited.

Exhibition of Early American Paintings, Brooklyn Institute, 1917.
On exhibition at the Rhode Island School of Design, Providence.

Reproduced.

(1) *Bulletin of the Rhode Island School of Design*, Vol. V, No. 1, January, 1917.

(2) *Brooklyn Museum Quarterly*, Vol. IV, No. 2, April, 1917.

(3) *Early American Paintings:* Catalogue of an Exhibition held in the Museum of the Brooklyn Institute of Arts and Sciences, Brooklyn, 1917.

(4) F. W. Bayley, *Five Colonial Artists of New England.* Boston, 1929.

CHARLES APTHORP

Subject.

Charles Apthorp was born in England about 1698. He came to Boston in 1726 and married Grizzell Eastwick, by whom he had eighteen children. He was paymaster and commissioner of the British naval military forces which had their headquarters at Boston, and became a prominent merchant and a man of great wealth. He died November 11, 1758.

Description.

Apthorp is shown standing, three-quarters length and three-quarters front, with his left shoulder toward the spectator, his left hand on his hip in the conventional pose so often used by Smibert, Feke, and other painters of the day. His right hand rests upon papers on a table. In the left background a ship is seen.

"Feke shows Apthorp nearly to the knees, standing in an easy dignified pose, his left hand resting on his hip, his right outstretched upon an unfolded letter which lies upon a table covered with a cloth of an old-rose shade. He wears a powdered wig, a suit of dull olive-green, lined with fawn-colored satin, the hand holding back the long coat from an equally long waistcoat with its large pocket lapel. His brown eyes directed to the spectator are keen and penetrating, his mouth firm, and his whole attitude is that of a man accustomed to command and to be obeyed, yet his face is not without an expression of kindness. In the background to the right is a large gray-stone column, and to the left, below a dull sky, is shown Boston harbor with a departing vessel doubtless intended to represent one of his own large fleet of ships bound for some foreign port. The picture is very typical of Feke's work both in pose and method, and while low in key and without the pearliness of many of his portraits, the composition is strong and the coloring harmonious, producing an effect of distinct decorative charm." [1]

Date.

The portrait is signed and dated "R. F. 1748," and was presumably painted in Boston.

Size.

Height 50 inches; width 20 inches.

Ownership.

At the beginning of this century this portrait, that of Mrs. Apthorp, and that of their daughter Grizzell, Mrs. Barlow Trecothick, were owned by Mrs. Sarah A. C. Bond of Cambridge, to whom they had descended. Mr. Thomas B. Clarke of New York purchased the portrait of Charles Apthorp a few years ago for "The Brook," New York, but exchanged it for another picture from the Cleveland Museum of Fine Arts in 1919. The Cleveland Museum now owns it.

Exhibited.

Boston Museum of Fine Arts, 1909–14, and now at the Cleveland Museum.

Reproduced.

(1) With a description by Lawrence Park, quoted (in part) above, in the *Bulletin of the Cleveland Museum of Fine Arts*, No. V, June, 1919.

(2) F. W. Bayley, *Five Colonial Artists of New England*. Boston, 1929.

MRS. CHARLES APTHORP (Grizzell Eastwick)

Subject.

Grizzell, daughter of John Eastwick, by his wife, Grizzell, daughter of James Lloyd of Boston; born in Jamaica, August 10, 1709; came to Boston in 1716; married Charles Apthorp, January 13, 1726; died in Quincy, Massachusetts, August 16, 1796.

Description.

The subject is shown nearly full length, half-front, her left shoulder to the spectator, her face turned nearly full front. She is a large woman, sitting very erect against a dark blue-green curtain which

---

[1] Lawrence Park, *Bulletin of the Cleveland Museum of Fine Arts*, No. V, June, 1919.

hangs by the base of a large column. Beyond the column, to the left, is a glimpse of fields, trees, and sky. She has dark hair and eyes, and a fresh complexion, though the flesh tints on her arms and breast have somewhat faded. She is dressed in a golden-brown satin gown, trimmed with muslin, with jewelled pins in the bodice and catching up the sleeves inside the elbow. Her right arm rests on the parapet from which the column rises; her left hand lies in her lap, holding an open copy of *Paradise Lost*.

The portrait is painted in subdued tones, and makes a worthy companion piece to the portrait of Charles Apthorp, now in the Cleveland Museum, but it has not the unusual charm of her daughter's picture.

Date.

Signed on the right edge of the picture, on a level with the left elbow: "R. F. 1748."

Size.

Height 48½ inches; width 39 inches.

Ownership.

This portrait descended with that of Charles Apthorp to Mrs. Sarah A. C. Bond of Cambridge, who sold it to Mr. Isaac Thomas of Boston, also a descendant, who gave it to his daughter, the present owner, Mrs. Ben P. P. Moseley, Boston.

Exhibited.

Boston Museum of Fine Arts, 1909–14.

Loan Exhibition of Portraits by American Painters before the Revolution, Copley Society, Boston, March, 1922.

Reproduced.

F. W. Bayley, *Five Colonial Artists of New England*. Boston, 1929.

ROBERT AUCHMUTY II

Subject.

Robert Auchmuty II, son of Judge Robert Auchmuty; born in Boston about 1722; married Deborah Cradock of Boston, in King's Chapel, 1751; died in London, 1788. He was a distinguished lawyer; was counsel for the defense, with Adams and Quincy, in the trial of the British soldiers after the "Boston Massacre"; and was Judge of the Court of Admiralty from 1767 until the Revolution. Being a loyalist, he then went to England, whence he never returned.

ROBERT AUCHMUTY, JR.

Description.

The head and bust of young Auchmuty are shown enclosed in a painted oval against a shaded brown background. His figure is half-front, the right shoulder toward the spectator, the handsome and intelligent face turned right, full front. He has abundant dark hair, brushed back, and falling in short curls above his coat; dark brown eyes; a clear complexion and fine features. He wears a light-gray coat and a pink silk waistcoat, both heavily ornamented with gold braid. The waistcoat is buttoned to the top, but the white linen neckband and a small amount of ruff show above it. The picture is in the original frame and is in excellent condition. It is simply done, but has exceptional charm.

Date.

Signed and dated "R. F. Pinx, 1748" (on the right side above the left sleeve).

Size.

Height 30 inches; width 25 inches.

Ownership.

At the time of the Revolution the portrait appears to have been in the possession of Robert Auchmuty's brother, Rev. Samuel Auchmuty, Rector of Trinity Church, New York. After Washington entered New York, in 1776, Dr. Auchmuty left the city with his family and a few possessions, including portraits, taking refuge with friends in New Jersey. Later, when the British again took possession of New York he returned, to find his church and house burned. He died soon after and the family portraits remained in the care of his parishioner, Mrs. Rebecca Moore of Perth Amboy, and were never reclaimed. This portrait passed to her descendants, who kept it until 1930. It is at present owned by Mr. Robert C. Vose of Boston.

DR. PHINEAS BOND

Subject.

Phineas Bond was born in 1717; married Williamina Moore in 1748; died in 1773. He was a prominent physician in Philadelphia.

Description.

Dr. Bond is shown half-length, half-front, his left shoulder turned toward the spectator, his face turned nearly full front. He has dark

brown eyes and eyebrows, and a pleasing and intelligent countenance. He wears a full white wig, a black coat lined with red silk,
black waistcoat, ruffled shirt and ruffles at the wrists. His left hand
rests against his hip, four fingers showing; his right arm rests upon a
low wall, the hand holding a gold-headed cane. A gilded sword hilt
shows beneath his coat in the lower right corner of the picture. The
background is dark on the right, with trees and sky showing faintly
on the left. Mr. Albert Cook Myers, in his list of illustrations in
Hannah Logan's Courtship, states that the picture was painted in
1765. If that be true it obviously cannot be the work of Feke, but
the portrait clearly represents a young man, nearer the thirty-three
years which Dr. Bond would have attained in 1750 than the forty-
eight years which he would have reached in 1765. While the picture
might have been painted as early as 1746 the apparent age of the
subject makes 1750 the more probable date. Dr. Bond married, in
1748, Miss Williamina Moore, (q. v.) whom Feke had painted in
1746. It would, therefore, have been entirely natural for him to
have employed Feke to paint a companion portrait when the artist
returned to Philadelphia on his last visit. Finally, the portrait is so
strongly reminiscent of Feke's pictures of William Bowdoin, of
John Channing, and of Tench Francis, No. 2, that it is difficult to
believe that it was not painted by the same hand. It is an unusually
fine portrait.

Size.
Height 38½ inches; width 32½ inches.

Ownership.
Miss Fanny Travis Cochran, Philadelphia.

Reproduced.
A. C. Myers (ed.), *Hannah Logan's Courtship*. Philadelphia, 1904.

JAMES BOWDOIN II (No. 1)

Subject.
James, son of James Bowdoin I by his second wife, born in Boston,
August 8, 1727; was graduated from Harvard in 1745; married
Elizabeth Erving, September 15, 1748; died November 6, 1790. He
was delegate to the First Continental Congress; governor of Massa-
chusetts; first president of the American Academy of Arts and
Sciences; Fellow of the Royal Society of London and Dublin.

DR. PHINEAS BOND

Description.

This charming portrait depicts a tall, slender boy, who might be between twelve and fourteen years of age, standing against a lovely and delicately painted background showing a meadow with a winding stream, woods, distant hills, and clouds. He stands half-front, his right shoulder toward the spectator, his face turned right nearly full front. He has light brown, curling hair, hanging to his shoulders; brown eyes; and a pleasant, boyish face with a dimpled chin. He is dressed in a green silk coat and waistcoat, with white neckband, shirt-ruffles, and wristbands. His left hand grasps a strung bow, while his upraised right hand holds an arrow. The drawing is good, the pose and expression of the young archer are natural, and the background is particularly pleasing.

There is no reason to doubt the identity of the subject, both because the portrait came straight from the Bowdoin family to Bowdoin College, and because the boy here depicted closely resembles the young man of twenty-one shown in Feke's portrait of James Bowdoin II, painted in 1748. Tradition has attributed the earlier portrait to Smibert, but the attribution rests on no documentary evidence, and has no better foundation than the attribution to Smibert of the portrait of General Waldo, also in the Bowdoin Collection. The picture does not look like the work of Smibert, who hardly attained so large a measure of charm. On the other hand it has many resemblances to the later work of Feke, who was certainly in Boston in the summer of 1741, painting the Royall group. James Bowdoin II was fourteen in August of that year, and might easily have looked as young as he does in this picture. The chief argument against the attribution of this portrait to Feke is that it is a more accomplished and delightful piece of work than it has hitherto been supposed he could do at this period. But the reasons for assigning it to Feke seem so strong as to indicate that his accomplishments as a painter have been underestimated.

Date.

Probably painted at Boston in the summer of 1741.

Size.

Height 33⅝ inches; width 25¾ inches.

Ownership.

The portrait was bequeathed, with other family pictures, to Bowdoin College, in 1811, by James Bowdoin III.

Exhibited.

Bowdoin Museum of Fine Arts, Brunswick, Maine.

JAMES BOWDOIN II (No. 2)

Description.

In this portrait James Bowdoin is shown as a youth of twenty-one, three-quarters length, half-front, with his left shoulder toward the spectator, his handsome face turned nearly full front. His hair, which is apparently his own and not a wig, is carefully curled and powdered gray. He wears a tobacco-brown coat, lined with gray silk, and a long, light gray, brocaded silk waistcoat, against which his left hand rests, with two fingers extended, while his right hand is thrust into the waistcoat. The background shows woods, hills, and sky. The portrait is one of Feke's finest and most careful works, but the flesh tints have faded.

Date.

Signed, lower left, "R. F. Pinx, 1748." Probably painted at Boston.

Size.

Height 48¾ inches; width 39¼ inches.

Ownership.

The portrait was bequeathed to Bowdoin College in 1811 by James Bowdoin III.

Exhibited.

Bowdoin Museum of Fine Arts, Brunswick, Maine.

Reproduced.

(1) W. Updike, *History of the Episcopal Church in Narragansett,* I, 466.

(2) *Catalogue of Exhibition of Colonial Portraits,* Metropolitan Museum of Art. New York, 1911.

(3) W. Dunlap, *History of the Arts of Design in America.* 1918.

(4) *Connoisseur,* LXVIII (January–April, 1924), 128.

(5) *International Studio,* LXXVII (July–September, 1923), 431.

(6) F. W. Bayley, *Five Colonial Artists of New England.* Boston, 1929.

MRS. JAMES BOWDOIN (Elizabeth Erving)

Subject.

Elizabeth, daughter of John Erving, born September 14, 1731; married James Bowdoin II, September 15, 1748; died May 5, 1803.

Description.

This portrait is a companion piece to that of James Bowdoin, No. 2, whom the subject married in the same year that the picture was painted. She is represented at three-quarters length, nearly full front, seated against a background which is dark on the left, but which shows open country and sky on the right. She has brown hair and eyes. Her gown is of light blue satin with white trim, bodice, and sleeves. A jewelled pin, catching up the right sleeve inside the elbow, is shown. She holds a basket of roses in her lap with her right hand, and is tucking a rose into her bodice with her left hand.

"The blue satin demonstrates Feke's ability to render fabrics. Its tones echo the blue of the distant sky in the background. The flesh tints are warm and vibrant." [1]

Date.

Signed, right-hand side, "R. Feke Pinx. 1748." Presumably painted at Boston.

Size.

Height 48¾ inches; width 39 inches.

Ownership.

Bequeathed to Bowdoin College in 1811 by James Bowdoin III.

Exhibited.

Bowdoin Museum of Fine Arts, Brunswick, Maine.

Reproduced.

(1) W. Dunlap, *History of the Arts of Design in America.* 1918.
(2) *International Studio*, LXXVII (July–September, 1923), 431.
(3) F. W. Bayley, *Five Colonial Artists of New England.* Boston, 1929.

WILLIAM BOWDOIN

Subject.

William, son of James Bowdoin I by his first wife, and half-brother of James Bowdoin II; born in 1713; married Phoebe Murdock, July 3, 1739; died February 24, 1778.

---

[1] Virginia Robie, *International Studio*, LXXVII (July-September, 1923), 431.

Description.

This is a very handsome, full-dress portrait. The subject is shown standing, three-quarters length, three-quarters front, his left shoulder toward the spectator, his face turned left nearly full front. His left hand, with index finger straight, rests against his waistcoat, holding back his coat. His right arm rests upon the top of a masonry wall, the hand holding a gold-headed cane with a blue ribbon. Rough masonry rises behind him, and to his right is a vista showing distant hills.

He is dressed in a dark brown coat lined with white silk, and a pink waistcoat elaborately trimmed with gold lace, with white ruffles at wrists and throat. His hair is curled and powdered. He has brown eyes. The flesh tints are somewhat faded.

Date.

Signed and dated, lower left, "R. F. Pinx, 1748." Probably painted at Boston.

Size.

Height 49⅛ inches; width 38⅞ inches.

Ownership.

Bequeathed to Bowdoin College in 1811 by James Bowdoin III.

Exhibited.

Bowdoin Museum of Fine Arts, Brunswick, Maine.

Exhibition of Colonial Portraits at Metropolitan Museum of Art, New York, November 6 to December 31, 1911.

(On page 57 of the catalogue of this exhibition this picture is said to have been painted at Newport. No authority is given for the statement.)

Reproduced.

(1) W. Updike, *History of the Episcopal Church in Narragansett,* I, 376.

(2) *Art and Progress,* III (February, 1912), 347.

(3) *International Studio,* LXXVII (July–September, 1923), 432.

(4) F. W. Bayley, *Five Colonial Artists of New England.* Boston. 1929.

MRS. WILLIAM BOWDOIN (Phoebe Murdock)

Subject.

Phoebe Murdock; married William Bowdoin, July 3, 1739; died December 14, 1772.

Description.

The subject is shown at three-quarters length, three-quarters front, her left shoulder toward the spectator, her face turned left nearly full front. She is seated with her right elbow resting on the top of a low masonry wall, her left hand in her lap, the two hands holding between them an upright, closed book. She is dressed in a beautifully painted light gray silk gown, with white lawn trim about the bodice, and undersleeves of the same material, with jewels at the bodice and on the inside of the elbows. The masonry wall rises in the background on the spectator's right, while behind Mrs. Bowdoin and to the left is a vista of trees and sky.

Date.

Signed, lower left, "R. Feke." Probably painted in Boston.

Size.

Height 49⅛ inches; width 38⅞ inches.

Ownership.

Bequeathed to Bowdoin College in 1811 by James Bowdoin III.

Exhibited.

Bowdoin Museum of Fine Arts, Brunswick, Maine.

Reproduced.

F. W. Bayley, *Five Colonial Artists of New England.* Boston, 1929.

REV. JOHN CALLENDER

Subject.

Rev. John Callender, born in Boston in 1706. He was a son of Rev. Ellis Callender, pastor of the First Baptist Church of Boston (1708–26). He was graduated from Harvard in 1723; was pastor of the Baptist Church at Swansea, Rhode Island, August, 1727–February, 1730; in October, 1731 he became the colleague of Rev. William Peckham, pastor of the First Baptist Church of Newport, whom he succeeded. He married Elizabeth Hardin of Swansea, February 15, 1730. Their daughter became a prominent member of the

Society of Friends in Newport. He died at Newport, January 26, 1748.

Description.

The portrait shows Mr. Callender in a Geneva gown and bands, the body turned three-quarters front, with the left shoulder advanced, the face turned nearly full front. The figure is set in the lower half of a painted oval, very high in the picture, the head not being as well centred as in some other of Feke's portraits. The subject wears a white curled wig, and has a gentle face of exceptional charm and attraction.

The head is a beautiful one, but the picture is sadly overlaid by dirt and varnish.

Date.

Signed "R. Feak, Pinx. A.D. 1745." Painted in Newport.

Size.

Height 28 inches; width 24 inches.

Ownership.

This picture, with its companion portrait of Rev. Thomas Hiscox, was painted on commission for Henry Collins of Newport. It was purchased from his heirs, and was given in 1847 to the Rhode Island Historical Society, Providence, by Henry Bull of Newport.

Reproduced.

There is a poor copy by Miss Jane Stuart in the Redwood Library, Newport, made about 1844 (see *Redwood Library Annals*, p. 165), and another, even poorer, made by Herring about 1860, in the Newport Historical Society.

Bibliographical References.

Callender's *Historical Discourse on Rhode Island* is reprinted, with notes, in the *Collections of the Rhode Island Historical Society*, Vol. IV.

JOHN CHANNING (No. 1)

Subject.

John Channing, born in Newport 1714; merchant; married Mary Chaloner, 1746; died in Newport, 1771. He was the grandfather of the famous clergyman, William Ellery Channing.

JOHN CHANNING (No. 1)

Description.

The subject is represented standing, half-front, with his right shoulder toward the spectator, his face turned nearly full front. He is a man in his thirties, with a full, well colored face and dark eyes. He does not wear a wig, but his own dark curled hair falls to his shoulders. He is dressed in a dark bottle-green coat lined with red silk, and a black waistcoat, with the usual linen ruffles at his neck and wrists. His right hand, resting on his hip, with the forefinger extended, holds back his coat. His left hand, resting upon a stone parapet, holds a gold-headed cane with a black cord in the same manner shown in the portraits of Phineas Bond and William Bowdoin. The background behind the figure is brown, but to the right are shown sky and clouds painted in low tones. The portrait is a typical example of Feke's work and the figure is well posed, but the face is heavy and not very well modelled.

Date.

Unsigned and undated. Probably painted in Newport some time between 1746 and 1749.

Size.

Height 50 inches; width 30 inches.

Ownership.

The portrait descended to William Ellery Channing, and is now owned by the latter's grandson, William E. C. Eustis, Esq., of Milton, Massachusetts.

JOHN CHANNING (No. 2)

Subject.

The owner of the portrait of Mrs. John Channing, No. 2, states that the family owned a companion piece representing John Channing, but that the picture was lost many years ago. No description of it is available, but it may be assumed to have been a bust portrait, with spandrels in the lower corners, approximately 30 inches by 24 inches in size. It is not known whether the portrait is still extant.

MRS. JOHN CHANNING (Mary Chaloner) (No. 1)

Subject.

Mary Chaloner, born in Newport, 1721; married in 1746 to John Channing; died in Newport, 1790.

Description.

Mrs. Channing is shown seated in a carved wooden chair uphol-
stered in red silk, three-quarters front, with her left shoulder toward
the spectator and her face turned left full front. She has a rather
full, well colored face, with gray eyes and brown hair, a curl of which
falls over her left shoulder. She wears a green silk dress, trimmed
with white muslin. Her sleeves are caught up, inside the elbows,
with crystal pins. Her right arm rests on a table with a marble top,
partly covered with a red cloth. Her left hand rests in her lap,
holding a spray of flowers. The background behind the figure is
brown, but to the left a red curtain is shown. She is a robust
woman, apparently between twenty-five and thirty years old.

Date.

Unsigned and undated. Probably painted in Newport between
1746 and 1749.

Size.

Height 50 inches; width 30 inches.

Ownership.

This portrait, with that of her husband, descended to their grandson, William Ellery Channing. It is now owned by the heirs of the
late F. A. Eustis, and hangs, with its companion picture, in the
house of William E. C. Eustis, Esq., Milton, Massachusetts.

MRS. JOHN CHANNING (Mary Chaloner) (No. 2)

Description.

This portrait shows the head and bust of Mrs. Channing, nearly full
front, with her face turned a little to the left. She is dressed in a
plain gown of old-rose silk, cut low, and with white muslin trim
about the bodice. A dark blue scarf is thrown about her shoulders.
The background is dark brown and there are brown spandrels in the
lower corners. In face and pose this portrait is very similar to the
picture listed as Mrs. John Channing (No. 1). The subject appears
to be a little older, however, so that perhaps this portrait, and the
companion piece, now lost, representing her husband, may have
been painted at Newport about 1750.

Size.

Height 29¼ inches; width 24 inches.

MRS. JOHN CHANNING (No. 2)

Ownership.

The portrait has descended to Miss Edith Bangs, 355 Beacon Street, Boston, a great-great-granddaughter of the subject.

REV. NATHANIEL CLAP

Subject.

Rev. Nathaniel Clap, born in Dorchester, Massachusetts, in 1668; was graduated from Harvard College in 1690; went to Newport in 1695, where he gathered a group of Congregationalists to whom he preached for twenty-five years before organizing the First Congregational Church in Newport and being ordained as minister thereof in 1720; died October 10, 1745. In 1728 a group unable to accept Mr. Clap's very rigid Calvinism and dogmatic personality split off and formed the Second Church. After Clap's death the two churches came together again under the title of the United Congregational Church of Newport.[1]

Description.

The portrait shows, against a dark brown background and within a painted brown oval, the stooping shoulders and the head of an old minister, approaching seventy years of age. He is dressed in a black gown or coat indistinctly painted, with a white neckcloth, above which his face looks out nearly full front. His silvery hair, parted in the middle, reaches to his shoulders. The countenance has brown eyes, a large nose, a straight thin upper lip and a rather full lower one. The skin is brown and wrinkled. The face looks like that of an intolerant and narrow-minded man, bearing out the account given of him in the record of his church. It should be noted, however, that both Berkeley and Whitefield spoke very highly of him.

There is no doubt as to the identity of the subject, since across the lower part of the picture is painted an eighteenth-century inscription:

Rev. Nathaniel Clap, A.M.

ob. Oct. 10, 1745, Aetat 78, Pastoratus 25, Min. 50.

There is no indication, however, as to the painter. From the apparent age of the subject it would seem that the portrait must have been painted between 1730 and 1740. The only painters known to have been working in Newport about that period are Smibert and

[1] See *Manual of United Congregational Church,* 1921.

Feke. Smibert removed to Boston late in 1729, though he probably made one or two excursions to Newport after that date. We do not know when Feke began painting in Newport, though he had certainly taken up his residence there before his marriage in September, 1742, and may have been there, at least from time to time, for as much as a decade and a half previously. The portrait in question is decidedly inferior to those of Rev. John Callender and Rev. Thomas Hiscox, though its dilapidated condition makes it difficult perhaps to pass fair judgment on it, but the head is painted with a good deal of ability. It therefore seems reasonable to believe that the picture may be the work of Feke, done at an early stage of his residence in Newport, some time in the seventeen-thirties.

Size.

Height 25 inches; width 23 inches.

Ownership.

The portrait is now owned by the United Congregational Church of Newport. It is supposed to have been painted for Henry Collins, but there is no record of its history. No other portrait of Clap is known to exist.

LEVINAH ("PHIANY") COCK

Subject.

This portrait is believed to represent Levinah Cock, whose nickname, "Phiany," obviously arose from the child's mispronunciation of her given name. She was the eldest child of Deborah Feke, younger sister of Robert "the Painter," who married James Cock, into whose family two of her aunts had already married. James Cock was born at Matinecock, Long Island, in 1708 and died in 1746. The date of his wife's birth is not known, nor the date of their marriage, but she is not likely to have been older than he. After his death Mrs. Cock married again, and in 1755 is recorded as owner of two slaves. In *The Cox Family in America* the date of "Phiany's" birth is given as "about 1730." "Phiany" Cox died, unmarried, in 1778. She was a birthright member of the Society of Friends, but in 1772 was disowned as having "gone to the Baptists."

Description.

The picture shows a small child, not more than two or three years old, framed in a painted oval, who is shown from the waist up, undressed, but with a loose garment which is black on the outside and white on the inside thrown over her left shoulder and partly wrapped round her waist. She is sitting against a very dark background, three-quarters front, her uncovered right shoulder and arm toward the spectator, her face turned right, nearly full front. She has a round, ruddy face, and auburn hair parted in the middle and falling to the shoulders. The eyes were probably brown, but many years ago a superstitious servant, who claimed that the child's eyes were "following her round the room," dug them out with a sharp instrument, and they have since been repainted.

While the figure of the child is stiff and crude it is easy to undervalue the picture. The coloring is still fresh and lifelike, and the drawing is little worse than may be seen in portraits of small children by Smibert or Blackburn. In any case the picture has value as being the earliest known work of Robert Feke, except his early self-portrait.

The picture is painted on a wooden panel, now somewhat warped. On the back of the panel, in ink, are the words

> To Robert Feke
> at Mr. Judea Hayes
> in Newyork.

Date.

Probably painted about 1732 or 1733 at Oyster Bay or Matinecock.

Size.

Height 20 inches; width 17 inches.

Ownership.

It descended in the family of James Cock to the late George W. Cocks, of Oyster Bay, and is now owned by his son, Robert Feeks Cox of Media, Pennsylvania.

MISS RUTH CUNNINGHAM (MRS. JAMES OTIS)

Subject.

Ruth, daughter of Captain Nathaniel Cunningham, born in Boston, January 15, 1728; married James Otis in 1755; died in Boston, November 15, 1789. Both she and her husband, the distinguished lawyer and patriot, were painted by Blackburn in 1755.[1]

---

[1] See Lawrence Park, *Joseph Blackburn*, pp. 40–41.

Description.

The subject is shown full front against a brown background, seated in a chair covered with red damask. Her right hand lies in her lap; her left rests upon a bare table at her side, holding down an open book. She is dressed in bright blue silk, trimmed with white muslin, and with unusually ample white muslin undersleeves. An old-gold scarf with a heavy gold fringe crosses her left shoulder and is fastened to her corsage. The face is well colored, well modelled and expressive. She has brown eyes, well-arched eyebrows, and abundant brown hair piled high upon her head and falling in a heavy curl over her left shoulder.

The portrait is a fine one, well studied and attractive, in Feke's latest and most sophisticated manner, though less typical of his work than most of his portraits, owing perhaps to the outstanding individuality of the subject.

Date.

Signed and dated "R. Feke Pinx 1748." The signature appears across the top of the left-hand page of the book held open upon the table by Miss Cunningham's left hand. It is in small, flowing script, rather awkwardly done, as though painted upside down. Across the top of the right-hand page is the word "Spring," which may possibly note the season of the year in which the portrait was painted. No doubt it was executed during Feke's visit to Boston in 1748.

Size.

Height 37 inches; width 28¾ inches.

Ownership.

The picture was inherited by Susanna Cunningham, niece of Mrs. Otis and wife of John Henry Mills, then by her son John Mills, then by his daughter Frances Mills, who married G. W. Lord, then by her daughter Georgiana, who married J. M. Hall. It is now owned by Thomas B. Clarke, Esq., 22 East 35th Street, New York City.

Exhibited.

Union League, New York City, January, 1923; Exhibition of Paintings by Early American Portrait Painters, Century Association, New York City, November, 1926; Exhibition of Portraits of Early American Artists, Philadelphia Museum of Art, 1928.

Reproduced.

Art in America, II (October, 1923), 329.

ROBERT FEKE (Early Self-Portrait)

Description.

This self-portrait of the subject of this biography represents him as a serious youth of about twenty years of age, standing against a plain brown background. The body is shown nearly profile, the right shoulder toward the spectator, the face turned nearly full front. The subject has a thin, rather long, pale face; pointed nose and chin; thin, rather straight lips; large, dark eyes with arched eyebrows; very abundant, nearly black hair falling in curls to his shoulders.

The portrait perfectly fits the description of Feke given by Dr. Alexander Hamilton in 1744: "This man had exactly the phiz of a painter, having a long pale face, sharp nose, large eyes with which he looked at you steadfastly; long curled black hair, a delicate white hand, and long fingers."

He is dressed in a plain coat, probably originally of green-blue, now rather green-gray, with a white neckscarf. His left hand is thrust into his black waistcoat, only the wrist and white linen showing.

Date.

Probably painted about 1725.

Size.

Height 30 inches; width 26 inches.

Ownership.

This portrait has been handed down for several generations in the family owning the portraits of Hannah and Gershom Flagg IV, to Henry Wilder Foote, Belmont, Massachusetts, the present owner.

In addition to the fact that the portrait perfectly fits the description of Feke given by Dr. Alexander Hamilton, and unmistakably represents the same individual as the late self-portrait of Feke owned by the Misses Bullock, there has been an unquestioned tradition in the family that this picture represented Feke, the painter of the portraits of Hannah and Gershom Flagg IV, although nothing further was known about him. There is no family tradition as to how the Flaggs came into possession of the picture.

Reproduced.

(1) W. Dunlap, *History of the Arts of Design in America.* 1918.

(2) F. W. Bayley, *Five Colonial Artists of New England.* Boston, 1929.

ROBERT FEKE (Late Self-Portrait)

Description.

In his late self-portrait Feke has painted himself sitting in a mahogany chair, the curved back of which is indicated against a dark
background. His body is nearly in profile, with the right shoulder
toward the spectator, the face turned to the right, three-quarters
front. Feke is said to have completed the upper half of the figure,
including the head and shoulders, but the lower half, including the
body, hands, and legs to below the knees, were only sketched in outline. His wife's companion portrait was left in the same unfinished
state. Unfortunately both were "completed," some time after 1878,
by Mr. James S. Lincoln. The left hand, which is barely indicated,
holds the painter's palette, the right hand holds a brush. The head,
set high in the picture, and painted from almost the same point of
view as that of Feke's earlier self-portrait, is unmistakably that of
the same individual when twenty-five years older. He has the same
sharp nose, large, dark eyes and arched eyebrows, but the face is a
good deal fuller and the long, curling, dark hair is less abundant.
The head is very well done and the coloring of the cheeks, ruddy
above and dark where shaven, is fresh and good. He wears a plain
dark coat with a wide cuff, dark knee-breeches, and a simple white
neckband and undersleeves.

"Feke's own portrait and that of his wife are now in the possession
of his descendants, Misses Ann and Rhoda Bullock of Providence.
Feke left his own portrait practically completed. He drew his
wife's but painted fully only the face. Some years ago the painting
was completed by the late Mr. James S. Lincoln. We regret that the
pictures were not allowed to remain as the original artist left them.
What we can learn of him through them is still of great value to us,
but much of their documentary evidence has necessarily departed.
We are perhaps justified in assuming that these works were among
the very last which Feke painted, and that, doing his work in haste,
when on the eve of his departure to Bermuda, fearing he might not
return, he took pains to complete the faces, while he was forced to
leave the rest incomplete. He appears before us in his portrait,
palette in hand. 'Mariner' though he is, he intended to be remembered as a painter. His expression is lively and genial. We

feel that we are in the presence of a man whom it is a pleasure to know." [1]

Date.

Presumably painted at Newport in 1749 or 1750.

Size.

Height 50 inches; width 40 inches.

Ownership.

The Misses Ann and Rhoda Bullock, 201 Angell Street, Providence. These ladies are descended from Feke through their mother. Their portraits of Robert Feke and his wife have not been handed down, however, in this branch of the family, but were bought by their father, William Peckham Bullock, about 1857 from some ladies in Philadelphia, whose names the present owners do not recall, to whom the pictures had descended through another branch of the family. The portraits were then in their unfinished condition, and so remained until after 1878, since in the *History of Rhode Island*, published in that year by Hoag, Wade and Co., in the brief biographical sketch of Feke [2] it is noted that the portraits of Feke and his wife "remain incomplete." Probably not long afterwards Mr. Bullock, not liking the pictures in their uncompleted state, had them finished by Mr. Lincoln. There is no reason to doubt the authenticity of the portraits, as Mr. Bullock only purchased them because they were painted by Feke himself. Furthermore, the resemblance of Feke in this later portrait to the youthful self-portrait is unmistakable.

Reproduced.

A crude lithograph of this portrait is reproduced in the *History of the State of Rhode Island* published by Hoag, Wade and Co., 1878, p. 200.

---

[1] Poland, *Robert Feke, the Early Newport Portrait Painter*, p. 22. I think that Professor Poland has overstated the degree of incompleteness in which Feke left his self-portrait, though a more careful examination than I have been able to make would be necessary to determine the degree of over-painting by Mr. Lincoln. Note also that Professor Poland assumes that Feke died in Bermuda.

[2] Pp. 353–354.

MRS. ROBERT FEKE (Eleanor Cozzens)

Subject.

Eleanor, daughter of Leonard Cozzens, born in 1718, married Robert Feke in 1742 at Newport; died at Newport, 1804.

Description.

Mrs. Feke is shown as a large, vigorous, and capable woman, looking rather older than her thirty-two years, sitting very erect in a mahogany chair similar to that in her husband's picture. Her figure is three-quarters profile, left shoulder toward the spectator, her head turned to the left, three-quarters front. She wears a white cap tied under the chin and a somewhat elaborate gray silk gown, with a white scarf about her neck fastened to the bodice. A blue insert in the gray silk skirt looks like a later addition. Her right arm rests on a table covered with a blue cloth, the hand holding what appears to be a fan. Her left hand is by her side. She has dark hair and eyes, and a face which, while not beautiful, is indicative of strong character. She well represents a typical middle-aged Quakeress of good estate in the eighteenth century. It is said that one of her descendants of the present day strongly resembles her.

The head and shoulders were finished by the painter and seem not to have been retouched. The rest of the picture was only sketched, and was "completed" by Mr. Lincoln at the same time that he did her husband's picture (q. v.).

Date.

Presumably painted at Newport in 1749 or 1750.

Size.

Height 50 inches; width 40 inches. The picture has been relined.

Ownership.

The Misses Ann and Rhoda Bullock, 201 Angell Street, Providence, who inherited it with the late self-portrait of Robert Feke (q. v.).

EBENEZER FLAGG

Subject.

Ebenezer Flagg, born in Boston, October 27, 1710; merchant; settled in Newport; married Mary, daughter of Governor Richard Ward, in Newport, February 8, 1741; died in Newport, September 3, 1762.

Description.

The subject is shown standing nearly three-quarters length, half-front, right shoulder toward the spectator. He is represented as a man approaching forty years of age, with a full, ruddy face and brown eyes, handsomely dresssed in a white wig, long black waist-coat, and a light-gray coat lined with red silk. The partly unbuttoned waistcoat reveals the white ruffles of the shirt, and the wide cuffs on the coat are turned back to show the full, white ruffled cuffs. His right hand, which holds back his coat, rests upon his hip, the forefinger nearly straight, the other fingers turned under. The other hand rests upon the plinth of a column. The background behind the figure is a dull brown but between the figure and the column is a vista showing distant trees and clouds. This portrait has been attributed to Copley, but from the apparent age of the subject it must have been painted in the late seventeen-forties, when Copley was still a child. On the other hand Feke, during these years, was doing his best work in Newport and this portrait is an exceptionally fine piece, with all the characteristics of his later work. It should also be noted that Gershom Flagg IV, of Boston, whom Feke painted in 1748, was a brother of Ebenezer Flagg.

Date.

Unsigned and undated; probably painted in Newport a little before 1750.

Size.

Height 49¼ inches; width 39¼ inches.

Ownership.

The portrait descended from Ebenezer Flagg to his son Henry Collins Flagg, to his son Henry Collins Flagg, Jr., to his son William J. Flagg, to his niece Alice Gwynne Vanderbilt (Mrs. Cornelius Vanderbilt) of New York City, the present owner.

Reproduced.

N. G. and L. C. S. Flagg, *Family Records of the Descendants of Gershom Flagg.* 1907.

E. Flagg, *Genealogical Notes on the Founding of New England.* 1926.

MRS. EBENEZER FLAGG (MARY WARD)

Subject.

Mary, daughter of Governor Richard Ward of Rhode Island, born in Newport in 1713; married Ebenezer Flagg, 1741; died, 1781.

Description.

Mrs. Flagg is shown seated, three-quarters front, her left shoulder toward the spectator, her face turned left nearly full front. She is a woman in her thirties, with fair hair parted in the middle, a curl falling over her right shoulder, a fair complexion and brown eyes. She is dressed in gray satin trimmed with white muslin, with the long waist and full skirt of the period. Her sleeves are caught up inside the elbows with jewels. Her right elbow rests on a table; her left hand lies in her lap, holding a spray of flowers. A faint vista of sky and clouds is to be seen in the right background. The portrait, like that of her husband, has been attributed to Copley, but from the apparent age of the subject it must have been painted in the late seventeen-forties, and, although inferior to the portrait of her husband as a work of art, and less strikingly characteristic of Feke, it is nevertheless clearly his work.

Date.

Unsigned and undated. Probably painted in Newport a little before 1750.

Size.

Height 48 inches; width 37 inches.

Ownership.

The portrait has come down, with that of her husband, by the same line of descent, to the present owner, Mrs. Cornelius Vanderbilt, New York.

Reproduced.

N. G. and L. C. S. Flagg, *Family Records of the Descendants of Gershom Flagg.* 1907.
E. Flagg, *Genealogical Notes on the Founding of New England.* 1926.

GERSHOM FLAGG III

Subject.

There were two persons named Gershom Flagg — father and son — born in Massachusetts in the seventeenth century, and no less than six persons of the same name born in various parts of New England during the eighteenth century, all being descendants, in various lines, from the original Gershom. The subject of the present portrait was Gershom Flagg III, son of Gershom II and grandson of Gershom I. He was born January 25, 1702, presumably on his father's farm at

Woburn, Massachusetts. He removed to Newport, and was twice married, leaving descendants by his first wife. The date of his death has not been ascertained. He was first cousin to Ebenezer Flagg and to Ebenezer's brother, Gershom Flagg IV, of Boston, both of whom Feke also painted.

Description.

The subject is shown seated in a stuffed high-backed chair covered with a dull red cloth. His left shoulder is toward the spectator and he sits half-front, his head turned toward the left. He has a rather full, ruddy face and fresh complexion, with brown eyes. He wears a white wig, dark waistcoat and breeches, white stockings, and a light gray coat lined with red silk. The costume is very similar to that shown in the portraits of Ebenezer Flagg and Isaac Stelle. His right arm lies on a table beside a book; his left hand rests upon his leg. The pose, as well as the foreshortening of the crossed legs, closely resembles that shown in the portrait of Philip Wilkinson, which must have been painted about the same time. The portrait is wholly characteristic of Feke's work and must be ascribed to his latest period in Newport.

Date.

Unsigned and undated, presumably painted at Newport a little before 1750.

Size.

Height 49¼ inches; width 39 inches.

Ownership.

The portrait has come down by the same line of descent as the portrait of Ebenezer Flagg to the present owner, Mrs. Cornelius Vanderbilt, New York.

GERSHOM FLAGG IV

Subject.

Gershom Flagg was born April 20, 1705, in Boston, son of John Flagg, grandson of Gershom Flagg I; married Hannah Pitson, July 4, 1737; died at Boston, March 23, 1771. He was an architect, and a prosperous landed proprietor in Boston and in Maine.

Description.

The subject is shown half-length in the lower half of an oval, three-quarters front, right shoulder toward the spectator, against a brown background. He is a full-faced man about forty years of age, with long, very dark hair, and dark eyes. The face is very well colored and lifelike, keen and intelligent in expression. He is dressed in a plain, dark blue coat and waistcoat, with white neckcloth.

Date.

Presumably painted in Boston in 1748.

Size.

Height 30 inches; width 25 inches.

Ownership.

The portrait has passed by descent from the Flaggs to the present owner Henry Wilder Foote, Belmont, Massachusetts.

Reproduced.

(1) A copy, painted about 1890, is owned by Dr. Wilder Tileston of New Haven, Connecticut.

(2) Mary Wilder Tileston (ed.), *Memorials of Mary Wilder White*, Boston, 1903.

(3) N. G. and L. C. S. Flagg. *Family Records of the Descendants of Gershom Flagg.* 1907.

MRS. GERSHOM FLAGG (Hannah Pitson)

Subject.

Hannah, daughter of James Pitson, was born in England in 1711. Her father, with his family, came to Boston in 1714. She married Gershom Flagg IV, in Boston, July 4, 1737, and lived there until after her husband's death. She died at Lancaster, Massachusetts, October 13, 1784.

Description.

The subject is shown half-length in the lower half of an oval, with a brown background, slightly shaded. Her right shoulder is slightly advanced, her face turned to the right to face her husband's portrait. She is a woman in her thirties. The face is well colored and life-like. The set of the head and painting of the eyes and eyebrows are very characteristic of Feke's portraits of women. Her dark hair is tied behind the neck, and a curl falls over her right shoulder. She is dressed in silk, "old red" in color, cut low, with a white ruffle about the bodice.

Date.

Presumably painted at Boston in 1748.

Size.

Height 30 inches; width 25 inches.

Ownership.

The portrait has passed by descent from the Flaggs to the present owner, Henry Wilder Foote, Belmont, Massachusetts.

Reproduced.

(1) A copy, made about 1890, is owned by Dr. Wilder Tileston of New Haven, Connecticut.

(2) Mary Wilder Tileston (ed.), *Memorials of Mary Wilder White.* Boston, 1903.

(3) W. Dunlap, *History of the Arts of Design in America.* 1918.

TENCH FRANCIS (No. 1)

Subject.

Tench Francis, son of Very Rev. John Francis, Rector of St. Mary's Church, Dean of Lismore, Ireland, was born in England or Ireland about 1690, was educated for the law, and emigrated to Maryland in 1710. He was admitted to the Maryland bar, became attorney for Lord Baltimore in Kent County, and clerk of Talbot County from 1726 to 1734. In 1734 he removed to Philadelphia to practice law, and became Attorney General of Pennsylvania. He died in 1758.

Description.

The subject is shown seated, half-front, in a chair, the back of which is faintly indicated, with his left shoulder toward the spectator, his face turned left about three-quarters front. He wears a white wig, claret-colored coat and light gray waistcoat, with white neckband and ruffles. His right hand is thrust into his waistcoat, his left hand is open in gesture. He has gray eyes and the face is well modelled and colored. He is unmistakably the same individual who is represented in the portrait of Tench Francis, No. 2, but several years younger, and both portraits must be from the same hand, since they are very similar in style and technique. The companion portrait of his wife still more closely resembles the portrait listed as Mrs. Tench Francis, No. 2, being almost identical in pose and style, with but a slight shifting of the position taken by the subject. Inasmuch as the portrait of Tench Francis, No. 2, is signed "R. Feke, 1746," it would seem clear that the earlier pair of portraits was also painted by Feke on a previous visit to Philadelphia. The late owner, Mr. Sidell Tilghman, who acquired them by purchase, accepted the family tradition which attributed them to Copley, as does the present owner, but Copley was not born until 1738, and could not possibly have painted Mr. and Mrs. Tench Francis at the age at which they are here shown. Other critics have ascribed them to Gustavus Hesselius, but Hesselius hardly produced work of this calibre and the resemblance of these pictures to the later portraits of Mr. and Mrs. Tench Francis, known to be by Feke, is so close that they must certainly be ascribed to him.

Date.

Unsigned and undated — probably painted in Philadelphia before 1740.

Size.

Height 36 inches; width 29 inches.

Ownership.

This portrait, with that of Mrs. Tench Francis, No. 1, was purchased a few years ago by the late Sidell Tilghman of Madison, New Jersey, from another branch of the family in which they had descended. Now owned by Mrs. Sidell Tilghman, Madison, New Jersey.

TENCH FRANCIS (No. 2)

Description.

In this later portrait Tench Francis is shown three-quarters length, standing with his left shoulder toward the spectator, three-quarters front, his head turned to the left. He wears a white wig, long, dark brown coat and a lighter brown waistcoat, with white ruffles at the neck and sleeves. His left hand is thrust into his coat, his right hand is open as if making a gesture, but is shown with only three fingers and the thumb, the index finger lacking. The strong, vigorous face shows a man in later middle life, full-fleshed and ruddy, with blue eyes. The background is dark on the right, with clouds and sky showing dimly at the left. This is undoubtedly the picture to which J. Francis Fisher refers as a "kit-kat by Robert Feke" in his letter in

Dawson's *New York Historical Magazine*, 1860 (See Appendix A).
The portrait, however, being three-quarters length, is too large to
be accurately described as a "kit-kat."

Date.
Signed "R. Feke, 1746."

Size.
Height 50 inches; width 40 inches.

Ownership.
Now owned by Dr. Henry M. Fisher, Alverthorp, Jenkintown,
Pennsylvania, who inherited it from his father, J. Francis Fisher,
who probably received it from his first cousin, Hon. John Brown
Francis, son of John Francis, son of Tench Francis, Jr.

Exhibited.
Pennsylvania Academy of Fine Arts, Philadelphia, 1910.

MRS. TENCH FRANCIS (Elizabeth Turbutt) (No. 1)

Subject.
Elizabeth Turbutt, daughter of Foster and Bridget Turbutt of Tal-
bot County, Maryland; born March 17, 1708; married Tench
Francis of Philadelphia, December 29, 1724; died at Philadelphia,
May 1, 1800.

Description.
The subject is a large, robust woman in her early thirties, seated
nearly full-front, with her left arm resting upon an uncovered table
by her side. She has dark eyes and hair, a curl falling over the left
shoulder. She wears a blue satin gown, cut low and showing an
ample bosom, with white muslin trim, and white undersleeves. The
blue silk sleeves are caught up inside the elbows by jewels. A
pink silk scarf hanging rather awkwardly from her right shoulder
covers her right arm. The late owner supposed this portrait, like
that of her husband Tench Francis, No. 1, to be by Copley. But
the portrait is strikingly similar to that known as Mrs. Tench
Francis, No. 2, except that it is of smaller dimensions, and that the
subject is shown at a somewhat earlier age. The pose and manner of
painting of the head and bust are identical, and the subject has
simply moved her arms.

Date.

It would seem certain that this picture was painted by Feke in Philadelphia, probably before 1740.

Size.

Height 36 inches; width 29¼ inches.

Ownership.

Owned by Mrs. Sidell Tilghman, Madison, New Jersey.

MRS. TENCH FRANCIS (No. 2)

Description.

This later portrait of Mrs. Francis shows her in a pose similar to that in her early portrait, nearly full-front, three-quarters length. Her left shoulder is slightly advanced toward the spectator; the head is turned toward the left. She has dark brown hair, one curl of which falls over her left shoulder, dark gray eyes, and a well colored but not very expressive face. She wears a blue silk or satin dress with the long, tightly laced waist and very full skirt of the period, with white muslin trim around the bodice and white muslin sleeves. The silk sleeves of her gown are caught up inside to the elbow by crystal buttons. Her right elbow rests upon an indistinct object, perhaps a cloth-covered table or possibly gray stone masonry; her left hand hangs by her side holding an old-rose silk scarf. Behind the figure is a dark mass apparently intended to represent a wall of large rough stones or a brown curtain pulled aside to show at the right a vista of sky and landscape painted in low tones.

The portrait is by no means one of Feke's best. The figure is stiff and poorly drawn, but the face is better, being fairly well modelled, and the eyes and mouth are definitely characteristic of Feke's hand-work. The portrait is unsigned and undated, but it seems highly probable that it was painted as a companion piece to the Feke portrait of Tench Francis, although its dimensions are slightly smaller than that picture.

Date.

Unsigned and undated but presumably painted in Philadelphia in 1746.

Size.

Height 49 inches; width 39¼ inches. The picture has been relined.

MRS. TENCH FRANCIS (No. 2)

MRS. TENCH FRANCIS (No. 1)

Ownership.

This portrait was inherited by Margaret, daughter of Mr. and Mrs. Tench Francis, who married Edward Shippen, and has descended to Edward Shippen Willing, Bryn Mawr, Pennsylvania.

BENJAMIN FRANKLIN

Subject.

Benjamin Franklin, printer, scientist and statesman, born in Boston, January 17, 1706. He went to Philadelphia in 1723, and to London in 1726. Returning to Philadelphia he established a printing business. Founder of the Philosophical Society. A leading figure in the thought and life of the eighteenth century. He died in Philadelphia, April 17, 1790.

Description.

"The picture shows Franklin at about the time of his retirement from the printing business with what was for those days an ample fortune. He is shown standing, not quite to the knees, in an erect but easy pose, his shoulders thrown back and his head and body turned three-quarters toward his left, with his small, deep-set dark brown eyes, above prominent cheek-bones, calmly directed to the spectator. His well-developed but not yet corpulent figure is dressed in a long coat of neutral greenish black, unbuttoned and showing beneath it a very dark green waistcoat, unbuttoned to the waist, into which his left hand is partially thrust. The right arm hangs at his side, the short coat sleeve with a cuff, exposing the sleeve of his linen shirt, caught at the wrist by a wristband with crisp flaring ruffles, below which appears his opened hand with the index finger pointing downwards. He wears a dark [1] brown wig of small, tight curls which fall to his shoulders, a white neckcloth, and shirt ruffles, and the point of his three-cornered black hat held under his left arm, projects from the front line of his body. His expression denotes firmness and determination, particularly about the thin-lipped mouth and the strong, prominent jaw and long chin. It is these features which more nearly resemble those in the later portraits, but the whole face seems convincing as a likeness and looks much as one would suppose Franklin would look at this age. The

---

[1] Since Park saw the portrait it has been cleaned, and the wig is more accurately to be described as "light brown."

background shows two-thirds of the surface occupied by a plain dark brown wall against which the figure is placed, while at the right is an opening with a dull greenish sky and gray clouds with a distant landscape below. The picture is, it seems to me, the work of the early American artist, Robert Feke, conforming in every way as to drawing, color and pose with Feke's work. In my opinion it was painted by him in Philadelphia, in 1746, when both artist and subject were there and when Franklin was forty years old, which is his apparent age in the portrait.

"Although by this attribution the date of the picture is brought forward twenty years from the date previously assigned it, it still remains the earliest known portrait of Franklin."[1]

Size.

Height 49¼ inches; width 39¾ inches.

Ownership.

"The portrait, if not directly, at least very soon after it was painted came into the possession of Franklin's older brother, John Franklin (1690–1756). Indeed the picture may have been painted on his order. In a codicil to his will dated January 24, 1756, and probated February 6 following, he bequeathes to his 'well-beloved wife . . . my Brother Benjamin Franklin's picture during her natural Life.' At her death he stipulates that it is to go to his nephew, James Franklin of Newport. James Franklin died childless in 1762 and as Mrs. John Franklin survived until 1768 it is probable that his uncle's portrait never passed into his hands. John Franklin's widow does not mention the portrait in her will nor does it seem likely that it is included among the twenty-nine pictures appraised at twenty-six shillings and six pence in the inventory of her estate. When John Franklin married her, she was the widow of John Hubbert, or Hubbard, of Boston, and by her first husband had five children, one of

[1] Lawrence Park in *Art in America and Elsewhere*, Vol. XII, No. 1, Dec. 1923 (abbrev.). The correctness of Mr. Park's attribution of the portrait to Feke has been questioned on the ground that the picture is not particularly characteristic of Feke's style. While this is true, the picture is sufficiently like his other work to make the attribution not unreasonable on the ground of style alone. Certainly it more resembles his work than it does that of Hesselius or Smibert or Pelham, who were the only other painters in Philadelphia or Boston upon whom Franklin could have called to execute the commission in 1746. When this consideration is added to the links connecting Franklin with Feke (cited on pp. 67–68) there seems no adequate ground for doubting the attribution.

whom, Thomas, became the father of Elizabeth Hubbard who married at Weston, Massachusetts, in 1793, Thomas Waldron Sumner of Boston and Brookline, who was the owner of the portrait in 1840. In fact, as we learn from the inscription on a label in Mr. Sumner's handwriting, pasted on the back of the canvas, he acquired it July 21, 1837. Mr. Sumner died in 1849, and the portrait was purchased from his estate by Dr. John Collins Warren (1778–1856). Dr. Warren had the portrait in his house at 2 Park Street, Boston, until his death and the following letter found in the Corporation Records of Harvard College explains its subsequent history:

'Gentlemen:

My father, Dr. Warren, directed an original portrait of Dr. Franklin executed in London in 1726, [sic] to be given to Harvard College. This picture is large and the frame fragile. Will you be kind enough to take charge of the same or give me your directions concerning it, and oblige

Your very obt. servant
J. S. Warren

2 Park Street, Boston Mass.
May 13, (1856.)
To the President and Fellows of Harvard University.'

"This bequest was gratefully accepted by the college which had given Franklin one hundred and three years earlier the degree of Master of Arts."[1]

Because of its purchase from Mr. Sumner, noted above, the picture is sometimes called the "Sumner portrait" of Franklin.

Reproduced.
(1) Jared Sparks (ed.), *The Works of Benjamin Franklin*, Vol. I. 1840.
(2) Stevens, *Benjamin Franklin's Life and Writings.*
(3) James Parton, *Life and Times of Benjamin Franklin.* 1864.
(4) Justin Winsor, *Memorial History of Boston.* 1881.
(5) Scharf and Westcott, *History of Philadelphia.*
(6) C. W. Bowen, *Centennial Celebration of Washington's Inauguration.* 1892.
(7) *The Century Magazine*, November, 1898.
(8) Sidney George Fisher, *The True Benjamin Franklin.* 1899.

---

[1] Lawrence Park, op. cit.

(9) John Fiske, *The Dutch and Quaker Colonies in America.* 1903.
(10) *Art in America and Elsewhere*, Vol. XII, No. 1 (December, 1923) opp. p. 29.

Bibliographical References.

Art in America and Elsewhere, Vol. XII, No. 1, December, 1923. An important article by Lawrence Park, in which he describes the picture and gives its history (as quoted above in abbreviated form), and discusses his reasons for rejecting the tradition that it was painted in London in 1726, assigning it instead to Robert Feke.

JOHN GIDLEY, JR.

Subject.

John Gidley, Jr., merchant, of Newport, Rhode Island, 1700–44; son of Judge John Gidley, 1667–1718. The picture has been re-lined, but on the back is painted the following inscription, perhaps copied from the original canvas: —

> J^{no} Gidley, Esq., Captain of Newport Ar^{ty} Co. mar.
> Sar^h Shackmaple, Sept. 17th 1726. Killed Sept. 30th
> 1744. aet. 44. His son Midship^m R.N.

Description.

The subject is shown standing half-front, with his right shoulder toward the spectator, his face turned to the right three-quarters front. He wears a gray wig and is handsomely dressed in a blue coat, fawn-colored waistcoat with gold braid trimming, white neckcloth and ruffled shirt which shows through the loosely buttoned waist-coat, and white sleeve-ruffles. His left hand rests on a table, his right is placed in conventional pose against his waistcoat pocket, holding back his coat.

He stands against a dull brown background which opens on the right into a dim vista of trees and sky. He has a full, round face, rather pensive in quality, and not unlike that of his father.

The portrait was evidently done as a companion piece for the older portrait of the subject's father, Judge Gidley, which is also in possession of the Newport Historical Society, as the dimensions of the two pictures are identical (as is the early nineteenth century style of framing). The portrait of the judge is by an unknown hand, and is crudely done. The portrait of John Gidley, Jr., is reasonably assignable to Feke.

Date.

Unsigned and undated, but Gidley's death in 1744 fixes the latest possible date. Presumably the portrait was executed at Newport in the late seveenteen-thirties or early seventeen-forties.

Size.

Height 45⅝ inches; width 34¾ inches.

Ownership.

Newport Historical Society, Newport, Rhode Island.

COL. THOMAS GOLDTHWAIT

Subject.

Thomas Goldthwait, born in Boston, January 15, 1717–18; married (1) August 26, 1742, Esther, daughter of Epes Sargent of Gloucester; (2) February 19, 1746, Katharine Barnes. He was a merchant in Boston, but in 1750 moved to Chelsea, nearby, representing that town for seven years in the General Court. He took part in the French and Indian ar, Was paymaster. In 1763 he signed an order as "Secretary at War" for the Province. From that year until 1774 he was in command at Fort Pownal on the Penobscot River, Maine, and acquired a large tract of land there. When the Revolution broke he went to England and settled at Walthamstow, where he died August 31, 1799.

Description.

This is a very pleasing portrait of a young man not much over thirty years of age, shown at half-length, standing half-front, his right shoulder toward the spectator, his face turned right nearly full front. He is dressed in a white wig, gray cloth coat lined with pink silk, and pearl-gray silk waistcoat trimmed with handsome silver braid. His left hand is inserted into the waistcoat; his right, posed on his hip, the index finger extended, holds back the coat. His black cocked hat is held against his body by his left arm. He has gray eyes, level eyebrows, and a pleasing expression. The figure is set against a dark background.

The present owner, who inherited the fine portraits of Ezekiel Goldthwait (brother of Thomas) and his wife, which Copley painted in 1771, believes this portrait also to be by Copley, and bought it as his work. It is listed in *The Life and Works of John Singleton Copley,* by F. W. Bayley (Boston, 1915), p. 113, and might be considered to be an early work of his. It would appear much more probable, however, that it was painted by Feke during his Boston visit of 1748. The subject would have been thirty-one that year, which is his apparent age in the picture, whereas Copley was not old enough to produce work of this excellence until about a decade later. Goldthwait was a friend and associate of a number of the people whom Feke certainly painted in that year. The costume is that of the seventeen-forties. And finally, the portrait has all the characteristics of Feke's workmanship, of which it is a very good specimen.

While admitting the possibility of doubt, the probabilities strongly favor the attribution of the picture to Feke.

Size.

Height 34 inches; width 26 inches.

Ownership.

The present owner is Dr. John T. Bowen of Boston, a descendant from Thomas Goldthwait's brother Ezekiel. He bought the portrait some thirty years ago from a dealer who had acquired it from a Mr. Caldwell of Charlestown, Massachusetts. When Thomas Goldthwait went to England he probably left the portrait with his daughter Mary, who had married Francis Archibald. Their daughter Catherine married Stephen Caldwell, and their sixth child was Thomas Goldthwait Caldwell who was living in Charlestown in 1899.

Reproduced.

Charlotte Goldthwaite, *Descendants of Thomas Goldthwaite.* 1899.

REV. THOMAS HISCOX

Subject.

Rev. Thomas Hiscox, born 1686, son of "Elder" William Hiscox, first pastor of the Seventh-Day Baptist Church at Newport, Rhode Island. Thomas Hiscox moved to Westerly, Rhode Island; was chosen deacon in 1716, and ordained as an evangelist in 1732 at Newport. He twice refused appointment as an "Elder," but in 1750, at sixty-four years of age, consented and served Westerly as pastor until his death on May 20, 1773. He was also Justice of the Peace, Town Clerk and Town Treasurer, holding the latter office for sixty years.

THOMAS GOLDTHWAIT

Description.

The portrait shows a large, vigorous man painted nearly full front against a plain dark background, with his head turned a little to his right. He is about sixty years of age and wears his own abundant white hair. He has keen, brown eyes under straight, thick gray eyebrows; a sharp nose and straight, thin lips, above an uplifted and slightly dimpled chin. The well-colored face lacks the sweetness and charm shown in the companion portrait of Rev. John Callender, but it is not unkindly, and well portrays the rugged force of a strong personality. He is plainly dressed in a white shirt and neckcloth with clerical bands hanging over his plain black coat, which is left unbuttoned to show the waistcoat beneath. There are spandrels in the lower corners. For many years the identity of the subject was forgotten and the picture was supposed to represent John Callender, until identified a few years ago as a likeness of Hiscox.

Date.

Signed "R. Feak, A.D. 1745." Presumably painted in Newport.

Size.

Height 28¾ inches; width 24¼ inches.

Ownership.

This portrait, like that of Rev. John Callender, was commissioned by Henry Collins of Newport. When Collins died unmarried it passed to Henry Collins Flagg, son of Ebenezer Flagg and of his wife Mary, who was a daughter of Collins' half-brother, Richard Ward; thence to Henry Collins Flagg, Jr., thence to William J. Flagg, thence to his niece Mrs. Cornelius Vanderbilt, in whose house at Newport, Rhode Island, it now hangs.

Reproduced.

(1) A mezzotint engraving (6$\frac{10}{16}$ inches by 5$\frac{11}{16}$ inches) of the portrait by Samuel Okey of Newport was published after Hiscox's death with the following inscription:

The Rev^d. M^r. Thos. Hiscox,

late Pastor of the Baptist Chuch in Westerly, taken from an Original Picture painted by Mr. Feke

Published by Feak and Okey, Printsellers and Stationers on the Parade, Newport, Rhode Island, October 22, 1775.

This is the earliest known reproduction of any of Feke's paintings and the first appearance of his name in print.

(2) *The Seventh-Day Baptist Memorial*, Vol. I, No. 2 (New York, April, 1822), contains a biographical sketch of Hiscox with a lithographic reproduction of the portrait made by Sarony and Major of New York. It is a softened copy of Okey's engraving, printed in reverse. A note says that Feke's original portrait "is supposed to be in the possession of some one of the descendants of Governor Collins, of Newport, who was a great admirer of him and who had it painted at his own expense."

(3) Okey's engraving is also reproduced in photogravure in *Seventh-Day Baptists in Europe and America. Historical Papers*, Vol. II, p. 620, published by the American Sabbath Tract Society, Plainfield, New Jersey, 1910, and in *American Engravers upon Copper and Steel*, by David McNeely Stauffer, Part I (Grolier Club, New York, 1907), p. 70.

Bibliographical References.

See *Seventh-Day Baptists in Europe and America*, cited above, for information about Thomas Hiscox. See D. M. Stauffer, *American Engravers upon Copper and Steel*, Part II, p. 392, for catalogue description of the engraving.

THOMAS HOPKINSON

Subject.

Thomas Hopkinson, born in London, England, April 6, 1709; came to America in early life; died in Philadelphia, November 5, 1751. He was Judge of the Admiralty Court of the province of Pennsylvania; member of the Provincial Council; one of the founders and the first president of the American Philosophical Society, of which Benjamin Franklin was the first secretary; one of the founders of the Philadelphia City College (afterward the University of Pennsylvania); one of the founders of the Philadelphia Public Library. He was the father of Francis Hopkinson, Judge of the Admiralty Court and a signer of the Declaration of Independence, and was the grandfather of Judge Joseph Hopkinson, the author of "Hail Columbia."

Description.

Thomas Hopkinson is shown standing three-quarters length, half-front, with his right shoulder toward the spectator, and his head,

REV. THOMAS HISCOX

which is highly lighted from the spectator's left, turned nearly full front. He has dark brown eyes and well pencilled eyebrows. He wears a white wig, white neckcloth and ruffled shirt which shows through the partly unbuttoned waistcoat, and white ruffled sleeves. His dark wine-colored coat, lined with a lighter shade of satin, is held back by the right hand, which is placed against the pocket of the long, blue waistcoat. His left hand rests on the table by his side. The background behind the figure is a dull brown curtain drawn aside to show, at the right, trees and sky faintly painted.

Date.

Unsigned and undated; presumably painted in Philadelphia. The face is that of a man forty-one rather than thirty-seven years of age, so that it would seem probable that Feke painted it on his visit to Philadelphia in 1750, rather than in 1746.

Size.

Height 50 inches; width 40 inches.

Ownership.

The portrait was inherited by his daughter Anne, wife of Dr. Samuel Stringer Coale, and descended from her to George Buchanan Coale of Baltimore. It then passed to Mrs. Francis T. Redwood of Baltimore, who presented it to the National Gallery of Art, Smithsonian Institution, Washington, D. C. in 1926.

Reproduced.

(1) Alice Morse Earle, *Two Centuries of Costume in America.* Macmillan, 1903, p. 342.

(2) A poor copy painted by Herman Deigendesch in 1910, is owned by the American Philosophical Society, Philadelphia.

RALPH INMAN

Subject.

Ralph Inman, born about 1710. He married Susannah Speakman, and lived in Cambridge, in a house which stood just behind the site of the present City Hall. His name is perpetuated in Inman Street. He was one of the original subscribers to the fund for erecting Christ Church, Cambridge, 1759. During the Revolution he was a Royalist. He died in Cambridge in May, 1788.

Description.

He is shown at a little more than half-length, three-quarters front, with his right shoulder toward the spectator and his head turned to the right. His right elbow rests on a table, his hand holding a paper. He has blue eyes and a ruddy complexion. His rather abundant curly hair is brushed back and powdered. He wears a tobacco-brown coat, white waistcoat and white stock. The background is a grayish-brown at the left, showing blue sky at the right.

Date.

Presumably painted in Boston or Cambridge in 1748.

Size.

Height 36 inches; width 29½ inches.

Ownership.

William Amory, Boston.

Exhibited.

Fogg Art Museum, Harvard University, Cambridge, 1928.
Boston Museum of Fine Arts, 1930.

Reproduced.

(1) A. R. Cunningham (ed.), *Letters and Diary of John Rowe.* Boston, 1903.

(2) J. W. Linzee (ed.), *History of the Linzee Family.* Boston, 1917. Vol. I.

(3) F. W. Bayley, *Five Colonial Artists of New England.* Boston, 1929.

MRS. RALPH INMAN (Susannah Speakman) (No. 1)

Subject.

Mrs. Ralph Inman was Susannah Speakman, and was born in Boston in 1725. She is said to have been a twin sister of Mrs. John Rowe. She married Ralph Inman as his first wife, and died in Cambridge, June 30, 1761.

Description.

In this companion piece to the portrait of Ralph Inman, his wife is shown at half-length, three-quarters front, with her right shoulder toward spectator, her head turned to the right. She has brown hair and eyes, and wears a blue silk dress with white trimming around the neck and sleeves, with a light rose scarf thrown loosely about her. The background is reddish-brown at the left, perhaps intended to represent a curtain, but at the right a distant landscape of water, trees, and a hill is shown, rather dully painted. The portrait is in rather poor condition, and is not one of Feke's best. The portrait closely resembles that of Mrs. John Rowe (q. v.).

Date.

Unsigned. Presumably painted at Boston in 1748.

Size.

Height 36 inches; width 29½ inches.

Ownership.

William Amory, Boston.

Exhibited.

Fogg Art Museum, Cambridge, 1928.
Boston Museum of Fine Arts, 1930.

Reproduced.

(1) A. R. Cunningham (ed.), *Letters and Diary of John Rowe.* Boston, 1903.

(2) J. W. Linzee (ed.), *History of the Linzee Family.* Boston, 1917. Vol. I.

(3) F. W. Bayley, *Five Colonial Artists of New England.* Boston, 1929.

(The portrait is there listed as that of Hannah Speakman, the sister of Mrs. Inman, who married John Rowe, and Mrs. Rowe's picture is listed as that of Mrs. Inman.)

MRS. RALPH INMAN (No. 2)

Subject.

This portrait is said by tradition to represent Susannah Speakman, who married Ralph Inman, and comparison with the picture listed as Mrs. Ralph Inman, No. 1, seems to verify the identification, though the costume and pose are quite different.

Description.

The subject is a young woman shown seated, nearly full front, against a dark brown background, which on the left opens to a vista of trees and sky. She has dark eyes, and dark hair, a curl of which falls on her right shoulder. She is dressed in blue silk, trimmed with yellow, a white muslin bodice and undersleeves, and about her is thrown an old-rose scarf. Her hands are folded in her lap.

The painting has been attributed to Blackburn, but does not look at all like his work. It is not particularly characteristic of Feke, but it is difficult to attribute it to anyone else. Possibly it was painted for Mrs. Inman's twin sister, Mrs. Rowe (q. v.).

Date.

Unsigned and undated; presumably painted in Boston or Cambridge in 1748.

Size.

Height 33½ inches; width 26¼ inches.

Ownership.

It has descended in the family, through Susannah, daughter of Mrs. Inman, who married Captain John Linzee; to their daughter, Hannah, who married Thomas Amory; to their daughter Susan, who married William H. Prescott; to his son William Gardner Prescott; to his son Linzee Prescott; and to his daughter, Mrs. Leonard Opdycke, of Boston, the present owner.

Exhibited.

Copley Society Loan Exhibit, Boston Art Club, March, 1922. (No. 15, listed, "Artist Unknown.")

MRS. BENJAMIN LYNDE, JR. (MARY BOWLES GOODRIDGE)

Subject.

Mary, daughter of John Bowles, born in Roxbury, Massachusetts, September 6, 1709; married (1) Walter Goodridge, (2) Benjamin Lynde, Jr., November 1, 1731; died Salem, Massachusetts, May 31, 1790. Her husband (born in Salem, 1700; died in Salem, 1781), who was a distinguished lawyer, was made Chief Justice of Massachusetts in 1771, a position which his father, of the same name, had held before him.

Description.

The bust of the subject rises from painted spandrels in the lower corners, without the hands being shown. The figure is shown half-front, with the left shoulder turned toward the spectator, the head turned left, three-quarters front. She is a robust woman in her late thirties, with dark hair falling behind her back but without the usual curl over one shoulder, and with dark eyes and rather level eyebrows. The face is expressive and is unusually well modelled and colored, one of the best of Feke's portraits of women. She wears a well-painted red velvet dress, simply trimmed with white muslin about the bodice. The background is a fairly uniform dark brown. This simple but effective picture is much like that of Hannah Flagg in color and manner, but the pose of the figure is more like that shown in the portraits of Mrs. William Peters and Mrs. Tench Francis.

Family tradition has ascribed the portrait to Smibert, but it is thoroughly characteristic of Feke's work and fits well into the date of his second Boston visit. Furthermore comparison with the companion portrait of her husband, which is certainly Smibert's, reveals certain discrepancies. The portraits are not quite identical in size; the figure of Benjamin Lynde, Jr., is set in a painted oval of a quite different style; and Smibert's portrait, while of fair quality, is decidedly inferior in characterization and in the painting of the fabrics. From the age of the subject it must have been painted about the same time, near the end of Smibert's career, and one may surmise that the sitter, being either dissatisfied with the result, or unable to secure Smibert's services to paint his wife's portrait, commissioned Feke to do so.

Date.

Presumably painted in Boston in 1748.

Size.

Height 29 inches; width 24¾ inches.

Ownership.

The portrait, with those of Mrs. Lynde's husband and parents-in-law, was inherited by the Oliver family, into which a daughter married. In 1910 Mrs. Fitch E. Oliver sold them to the present owner, Mr. F. E. Moseley of Boston, whose wife was also a descendant of the Lyndes, keeping in their place copies made in that year.

Exhibited.

Exhibited at the Copley Society Loan Exhibition, Boston Art Club, March, 1922, where it was described as "Formerly attributed to John Smybert; attributed to Feke by Lawrence Park."

Reproduced.

(1) A copy painted in 1910.
(2) F. W. Bayley, *Five Colonial Artists of New England.* Boston, 1929.

JOSIAH MARTIN

Subject.

Josiah Martin was born in Antigua, West Indies, in 1699; settled at Hempstead, Long Island, about 1730, though retaining his estate in Antigua, which he visited from time to time; purchased "Rock Hall," Rockaway (now Lawrence), Long Island, in 1767, where he died in 1778. He married, in 1735, as his second wife, Mary Yeamans.

Description.

The subject is shown three-quarters length, half-front, with his right shoulder toward the spectator and his head turned right. He stands with his right hand resting on a table by his side, his left hand outstretched with open palm. He is a somewhat florid, full-fleshed man in his forties, with very erect pose. He wears a white wig; a coat which now appears black but which seems originally to have been dark green, lined with white satin; a long, white brocade waistcoat; white neckband and ruffles edged with lace, showing through a partly unbuttoned waistcoat, and white wristbands. The background behind the figure is a dull brown; to the right is a vista painted in low tones showing a bay with houses at the water's edge, behind which rises a hill with trees, and clouds in the sky above.

It seems probable that the view is intended to represent the shores of what was then called Cow Bay, now known as Hempstead Harbor, where Josiah Martin had his residence at the time that the picture must have been painted. An almost identical vista is shown in his wife's portrait. The site of Martin's house on the shore of Hempstead is unknown so that the vista depicted may be intended to represent either the view looking toward the house or the view from it.

The portrait, like that of Mrs. Martin, is apparently the work of Feke in his maturity. In view of the fact that Martin lived only a few miles from the residences of the painter's father and grandfather it would seem probable that the Martin portraits were painted during one of Feke's visits to his childhood home at Oyster Bay. We have no knowledge of how frequently such visits occurred but it seems reasonable to suppose that he may have stopped at Oyster Bay on his way to or from Philadelphia on one of his expeditions thither. It is, therefore, not unreasonable to assign a provisional date of 1746 to these portraits.

MRS. JOSIAH MARTIN

JOSIAH MARTIN

Size.

Height 50¼ inches; width 40¾ inches.

Ownership.

Josiah Martin, 1746–78; to his son Samuel Martin, 1778–1806; to Alice and Rachel Martin (Bannister) his sisters, 1806–15; to Alice Hermione Pelham Bannister McNiel, 1815–23; gift to Mary and Thomas Hewlett, 1823–87; to George Hewlett, Brooklyn; but the picture hangs at "Rock Hall," Lawrence, Long Island.

MRS. JOSIAH MARTIN (Mary Yeamans)

Subject.

Mary, daughter of William Yeamans, born about 1720 in Antigua; married 1735 to Josiah Martin; died at "Rock Hall," Rockaway (now Lawrence), Long Island, 1805.

Description.

Mrs. Martin is shown seated, nearly full front, her head turned a little to the right. She is a ruddy faced woman approaching thirty, with dark hair, a curl of which falls over her shoulder, and dark eyes. She wears a pearl-gray satin gown, the sleeves of which are caught up with jewels inside the elbows. The bodice is trimmed with white muslin and she has white muslin undersleeves. The dress is cut low, with the long, tightly laced waist, and very full skirt of that period. Her left arm rests on a table by her side. Her right hand lies in her lap holding a bright red rose and rosebud. The background behind the figure is brown, and at the left shows a vista of bay, hillside, and clouds, closely resembling that shown in her husband's picture.

Size.

Height 50½ inches; width 40½ inches.

Ownership.

This portrait passed, with that of the subject's husband, to the present owner, George Hewlett, Brooklyn; but the picture is still at "Rock Hall," Lawrence, Long Island.

MRS. GEORGE McCALL (Ann Yeates)

Subject.

Anne, daughter of Judge Jasper Yeates of Philadelphia, born December 27, 1697; married George McCall in 1716; left a widow at his death, October 13, 1740. She died in June, 1746.

Description.

This portrait was destroyed by fire about forty years ago, but a photograph of it is herewith reproduced.

The subject is shown three-quarters length, full front, her face turned a little to her left. She is standing against a wall, with a curtain (?) to the right. She has dark hair, a curl of which falls over either shoulder. Her upraised right hand holds a spray of flowers; her left a drooping rose. She is dressed in a long, tight waist, around which is a cord with hanging tassels, very full skirts, and sleeve ruffles and buttons. Her dress is said to have been of yellow silk, and the picture is described as a beautiful one. In pose and costume this portrait markedly resembles the two pictures which have been supposed to represent Mrs. Clement Plumstead and Miss Margaret Willing, but which probably portray Miss Mary McCall, who later married William Plumstead, and another and unidentified member of the McCall family. The photograph of the portrait of Mrs. McCall is certainly reminiscent of these other two pictures.

Date.

The portrait clearly shows the characteristics of Feke's brush in his earlier years. The subject appears to be a woman of about forty years of age. Furthermore it seems probable that she would have been thus portrayed before her husband's death in 1740, rather than after that event. For these reasons the picture is best assigned to Feke's first visit to Philadelphia, a little before 1740, when he painted his first portraits of Mr. and Mrs. Tench Francis.

Size.

Probably about 50 inches in height by 40 inches in width.

Ownership.

H. B. McCall, on p. 126, in *Some Old Families* (privately printed, Birmingham, Watson and Ball, 1890) wrote: "Excellent portraits of him [George McCall] and his wife are [sic] in the possession of the late Hon. Peter McCall of Philadelphia." Peter McCall died in 1880. The portrait of George McCall is now owned by Miss Helen McCall of Chestnut Hill, Pennsylvania. It is clearly not the work of Feke, but was probably painted in the seventeen-thirties by Hesselius. The portrait of Mrs. McCall was inherited by Peter McCall's daughter Mrs. John M. Keating of Wawa, Pennsylvania, who owned it at the time it was burned.

MISS MARY McCALL (?) (MRS. WILLIAM PLUMSTEAD (?)
MRS. CLEMENT PLUMSTEAD, SO-CALLED)

Description.

This portrait shows a woman, three-quarters length, three-quarters front, with her left shoulder advanced, her face turned to the left toward the spectator. She wears a blue-green silk dress with a rose insertion in the front of the skirt and a gold cord with tassels around her waist. She holds a rose in her left hand. The bodice is tightly buttoned with crystal buttons and the sleeves caught up with similar buttons on the inside of the elbow. The neck is cut low and there are ruffles around the neck and sleeves.

The figure is stiff and awkwardly posed, apparently leaning against a stone parapet upon which her left elbow rests. While the pose is unsatisfactory, the head is very fine, representing a full-faced, vigorous woman of strong character, in her twenties. The coloring of the face is very good. She has dark eyes, and abundant dark hair with a curl falling over the right shoulder. The whole picture is in Feke's manner, and may well be attributed to his second or third Philadelphia visit.

The picture was bequeathed to the Pennsylvania Academy of Fine Arts by Helen Ross Scheetz, and is deposited by the Academy with the Historical Society of Pennsylvania, 1300 Locust Street, Philadelphia. It has been relined at a fairly recent period and on the back are painted the words "Mrs. Clement Plumstead painted by Sir Peter Lely." The attribution to Lely is obviously preposterous and the identity of the subject is uncertain. Clement Plumstead was a Philadelphia Quaker who died in 1745. His first wife was born in 1678, only two years before the death of Lely, was married in 1703 and died before 1707, when her husband married a second time. His third wife was married to him prior to 1722 and died in 1755.

Helen Henderson in *The Philadelphia Academy of Fine Arts and Other Collections in Philadelphia*, p. 359, appears to think that the portrait represents the first Mrs. Clement Plumstead, but that is impossible, since the subject is shown as a woman in her early twenties and in the costume of the seventeen-forties, when the first Mrs. Plumstead had been dead for many years, and would have been in her sixties had she been living.

The picture is listed as No. 341 in the printed *Catalogue of the Loan Exhibition of Historical Portraits*, Pennsylvania Academy of Fine Arts, December, 1887–January, 1888, with notes by the late Charles Henry Hart, as "Plumstead, Mrs. Clement. P. Lely." But in the notes Mr. Hart pointed out that Lely could not have painted the portrait of the first Mrs. Clement Plumstead and suggested that this picture might be the work of Hesselius, representing the second Mrs. Plumstead. The portrait does not look at all like the work of Hesselius, and the costume is not that of 1720. Finally, the subject is too young to be the third wife of Clement Plumstead; and the elderly wife or widow of a Quaker, if she had her portrait painted at all, which is most unlikely, would certainly not have been dressed like a lady of fashion in a blue-green silk dress with a rose insert and a gold cord around her waist.

A photograph of the portrait at the Frick Art Reference Library has the pencilled notation, "This is probably the picture called Mrs. Willing, No. 472 in the Loan Exhibition of Historical Portraits Catalogue, Pennsylvania Academy of Fine Arts, December, 1887–January, 1888, and there attributed to Benjamin West." The writer of this notation was mistaken, due to his having failed to observe that the portrait was duly listed in the Catalogue under the name of Mrs. Clement Plumstead.

The most plausible identification of the subject is discussed on pp. 90–93, where the theory is advanced that it represents Miss Mary McCall, daughter of George McCall, who in 1753 married William Plumstead, son of Clement, as his second wife. Miss Scheetz, who bequeathed the portrait, with that of William Plumstead, to the Pennsylvania Academy of Fine Arts, was the last living descendant of the couple.

See the descriptions of the portraits of Mrs. George McCall and of Miss Margaret Willing (so-called) for a discussion of the striking resemblance of this picture to those two portraits.

Size.
Height 49 inches; width 38¾ inches.

Ownership.
Pennsylvania Academy of Fine Arts, Philadelphia.

Exhibited.
Historical Society of Pennsylvania, Philadelphia.

MISS RICHEA MEYERS (or MEARS) (Mrs. Barnard Gratz)

Subject.

Richea, daughter of Sampson Meyers (or Mears); born 1731, died 1801. She married Barnard Gratz, a German Jew, said to have been born in Germany in 1738, who came to Philadelphia when about seventeen years of age.

Description.

The portrait shows the bust and head of a fine looking young Jewess of dark complexion, set in the lower half of a painted oval against a plain background. Her right shoulder is slightly advanced and her face turned a little to her right, nearly full front. She has large dark eyes, and abundant dark hair parted in the middle and falling in curls on either shoulder. She wears a dark red dress with the usual white muslin trim about the bodice, and two white ribbon bows in the corsage.

Date.

This portrait was known to Lawrence Park and he attributed it to Feke. The pose of the head and figure so strongly resemble other examples of Feke's workmanship as to make the attribution a reasonable one. If it be his, the latest date for it would be in the spring of 1750, when Miss Meyers was about nineteen years of age, although the portrait represents a woman who looks rather more mature than one would expect her to be at that age. Presumably, therefore, the picture was painted during Feke's latest Philadelphia visit.

Size.

Height 29½ inches; width 24½ inches.

Ownership.

Miss A. B. Hays, Philadelphia.

Reproduced.

Hannah R. London, *Portraits of Jews by Gilbert Stuart and Other Early American Artists.* 1927. (Under the name of Mrs. Barnard Gratz.)

MISS WILLIAMINA MOORE

Subject.

Williamina, daughter of Col. William and Williamina Wemyss Moore; born, 1727; married Dr. Phineas Bond of Philadelphia, 1748; died, 1809. Her father, Col. Moore, was a member of the Assembly, a judge, and Colonel of the Regiment of Foot. He had a country home, "Moore Hall," near Valley Forge, which was visited by Washington.

Description.

The subject is shown as a slender young woman, seated, facing nearly full front. She has dark hair and eyes. Her hair is parted in the middle, and is closely done up behind, so that the usual falling curl is absent. She wears a white lace cap with pink ribbons. She is dressed in a low-cut gown of golden-yellow brocade, trimmed with white muslin about the bodice, and white muslin undersleeves. Her right arm rests upon the lower folds of a dark blue curtain which is draped over a table by her side, her right fingers out-reached to touch a handful of roses and small white flowers which her left hand holds in her lap. The dark blue curtain forms the background at the spectator's left; in the centre is shown the base of a large column; and to the right a vista of trees and sky. On the edge of the table is clearly painted the inscription "R. F. Pinx, 1746."

The portrait is in a state of perfect preservation, and is unusually beautiful in its details and accessories. Miss Moore is shown with an ivory complexion, highly arched eyebrows, large nose and small mouth. She was evidently far from handsome, being decidedly plain of face and meagre in person, though the face is that of a woman of intelligence and character. Evidently the painter felt that he must exert all his skill to make up for what his subject lacked of personal charm. The result is one of his finest achievements in color and detail.

Size.

Height 36 inches; width 28 inches.

Ownership.

Inherited in the family of her uncle Col. John Moore of New York; passing to his daughter Frances, wife of Samuel Bayard; thence to their daughter Frances who married Philip J. Livingston; thence to their daughter Maria, who married Andrew Smyth; thence to their

son John Smyth II; thence to his daughter Georgiana Maria Smyth
Payne, from whose estate it was purchased in 1926 by the present
owner, Thomas B. Clarke, 22 East 35th Street, New York City.

Exhibited.

    (1) Loan Exhibition of Paintings by Early American Portrait
        Painters, The Century Association, New York, January 14–
        February 2, 1928.

    (2) Exhibition of Portraits of Early American Artists, Philadelphia
        Museum of Art, 1928.

WILLIAM NELSON

Subject.

William Nelson was the son of Thomas Nelson and Margaret Reid,
his wife. Thomas emigrated from Penrith, Cumberland, about 1690;
laid out Yorktown, Virginia, in 1705, and built the famous Nelson
House there. William was born in 1711, was a merchant and landed
proprietor, president of the Supreme Court of the Province, member
of the Governor's Council, and, as its president, was acting governor
of Virginia 1790–91. He married Elizabeth Burwell of Virginia, and
their son Thomas was a signer of the Declaration of Independence.
William Nelson died at Yorktown, November 19, 1792.

Description.

Nelson is shown as a man about forty years old, standing half-
front, his right shoulder to the spectator, his face turned right nearly
full front. His right hand rests on the edge of a stone parapet; his
left is thrust into his half-buttoned waistcoat. His left arm holds a
cocked hat against his side. He is dressed in a light coat and a long,
nearly white waistcoat, with the usual neckband and sleeve ruffles.
The background shows trees and sky. He has abundant dark hair
brushed back from his forehead, and a full face showing decided
vigor and character.

Date.

The picture is unsigned and undated. Mr. F. W. Bayley attributes
it, and its companion portrait of Mrs. Nelson, to Wollaston, who
was painting in Virginia in the seventeen-fifties. The general style
of the pictures, and the fact that Feke is not known to have gone
further south than Philadelphia (no other portraits by him have
been found in Virginia), lend support to Mr. Bayley's attribution.

On the other hand it would have been perfectly possible for the Nelsons to have visited Philadelphia in 1746 or 1750 when Feke was there, and both portraits strongly resemble other pictures attributed to Feke. For example, the right hand in the portrait of Nelson is so nearly identical with that shown in the portrait of Josiah Martin as to indicate that both pictures were painted by the same artist. While Wollaston, when in New York, might conceivably have painted Josiah Martin, the presumption on the ground of locality and the apparent age of the subject is strongly in favor of Feke. I have, therefore, felt justified in tentatively attributing the Nelson portraits also to Feke.

Size.

Height 50 inches; width 40 inches.

Ownership.

Mrs. Fanny Burwell Nelson Mercer of Richmond, Virginia.

Exhibited.

Virginia State Library Building, Richmond, Virginia.

MRS. WILLIAM NELSON (Elizabeth Burwell)

Subject.

Elizabeth Burwell, of Virginia, wife of William Nelson.

Description.

Mrs. Nelson is shown seated, nearly full front, her face turned toward her right but her eyes looking out of the picture. Her right arm rests upon a table at her side; her left hand, holding a rose, is in her lap. She wears the costume of 1750, with long, tight bodice, full skirt, and white lawn trim and sleeve ruffles. There are jewelled pins on the bodice and sleeves. The portrait is in poor condition.

Date.

From the age of the subject it is a reasonable assumption that the portrait may have been painted about 1750. It is unsigned and undated, and, like that of her husband, is attributed to Wollaston by Mr. F. W. Bayley, on the ground of style. The picture, however, shows many of the characteristics of Feke's work. In pose and in the way in which the right arm, with its sleeve and ruffle, is painted, it is nearly identical with Feke's portrait of Mrs. Ralph

WILLIAM NELSON

Inman, and in the treatment of the eyes and other details it closely resembles other portraits of women by him. The resemblances are so marked that it seems reasonable to assume that both this portrait and its companion piece may have been painted by Feke at Philadelphia during the painter's visit of 1750.

Size.

Height 50 inches; width 40 inches.

Ownership.

Mrs. Fanny Burwell Nelson Mercer of Richmond, Virginia.

Exhibited.

Virginia State Library Building, Richmond, Virginia.

WILLIAM PETERS

Subject.

William, son of Ralph Peters, born in Liverpool, England, 1702, emigrated to Philadelphia in 1735 or soon after. In 1741 he married his second wife, Mary Brientnall. He built a home called "Belmont" in what is now Fairmount Park, Philadelphia. He was Registrar of the Admiralty, Judge of the Court of Common Pleas, member of the Legislature from 1752 to 1756. Being a Tory he returned to England at the outbreak of the Revolutionary War and resided at Knutsford, where he died, September 8, 1789, but his son Richard Peters was prominent on the American side.

Description.

William Peters is shown in a bust portrait, nearly full front, with his right shoulder slightly advanced and his head turned slightly to the right. He wears a gray wig, brown velvet coat, brown satin waistcoat, white stock and shirt ruffle. The figure is set against a dark brown background with small, dark brown spandrels in all four corners. He has gray eyes, a well colored complexion, and shows the pleasing face of a man in his forties. In the catalogue of the Historical Society of Pennsylvania the portrait is attributed to Gustavus Hesselius but it is much more reasonable to assign it to Feke, of whose work it seems to be a rather mediocre specimen.

Date.

Probably painted in Philadelphia in 1750.

Size.

Height 30½ inches; width 25¼ inches.

Ownership.

Presented to the Historical Society of Pennsylvania, Philadelphia, in 1890 by a descendant, Mrs. John W. (Elizabeth Peters) Field, of Salem, Massachusetts.

Reproduced.

A copy painted about 1890 is in the possession of Richard Peters of Atlanta, Georgia. This copy has been reproduced in *Richard Peters, his Ancestors and Descendants* (1904), p. 60.

MRS. WILLIAM PETERS (Mary Brientnall)

Subject.

Mary, daughter of John Brientnall and Susannah Shoemaker of Philadelphia, married William Peters in 1741. She removed with him to Knutsford, England, at the time of the Revolution and is known to have died there at some time previous to his death in 1789.

Description.

The subject is shown nearly full front but with her right shoulder slightly advanced and with her head turned to the right. She is a robust woman with gray eyes and brown hair, a curl hanging over one shoulder. She wears a blue silk dress with white muslin trim around the bodice, and white muslin undersleeves. The silk sleeves are caught up with jewels inside the elbow. Her right arm leans upon the edge of a table. The background shows a dark brown curtain at the upper left. There are small, dark brown spandrels in the lower corners. In the catalogue of the Historical Society of Pennsylvania the portrait is attributed to Gustavus Hesselius, but the well modelled face, the painting of the eyes and of the figure, and the pose of the body which closely resembles that in the portraits of Mrs. Tench Francis, are all thoroughly characteristic of Feke. Mrs. Peters is shown as a matron approaching thirty years of age. In view of her marriage in 1741, and of the fact that her eldest child was born in 1744, it is more probable that the portrait was painted at the time of Feke's last visit to Philadelphia in 1750 rather than earlier.

Size.

Height 30 inches; width 25 inches.

Ownership.

Presented to the Historical Society of Pennsylvania, Philadelphia, in 1890, by a descendant, Mrs. John W. (Elizabeth Peters) Field, of Salem, Massachusetts.

Reproduced.

(1) *Cosmopolitan Magazine*, XVI (April, 1894), 651, in an article on "Some Colonial Women."

(2) A copy was painted about 1890 which is now in the possession of Richard Peters of Atlanta, Georgia. This copy was reproduced in *Richard Peters, his Ancestors and Descendants* (1904), p. 130.

WILLIAM PLUMSTEAD

Subject.

William Plumstead was born in Philadelphia, November 7, 1708; merchant; elected mayor of Philadelphia in 1750, 1754, and 1755. He was originally a member of the Society of Friends, but became an Episcopalian and served as vestryman and warden of St. Peter's Church. He died August 10, 1765.

Description.

The subject is shown at three-quarters length, nearly full front, against a very dark background. He wears a white wig, a tobacco-brown coat and waistcoat, with ruffles. His right hand rests upon a table of dark wood with a gray marble top. His left hand is thrust into his bosom. The face is well colored and expressive. He appears as a man in his forties. In the catalogue of the Historical Society of Pennsylvania the picture is attributed to Copley, but a pencil correction, perhaps in the hand of Lawrence Park, attributes the picture to Feke. It is thoroughly characteristic of Feke's work and may well have been painted in 1750, when Feke was in Philadelphia and when William Plumstead was forty-two years old and was serving his first term as mayor. While Plumstead lived long enough for Copley to have painted him, Copley would almost necessarily have represented him as an older man than is shown in this picture.

Date.

Probably painted in Philadelphia in 1750.

Size.

Height 49¾ inches; width 40 inches.

Ownership.

In the *Chronicles of the Plumstead Family*, by Eugene Devereaux, privately printed, Philadelphia, 1887, a footnote on p. 41 says, "A well painted, life-sized portrait of William Plumstead, said to have been by Copley, is now in the possession of Miss Helena R. Scheetz, a descendant who also possesses a full-length portrait of a handsome woman, said to have been painted by Sir Peter Lely and believed to have been the wife of Clement Plumstead and mother of William, but unfortunately there exists nothing to confirm this belief." The portrait of the woman referred to probably represents Mary McCall, second wife of William Plumstead, and is discussed on pp. 90–93. Miss Helena R. Scheetz was a great-granddaughter of William Plumstead and Mary McCall. She was the last of her family and bequeathed both portraits to the Pennsylvania Academy of Fine Arts, which has loaned them to the Historical Society of Pennsylvania.

Exhibited.

This is no doubt the portrait of William Plumstead which was exhibited by Miss Helena R. Scheetz at the Loan Exhibition of Historical Portraits, December 1, 1887–January 15, 1888. In the *Catalogue* of that exhibition it is attributed to Copley.

The portrait is now shown at the Historical Society of Pennsylvania.

Reproduced.

(1) A. C. Myers (ed.), *Hannah Logan's Courtship* (Philadelphia, 1904), p. 75.

(2) A crudely painted portrait of William Plumstead by J. Augustus Beck, now hanging in the building of the Historical Society of Pennsylvania, is apparently a copy of the head and shoulders of Feke's portrait.

(3) There is also a small lithographic reproduction of the bust and of William Plumstead's signature, by A. Rosenthal, in the Gilpin Collection of Eminent Americans, No. 19, at the Historical Society of Pennsylvania.

JOHN ROWE

Subject.

John Rowe was born in Exeter, England, November 16 (O. S.), 1715, and emigrated to America as early as 1736, in which year he purchased a warehouse on Long Wharf, Boston. In 1743 he married

Hannah Speakman. He was a successful merchant and a man of considerable eminence, frequently engaged in town affairs. During the Revolution he was a moderate, somewhat inclined to the Tory side, but came through the conflict without much loss of property, and afterwards represented Boston in the State Legislature. He also possessed property in his birthplace. He died in Boston in 1787, and was buried, with his wife, beneath Trinity Church, of which he was a communicant. His name is perpetuated in Rowe's Wharf. His letter book is preserved in the Boston Public Library; his journal in the Massachusetts Historical Society.

Description.

John Rowe stands behind a table covered with a green cloth, upon which his right hand rests. His body is almost in profile, the right shoulder toward the spectator, with his face turned right, nearly full front. It is that of a man in his early thirties, of pleasing expression though rather round and full. He has gray (hazel) eyes, level brown eyebrows and a rather fair complexion. He wears a gray, curled wig, but is simply dressed in a drab coat lined with light silk and a tobacco-brown waistcoat left partially unbuttoned to show the ruffles of the shirt. The plain background is shaded from dark to light to contrast with the lighting of the face. The portrait is very simple in composition and detail but is an attractive picture. Although it is unsigned it plainly bears the convincing marks of Feke's workmanship. There is a well established family tradition that Feke painted John Rowe and his wife, the latter being a sister of Mrs. Ralph Inman, whose picture Feke also painted twice.

Date.

Unsigned and undated. Presumably painted in Boston in 1748.

Size.

Height 35¾ inches; width 28 inches.

Ownership.

John Rowe had no children. His portrait passed to his nephew and namesake, John Rowe II, son of Jacob Rowe, and has been transmitted to his descendants. The present owner is Mr. J. Rowe Webster, Lexington, Massachusetts.

Exhibited.

Boston Museum of Fine Arts, 1929.

Reproduced.

A. R. Cunningham (ed.), *Letters and Diary of John Rowe, 1760–62 and 1764–79.* Boston, 1903.

MRS. JOHN ROWE (Hannah Speakman)

Subject.

Hannah Speakman (twin [?] sister of Mrs. Ralph Inman) born in Boston in 1725; married John Rowe of Boston; died in 1805.

Description.

Mrs. Rowe is shown seated, three-quarters front, her head turned right nearly full front. She wears a blue silk dress trimmed with white muslin, and a blue bow in her hair. Her right elbow rests upon a scarf which is thrown over a table at her side and is carried behind over her left shoulder and arm. She has a fresh complexion, dark eyes, and dark hair which falls to her shoulder. The background is dark behind, but to the right shows a landscape with a lake and sky painted in low tones. The portrait is strongly characteristic of Feke, and bears a very close resemblance to the portrait of the subject's sister, Mrs. Ralph Inman, No. 1. The present owner has believed the picture to be the work of Copley, since it was bought as such many years ago by her grandfather, Mr. Charles Amory of Boston, who was a descendant of Copley's. This attribution, however, seems certainly to be a mistaken one. The picture is clearly a companion piece to that of the subject's husband, John Rowe, which has descended in another line and has always been attributed to Feke. The subject is represented as a woman around twenty years of age, which would have been her age in 1748, when Feke was in Boston and when Copley was only eleven years old. Furthermore the picture too strongly resembles Feke's other works to allow of much doubt as to its being his work.

Date.

Presumably painted in Boston in 1748.

Size.

Height 35¾ inches; width 28½ inches.

Ownership.

The present owner is Miss Susan C. Amory of Boston, who inherited the picture from her grandfather, Charles Amory, who purchased the picture from an owner whose name is not now remembered. Presumably the portrait was inherited by John Rowe II, and was transmitted to his descendants.

Reproduced.
    (1) J. W. Linzee (ed.), *History of the Linzee Family.* Boston, 1917. Vol. I.
    (2) F. W. Bayley, *Five Colonial Artists of New England.* Boston, 1929 (but it has there been listed as Mrs. Ralph Inman, who was Susannah Speakman, Mrs. Rowe's sister, q. v.).

ISAAC ROYALL AND FAMILY

Subject.
On the back of the picture is an inscription,[1] painted in black, flowing letters, reading:

Drawn for
Mr. Isaac Royall whose
Portrait is on the foreside
Age 22 years 13th instant
His lady in blue
Aged 19 years 13th instant
Her Sister Miss Mary Palmer in (red) [2]
Aged 18 years 2nd of August
His sister Penelope Royall in Green
Aged 17 years in April
The (child his) [2] daughter Elizabeth
Aged 8 months, 7th instant
Finisht Sept. 15th, 1741
by Robert Feke.

The inscription, though now faint, is legible except for three words, in parentheses above. That it was painted by Feke himself seems probable both from the manner of painting and because no one but the artist is likely to have noted the exact day upon which the picture was finished. If this surmise be correct this portrait is the earliest known picture which he signed and the only one to which he put his full name.

---

[1] Since this description of the portrait was written the picture has been relined, covering the inscription, which, however, is reproduced in the accompanying illustration.

[2] Illegible; this is the probable reading.

It is also his only extant picture showing more than a single individual, and its size (height 54⅝ inches; width 77 11/16 inches), is exceeded only by the full-length portrait of General Waldo.

As the inscription indicates, the picture represents the following persons (right to left):

(1) Isaac Royall, Jr., son of Isaac Royall and Elizabeth Eliot, his wife. The father was a New Englander who made a fortune in Antigua where he lived nearly forty years and where it is probable that the son was born on September 13, 1719. In 1732 Isaac Royall, Sr., bought a handsome estate on the Mystic River in that part of Charlestown now known as Medford, and settled his family there. He died in 1739 and his son inherited the estate at the age of twenty. Isaac Royall, Jr. was a member of the Artillery Company in Boston, in 1750, and was appointed brigadier-general in 1761. He was also councillor 1752–74. He owned a pew in King's Chapel, Boston. He left Massachusetts on April 16, 1775, was proscribed as a loyalist, and his estate was confiscated in 1778. He died in England in October, 1781, bequeathing to Harvard College two thousand acres of land in Worcester County, Massachusetts, the proceeds of which were used to found its first professorship of law.

(2) Mrs. Isaac Royall, Jr. She was Elizabeth McIntosh, whose birthplace and parentage have not been traced. The date of her birth, if the painted inscription be correct, was September 13, 1722. She was married March 27, 1738, in King's Chapel, Boston. In the register her husband is described as "of Mystick," she as "of Boston." She died at Medford, July 14, 1770.

(3) Elizabeth Royall. In the Royall genealogies she is said to have been born June 7, 1740. If that date for her birth be correct she would have been more than fifteen months old when the picture was finished, and not "aged 8 months, 7th instant," as the inscription says. A child of eight months certainly could not sit up on her mother's lap, grasping a bauble, in the manner in which she is here portrayed, so it seems probable that Feke was mistaken as to her age. She died July 9, 1747.

Isaac Royall, Jr. and his wife had three other daughters; Mary McIntosh, born in 1744–45, a second Elizabeth, born in October, 1747, and Miriam. A portrait of Mary and the second Elizabeth, probably by Copley, is in the Boston Art Museum.

Lawrence Park, in his pamphlet on *Joseph Badger*, pp. 33–34, calls attention to a portrait found many years ago in the Royall

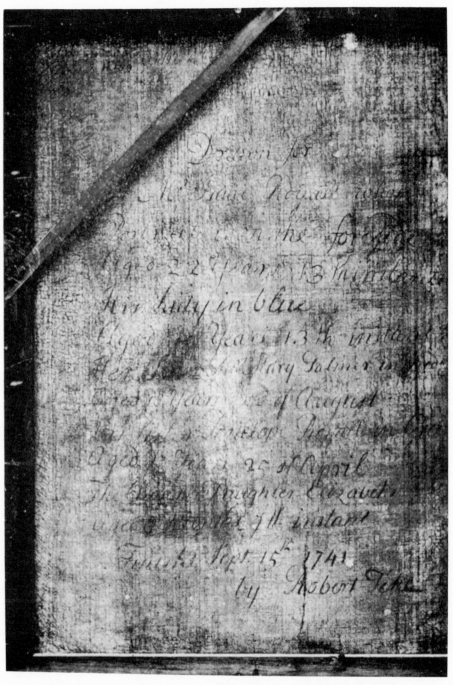

INSCRIPTION ON THE BACK OF THE PORTRAIT OF ISAAC ROYALL
(GREATLY REDUCED IN SIZE)

House in Medford, which is supposed to represent Mary McIntosh Royall at about the age of fourteen. He adds, "On the back of the stretchers is another canvas upon which is painted an unpleasant picture representing a young girl painted after death, with brown hair and closed eyes, wearing a white cap, and lying upon a pillow, with cold blue drapery above her. This may represent Mary Royall's older sister Elizabeth."

(4) Mary Palmer. The painted inscription describes her as Mrs. Royall's sister and gives the date of her birth as August 2, 1723. In view of the fact that there was only ten and a half months' difference in their ages, and that the difference in surnames indicates that they did not have the same father, the only interpretation of the inscription would seem to be that the mother of Elizabeth McIntosh had married as her second husband a man named Palmer who already had a daughter Mary by an earlier wife, so that the two girls were in reality stepsisters. No further information about Mary Palmer has come to light.

(5) Penelope Royall, sister of Isaac Royall, Jr. She was born in Antigua in April, 1724; married Henry Vassall of Cambridge, January 28, 1742, and died in Boston, November 19, 1800.

Description.

The youthful Isaac Royall stands at the end of a table, on the spectator's right, shown almost full length, to the middle of the calves of his legs. He stands half-front, his left shoulder toward the spectator, his face turned nearly full front. He wears a red velvet coat; dark brown or black waistcoat with a gold braid border; white neckband, ruffles, and undersleeves; white stockings and gray wig. His left hand rests upon his hip against the waistcoat pocket in conventional pose; his right hand holds a small book with red edges, bound in brown, gold-embossed leather, the middle finger thrust in to hold the place where he was reading. His right elbow leans on an invisible support.

Two women and a child sit behind the table, which is covered with a Turkish rug of highly colored design. The woman next to Royall is his wife, dressed in blue with a white guimpe and sleeve-ruffles. She has dark brown hair and blue eyes, and holds their daughter Elizabeth, dressed in a cream-colored dress and grasping a red, white and blue toy. The child also has brown hair and blue eyes. The second woman to the left is Mary Palmer, in a dress originally

red, now faded to a more orange tone, with white guimpe. She has
brown hair and brown eyes. At the end of the table farthest from
Isaac Royall sits his sister Penelope, in a dress which the painter
described as green but is now more brown, with a white guimpe.
She has dark brown hair and blue eyes, and holds a string of beads
in her hands. Isaac Royall stands against a window through which
is dimly seen a glimpse of trees and clouds. The rest of the background is dull brown save for a similar glimpse of country behind
Mary Palmer in the centre of the picture.

The three women and the child are painted nearly full front.
Their dresses are all alike, save for color, and the rendering of the
fabrics, except for Isaac Royall's costume, shows small skill. They
wear no jewels. Their hair is simply painted and none of them has a
curl hanging over the shoulder such as Feke showed in almost all
his later portraits of women.

The composition of the picture is unsatisfactory, with the three
heads of the women in a row, Mrs. Royall's slightly turned from her
husband, and Miss Palmer vainly trying to attract the child's attention by pointing to the upper left-hand corner of the picture.
The portraits of Mrs. Royall and Miss Palmer are flat and unin-
teresting, and the child is poorly drawn, stiff, and unnatural. On the
other hand, Isaac Royall is well drawn, easy and dignified in figure
and singularly attractive in face, well modelled and well colored.
Penelope Royall is much the best painted and most attractive of the
women, with Feke's characteristic tilt of the head and form of the
eyes. As a whole the picture is flat and stiff when compared to
Feke's later portraits, which exhibit a great advance in technical
skill. The similarities between this picture and Smibert's representation of Dean Berkeley and his household, now owned by Yale
University, are discussed on pp. 41–42.

There is no indication as to where this portrait group was painted,
but in view of the season of the year when it was finished it is probably a safe assumption that it was done at the Royall House in Medford.

Ownership.
Harvard University.

Exhibited.
Loan Exhibition of Portraits by American Artists before the Revolution, Copley Society. Boston, March, 1922.

Reproduced.

    (1) A copy of the figure of Isaac Royall, Jr. now hangs in the Royall House in Medford, and is reproduced in the descriptive pamphlet of the House.

    (2) F. W. Bayley, *Five Colonial Artists of New England.* Boston, 1929.

RICHARD SALTONSTALL

Subject.

Richard Saltonstall, born in Haverhill, Massachusetts, June 24, 1703; graduated from Harvard College, 1722; commissioned colonel in 1726; represented Haverhill in the General Court, 1728, and later; justice of the Superior Court, 1736–56; died October 20, 1756.

Description.

The somewhat portly subject is shown standing, three-quarters length, half-front, with his right shoulder toward the spectator, his full-fleshed face turned right nearly full front. He has a rather fair complexion, with brown eyes and level, light brown eyebrows, large nose and thin lips. The countenance, while not particularly pleasing, shows intelligence, dignity, and character. He wears a brown wig, tied behind with a black bow; a tobacco-brown coat lined with brown silk; a long, slate-gray waistcoat heavily adorned with gold braid, and the usual ruffles at neck and wrists. The background to the left is a brown wall or curtain, while behind him and to the right is a landscape painted in low tones, showing sky and clouds and two hills toward which a road winds across meadows, a vista strikingly similar to that in the portrait of Oxenbridge Thacher. His right hand is posed against his waistcoat pocket, holding back his coat, the index finger extended, while his left hand is extended in gesture, resembling the right hand in the portrait of Benjamin Franklin.

This fine portrait was attributed to Copley in the Saltonstall family genealogy, noted below, but the attribution can hardly be accepted. Copley was but little past his nineteenth birthday when Saltonstall died, and, though he had begun portrait painting at the age of sixteen, he had not attained at nineteen the power to produce work of this quality. In the second place Saltonstall is represented as a man in his forties (he would have been forty-five in 1748), rather than as he would have looked eight years later. In the third place the painting has all the characteristics of Feke's latest work, and closely resembles the portrait of William Bowdoin in pose, background, and the painting of the fabrics, especially of the gold braid on the waistcoat, which is almost identical with that worn by Bowdoin. There need, therefore, be no hesitation in assigning this work to Feke. It is one of his best works.

Date.

Presumably painted in Boston in 1748.

Size.

Height 49 inches; width 39 inches.

Ownership.

Mrs. R. M. Saltonstall, Chestnut Hill, Massachusetts.

Reproduced.

    (1) *Ancestry and Descendants of Sir Richard Saltonstall.* Riverside Press, 1897.

    (2) *Massachusetts Law Quarterly,* November, 1920.

STEPHEN SEWALL

Subject.

Stephen Sewall, born in Salem, Massachusetts, December 14, 1702. He was graduated from Harvard College in 1721; tutor and librarian at Harvard; lawyer; judge of the Superior Court, 1739; Chief Justice of the Colony, 1752; died September 1, 1760. Rev. Simon Bradstreet, of Marblehead, on a sermon preached after Judge Sewall's death, notes, "He was a Gentleman greatly beloved and respected and greatly lamented. And he deserved it. For he has left few or none behind him equal to him on all accounts; being eminent both in Gifts and Graces: above others, and yet remarkable for his Modesty and Goodnature to all."

Description.

Judge Sewall is shown three-quarters length, nearly full front, with his head turned a little to his left, standing against a dark background, with trees and sky showing dimly on the left and the base of a large column behind and to the right of the figure. His left elbow rests upon the corner of a table; his right hand, of which only a small part shows, is posed against his waistcoat, holding back the coat. He wears a full white wig, white ruffled shirt with a long, hanging white neckband and beautifully painted sleeve-ruffles, and mouse-gray (velvet?) coat and waistcoat, only three buttons of the

RICHARD SALTONSTALL

latter being fastened. The figure is dignified, the face rather full but intelligent and pleasing. All the mannerisms are eminently characteristic of Feke's work.

Date.

Signed and dated "R. F. Pinx. 1748" (in small red letters on the edge of the table). Presumably painted in Boston.

Size.

Height 44½ inches; width 35½ inches.

Ownership.

The portrait was painted for, or was at an early date acquired by James Otis (whose wife Feke also painted), and who was a close friend of Sewall. It descended with the portrait of Mrs. Otis to the latter's niece Susan Cunningham, who married John Henry Mills, thence to their son John Mills, to his daughter Francis Maria Mills, who married G. W. Lord of Boston, to their daughter Georgianna who married John Milton Hall, from whose estate it was purchased in 1929. It is now owned by Harvard University, Cambridge, Massachusetts.

EDWARD SHIPPEN, JR.

Subject.

Edward, son of Edward Shippen II, born in Philadelphia, February 16, 1729. He was great-grandson of Edward Shippen I, mayor of Philadelphia, and grandson of Joseph Shippen. He began the study of law with Tench Francis at the age of seventeen; went to England in 1748 to study at the Middle Temple, London; returned to Philadelphia, 1750. He married, November 29, 1753, Margaret, daughter of Tench Francis; was Judge of Vice-Admiralty, 1752; member of the Provincial Council, 1770–75; Chief Justice of Pennsylvania, 1799–1805. He died in Philadelphia, April 15, 1806. A fine portrait of him by Gilbert Stuart, painted about 1800, now hangs in the Corcoran Gallery at Washington.

Description.

This is a beautiful picture showing a handsome, slender youth of twenty or twenty-one years of age. He is represented standing, three-quarters length, half-front, with his right shoulder toward the spectator, his head turned right, nearly full front. He has a fair complexion, gray-blue eyes with fine arching brows, and a dimpled chin. He wears a gray, curled wig, a dark blue velvet coat lined with pink silk, a long, pearl-gray satin waistcoat, white neckband and shirt ruffles showing through the partly unbuttoned waistcoat, and full sleeve-ruffles. His right hand rests upon his hip above the waistcoat pocket holding back his coat, the index and middle fingers somewhat separated, the fourth and little fingers turned under. His left hand is thrust into his waistcoat, and the corner of his black cocked hat protrudes from under his left arm. The background behind the figure is a brown curtain drawn aside to show at the right a landscape of fields and trees, painted in very subdued colors. It is a charming picture of an aristocratic young gentleman, and in many respects strikingly resembles the portrait of young Isaac Royall, whom Feke painted at about the same age, although the Shippen portrait is painted with much superior technique.

Family tradition has it that this portrait was painted while Edward Shippen was a student in England in 1748–49. That tradition is not, however, supported by any documentary evidence, and appears to be nothing more than the guess of later generations who no longer recalled the painter's name. While it is possible that the tradition does represent the facts, it seems much more probable that the picture was painted by Feke early in 1750. A youth of twenty studying in England would not have been likely to have had his picture done, save under orders from his parents. Shippen had certainly returned to Philadelphia by 1750 and would have been only a little past his twenty-first birthday in April of that year, when Feke is known to have been in Philadelphia. Feke in 1746 had painted the portrait of Edward Shippen's aunt, Anne Shippen, wife of Charles Willing, as well as the portraits of Tench Francis and his wife, whose daughter Edward Shippen married, so that Feke was well known to young Shippen's family circle. Furthermore, the portrait is eminently characteristic of Feke's latest work in the whole pose, manner of painting, and the treatment of accessories. It therefore seems reasonable to ascribe it to Feke's third visit to Philadelphia in the spring of 1750, soon after Edward Shippen had returned from London. It is thus one of Feke's last works.

Date.

Presumably painted in Philadelphia early in 1750.

Size.

Height 46¾ inches; width 34⅜ inches.

Ownership.

This portrait, with that of Mrs. Tench Francis, No. 2, descended in the Shippen family. Both are now owned by Edward Shippen Willing, Bryn Mawr, Pennsylvania.

JOSEPH SHIPPEN

Subject.

Joseph, younger son of the second Edward Shippen (1703–81), of Philadelphia, and later of Lancaster, Pennsylvania, was born in 1732. He was graduated from Princeton in 1753; served as colonel in the French and Indian War; visited Europe; after his return in 1761 became secretary to the Provincial Council; appointed judge of the Lancaster County Court in 1789; died, 1810.

Description.

Joseph Shippen is shown as ι youth standing against a dark background, with the base of a column at the left. The figure is three-quarters length, half-front, the left shoulder toward the spectator, the round boyish face turned left nearly full front. He wears a dark coat, lighter silk waistcoat, white neckband, and full white ruffles at his wrists. His left hand is posed against his hip holding back his coat, the posture being almost identical with that of his brother Edward's right hand in Feke's portrait of him. Joseph's right hand hangs by his side holding a book.

The picture, which has unfortunately been destroyed by fire, was a charming one, though not so handsome as that of the subject's brother, Edward Shippen, to which it obviously was a companion piece. It must have been painted in the spring of 1750, when the subject was a freshman at Princeton. Family tradition attributed it to Benjamin West. It is true that at a later date Joseph Shippen took a warm interest in West's career as a painter, and is said to have assisted him to go to Europe in 1760. But West was not born until 1738, and could not possibly have painted Joseph Shippen at the youthful age at which this portrait represents him. Furthermore, the picture is a typical specimen of Feke's latest manner, and it may unquestioningly be assigned to him.

Ownership.

This picture was destroyed in the fire which burned the house of its owner, Prescott F. Huidekoper, Ruxton, Maryland, September 17,

1923. Mr. Huidekoper had inherited it from his uncle, Dr. Rush Huidekoper of Philadelphia, with whose family the Shippens had intermarried in an earlier generation. It is reproduced in *Hannah Logan's Courtship* (ed., A. C. Myers, Philadelphia, 1904), and in the Index of Illustrations in that book is attributed to Benjamin West, and is said to have belonged to the late Edward Willing, Walnut Street, Philadelphia. Either this statement is incorrect or else the portrait passed from the estate of Edward Willing into the hands of Dr. Huidekoper.

ISAAC STELLE [1]

Subject.

Isaac Stelle, merchant, born in 1714; came to Newport where he married Penelope Goodson, December 23, 1739. He was made a freeman of the Colony in 1743, and a warden of Trinity Church, Newport, in 1750. He died in Newport, May 4, 1763. His ledgers, now in the possession of the Newport Historical Society, disclose him as a prosperous merchant dealing in general merchandise and in sugar, molasses, and rum, with at least one venture in negroes. He visited Antigua in 1750.

Description.

The subject is shown three-quarters length, three-quarters front, his left shoulder toward the spectator, his head turned left nearly full front. He stands against a brown curtain drawn back to show a distant view of a sailless sea and faintly clouded sky, painted in subdued tones. He wears a gray, curled wig; white neckscarf, and ruffled shirt which shows through the loosely buttoned dark brown waist-

---

[1] It is a very curious coincidence that in the pamphlet *History of the Baptist Church in Oyster Bay*, by Charles S. Wightman, dated November 1, 1873, the author, after the reference to Robert Feke "the Preacher," which has been quoted on p. 28, speaks of his young colleague, Caleb Wright, and notes an *Elegy on the Death of that godly and eloquent young Preacher Mr. Caleb Wright, Of Oyster Bay, on Long Island, in the Province of New York, who departed this life the 27th of October, 1752, at six o'clock in the morning. Composed by Isaac Stelle of Piscataway, in New Jersey.* Isaac Stelle is a sufficiently unusual name, yet here is a second person thus designated, who certainly cannot be identified with the subject of Feke's portrait. It may also be noted that the name of one Benjamin Stelle is found with that of Robert Feke "the Preacher," in the list of subscribers to the fund for building a Baptist Meeting-house in New York in 1727 (see pp. 34–36). The relationship connecting the Newport Merchant whom Feke painted with the Stelle family which was resident in New Jersey and which had Baptist affiliations, has not been traced, but one is tempted to surmise that the Isaac Stelle who had migrated to Newport may have been a son or a cousin of the Isaac Stelle who wrote the *Elegy*.

JOSEPH SHIPPEN

coat; and a dark blue coat lined with red silk. The broad cuffs of the coat are turned back to show the white shirt-sleeves and wrist ruffles. His left hand rests against his hip in conventional pose, holding back his coat in the same manner as is shown in the portrait of Charles Apthorp. The full-fleshed face is well modelled and colored, showing a dimpled chin, brown eyes, and strongly pencilled eyebrows, but the expression is not altogether pleasant, suggesting a vain, shrewd, and perhaps unscrupulous man.

The picture, which has been relined, is thinly painted on a fine-woven canvas, in the manner characteristic of Feke's latest work. On the back the words "Touch up by W. O. Hathaway" have been painted. Hathaway was a Newport house-painter of the last century. He also "touched up," and nearly ruined the portrait of Mrs. Isaac Stelle (q. v.). In the case of her husband the "touch up" has not so seriously injured the portrait.

Date.

Signed "R. Fe(ke) P(inx)." (The letters in parentheses have been obliterated by abrasions.) Probably painted in Newport about 1749 or 1750.

Size.

Height 49 inches; width 39¼ inches.

Ownership.

The portrait, and its companion picture of Mrs. Stelle, was inherited by Christian, daughter of Isaac and Penelope Stelle, who married John Banister (or Bannister). In her will, dated March 7, 1831, she left the portraits of her father and mother to her friends Joshua and Anna W. Sayer, who seem to have occupied the Banister house. Their descendant, Miss Mary A. Sayer, gave both portraits to the Newport Historical Society in April, 1925.

MRS. ISAAC STELLE (PENELOPE GOODSON)

Subject.

Penelope Goodson, said to have been the daughter of John Goodson and Elizabeth Pelham, his wife; married Isaac Stelle, December 23, 1739.

Description.

The subject is seated, facing three-quarters front, her right shoulder toward the spectator, her face turned to the right. She wears a blue dress, with white guimpe and undersleeves. The outer sleeve is caught up with a brooch at the inside of the elbow. Her right hand lies in her lap, loosely holding a sprig of strawberries. Her left elbow rests on a now obliterated support, presumably a table, her hand raised to her cheek. The dark curtain which makes the background for the right half of the picture is pulled aside to show a tree, hills, and clouds in the distance, dully painted.

The portrait is now in very bad condition. It has at some time in the past been put into a smaller frame, the canvas having been folded back with resultant disintegration of the paint. It has several bad holes, which have been crudely patched. Like the portrait of her husband, it has been relined and repainted. On the back is the note, "Touch up by W. O. Hathaway, 5th 26, 1882." Hathaway was a Newport house-painter. In the case of this portrait his "touch up" has amounted to a ruinous repainting. The face is nothing but a mask, and hands and costume have also been daubed over. Only the vista in the background has escaped.

Under the circumstances it is difficult to form any judgment of the portrait. It is, however, obviously a companion piece to the portrait of Isaac Stelle, and therefore presumably from the same hand. Furthermore, the apparent age of the subject, the style and period of the costume, the pose, and the character of the untouched vista, are all in accord with the supposition that it was painted by Feke about 1750.

Size.

Height 49 inches; width 39⅝ inches.

Ownership.

With the portrait of her husband it was inherited by Christian Stelle, who married John Banister,[1] and was bequeathed by her to her friends Joshua and Anna W. Sayer, whose descendant, Miss Mary A. Sayer, gave it to the Newport Historical Society in 1925.

OXENBRIDGE THACHER

Subject.

Oxenbridge Thacher, son of Col. John Thacher and his wife Eliza Lillie, of Boston, and grandson of Rev. Peter Thacher of Milton,

---

[1] Portraits of John Banister and of Christian, his wife, holding a lap-dog and with a small boy at her side, hang in the Redwood Library. They were painted by Gilbert Stuart when he was fifteen years old, i. e., about 1770. The face of Mrs. Banister is painted from the same point of view as her father's in Feke's portrait, and there is a decided resemblance between the two.

Massachusetts; born in Boston, December 29, 1719, died in Milton, July 8, 1765. He was graduated from Harvard in 1738, became an eminent lawyer and an ardent advocate of the rights of the Colonies against the Crown, being a legal associate of James Otis. He represented Boston in the General Court.

Description.

The subject is shown three-quarters length, standing against a background which, on the right, is dark brown, representing a curtain or wall, and which on the left shows a landscape with a stream crossed by a road which winds through meadows with a few trees toward a hill in the distance. Possibly the view is intended to suggest Milton Hill, where Thacher lived. He stands half-front, his left shoulder to the spectator, his face turned nearly full front. His left hand, which is not shown, rests against his hip holding back the coat which covers it; his right hand rests upon the head of a black, white and tan foxhound, which looks up to his master's face from the lower corner of the picture. The dog is strongly reminiscent of the similarly posed spaniel in Feke's portrait listed as "The Unknown Man with a Spaniel."

Thacher is shown at about thirty years of age, with an attractive and intelligent face, sharp nose, and blue eyes. He wears a wig, a gray coat, and a dark blue (almost black) waistcoat, with white neckband and wrist-ruffles. A fine portrait, well preserved.

Date.

Signed and dated: "R. F. 1748" (lower left above the dog's back). Painted in Boston or Milton.

Size.

Height 50 inches; width 40 inches.

Ownership.

The portrait remained in the hands of his descendants. It is now owned by Col. Archibald G. Thacher of New York.

Reproduced.

F. W. Bayley, *Five Colonial Artists of New England.* Boston, 1929.

MRS. OXENBRIDGE THACHER (Sarah Kent)

Subject.

Sarah, daughter of John and Bathsheba Daggett Kent of Charlestown and Marshfield, Massachusetts; born December 25, 1724;

married Oxenbridge Thacher, July 27, 1741; died at Milton, Massachusetts, July 3, 1764.

Description.

Mrs. Thacher is shown seated, half-front, with her right shoulder toward the spectator, her head turned right nearly full front, against a background showing faintly painted sky and trees. She has brown eyes and dark hair, a curl of which falls over her left shoulder. Her left arm rests upon a masonry wall; her right loosely holds a red rosebud in her lap. She wears a gown of pearl-gray silk, with a long, stiff bodice, white muslin trim and undersleeves, with a large blue silk bow on the bodice, and smaller blue ribbons on the sleeves.

Date.

Signed and dated, "R. F. Pinx. 1749" (on the capstone of the wall on which her left hand rests).

Size.

Height 50 inches; width 40 inches.

Ownership.

The portrait, with that of her husband, was inherited by their descendants. It is now owned by Col. Archibald G. Thacher of New York.

Reproduced.

F. W. Bayley, *Five Colonial Artists of New England.* Boston, 1929.

MRS. JAMES TILGHMAN (Ann Francis) (No. 1)

Subject.

Ann, daughter of Tench Francis of Philadelphia; born, 1727; married in 1743 to James Tilghman; died in Philadelphia, December 18, 1771. Her husband was born December 6, 1716, was attorney to the Lord Proprietor and a member of the Council. He died in Philadelphia, August 24, 1793.

Description.

Mrs. Tilghman is shown standing, nearly three-quarters length, three-quarters front, her left shoulder toward the spectator, her head turned to the left. She is a robust young matron, with dark hair, a curl of which falls over her left shoulder; dark eyes; and rather high-colored complexion. The flesh tints both of face and

MRS. JAMES TILGHMAN (No. 1)

bosom are unusually good. She is handsomely dressed in pearl-gray satin, with white muslin about the bodice. The long, tight waist of the period is circled by a slender gold cord terminating in tassels. Her right hand hangs at her side, holding a dark gray scarf which crosses her skirt and folds over a table at her left, upon which her left elbow rests, her upraised hand holding a rose.

The background on the spectator's right is a dull brown, apparently representing a curtain, but behind her head and to the left is a faintly painted vista showing a hill, three small trees, and clouds.

Family tradition has ascribed to Copley this portrait and its replica (Mrs. James Tilghman, No. 2), but both are clearly from the same hand, and both have all the characteristics of Feke's work at the height of his career. The mannerisms with which the head is painted — the slight tilt, the eyes, and the mouth — closely resemble the picture of Hannah Flagg; the hands and the fabrics are painted like those seen in other portraits by Feke. Furthermore Feke painted Mrs. Tilghman's father and mother, to the latter of whom Mrs. Tilghman bears a strong resemblance. Finally, she is represented at too early an age for it to have been possible for Copley to have painted this picture. Possibly the portrait was painted in 1746, but her appearance indicates 1750, the year of Feke's last visit to Philadelphia, as the more probable date.

Size.
Height 38 inches; width 31½ inches.

Ownership.
Mrs. Sidell Tilghman of Madison, New Jersey.

MRS. JAMES TILGHMAN (No. 2)

Description.
This picture is a close replica of No. 1, apparently done by the same hand at about the same time. The present owner insists that it is the original portrait and that it is the work of Copley.

MRS. BARLOW TRECOTHICK (Grizzell Apthorp)

Subject.
Grizzell, daughter of Charles Apthorp, married Barlow Trecothick, in King's Chapel, Boston, March 2, 1746–47.

Description.

The subject is seated nearly full front before a brown wall across which a dark blue-green curtain is rather awkwardly draped. At the right the base of a column is shown, and a bit of sky and cloud. She is represented as a young woman, probably under twenty years, with a fresh complexion and dark brown hair and eyes. The flesh tints of the breast and arms are pallid, having faded rather badly. She is simply but elegantly dressed in pearl-gray satin trimmed with white muslin, and wears a jewel in her bodice. In her lap she holds a song-book, showing words set to three staves of music on each page. Her left arm rests on a red velvet cushion with a tassel, which, in turn, lies on a marble-topped table.

The portrait, though unsigned, is eminently characteristic of Feke's work. The figure is placed with unusual skill on the nearly square canvas, and, with the exception of the awkward handling of the curtain and the pallor of the arms and breast, it makes one of Feke's most delightful and charming pictures.

"A very beautiful picture with great harmony of color." (Pencil note by Lawrence Park in *Copley Society Catalogue* at the Frick Art Reference Library.)

Date.

Presumably painted at Boston in 1748, at the same time as the portraits of her parents.

Size.

Height 39¾ inches; width 39¼ inches.

Ownership.

This portrait has been transmitted with that of Mrs. Charles Apthorp to the present owner, Mrs. Ben P. P. Moseley, Boston.

Exhibited.

Boston Museum of Fine Arts, 1909–14. Loan Exhibition of Portraits by American Artists before the Revolution, Copley Society, Boston, March, 1922.

MRS. TWEEDY

Subject.

This picture was known only as that of "Mrs. Tweedy" when acquired by Mrs. Annie A. Ives of Providence, and was supposed to be the work of Smibert. Probably it represents the wife of a member of the Tweedy family of Newport. Before the revolution John and William Tweedy, of that city, are said to have been the largest importers of drugs into the Colonies, maintaining a branch office in New York. At the time of the British occupation of Newport some of the family moved to Providence, owning also a farm six miles away in what is now Cranston, Rhode Island. Some of them were buried in Providence. Presumably the portrait represents a member of this family.

The attribution to Smibert may be set aside, as the painting is superior to his workmanship, and furthermore, much resembles other paintings by Feke. Both the late Lawrence Park and Mr. F. W. Bayley attributed it to Feke. Probably it is one of his latest Newport paintings, dating from 1749 or 1750.

Description.

It is an exceptionally handsome portrait showing a woman, three-quarters length, standing nearly full front behind the corner of a table, her head turned slightly to her left. The plain background is shaded from dark to light, to balance the lighting of the face and figure. She appears to be a person of marked individuality, approaching thirty years of age. She has abundant dark hair, parted in the middle and falling with a curl over either shoulder; dark eyes beneath rather straight eyebrows; a clear complexion; straight nose; and a mouth which wears a faint suggestion of the smile of Mona Lisa.

She is dressed in a black silk gown, with red lining and gold tassels, and the usual white lawn guimpe and full undersleeves. Her right hand is raised to her bodice, and across the arm is thrown a red scarf which passes behind her and comes into view again upon the table at her left side, upon which her left hand rests, holding a heart-shaped silver patch-box. The whole costume and color scheme is more original than usual in Feke's portraits, but may be compared to the arrangements in the portraits of Miss Williamina Moore and Miss Ruth Cunningham.

Ownership.

It was bequeathed in 1909 to the Rhode Island School of Design, Providence, by Mrs. Ives' daughter, Mrs. Hope Brown Russell of Providence.

Reproduced.

F. W. Bayley, *Five Colonial Artists of New England*. Boston, 1929.

UNKNOWN MAN WITH A SPANIEL

Subject.

The unidentified subject of this portrait is shown half-front from the waist upward, within an oval of painted spandrels, his left shoulder toward the spectator, his face turned nearly full front. He wears a white wig, a lawn neckband, the ends of which show through the partly unbuttoned bright blue waistcoat ornamented with heavy gold embroidery, and a dark claret-colored coat lined with silk of the same color and decorated with gold buttons and gold-braided buttonholes. His hands are not shown. The background is brown, the spandrels rather inconspicuously indicated. The face is that of a man in his early forties, with brown eyes and strongly marked light brown eyebrows, suggesting auburn hair under his wig. The face rather full and well colored, with a large nose, and is pleasant in expression although not conspicuously intelligent. The noticeable peculiarity of the picture is the head and neck of a black spaniel painted over the lower left spandrel, looking up into the face of his master. Presumably the owner desired to have the dog shown in his portrait but did not wish to pay for a large picture, and the painter took this method of introducing him.

The portrait is unsigned. While it is not an exceptionally good picture, and might possibly have been done by another hand, the style and technique strongly suggest the work of Feke. The eyes and mouth, and the painting of the fabrics, especially the gold braid, are distinctly in his manner, and the wig and costume are those of the seventeen-forties. It is not unreasonable to regard the picture as one of Feke's less important works painted some time during the last decade of his life. There is no clue as to the identity of the subject or the place where the picture was painted. It has been relined and is in good condition, although it has been rather too much cleaned.

Size.

Height 28½ inches; width 23¾ inches.

Ownership.

The portrait is now owned by the Laura Davidson Sears Academy of Fine Arts, Elgin Academy, Elgin, Illinois, for which it was purchased in January, 1927, from the Ehrich Galleries of New York. The proprietors of the Ehrich Galleries bought the picture from some dealer and knew nothing of its origin.

UNKNOWN MAN WITH A SPANIEL

MRS. JOHN VINAL (Ruth Osborn)?

Subject.

This portrait is said on uncertain authority to represent Ruth Osborn, wife of Judge John Vinal. It is said that she was born in 1736, but this date is not compatible with the supposition that Feke painted the portrait during his Boston visit of 1748, since in that year she would have been only twelve or thirteen years old, whereas the young woman in the picture is nearly, if not quite, twenty years of age. If the picture is by Feke then either Ruth Osborn must have been born at least as early as 1730, or else the portrait represents another person. Otherwise the portrait must be accounted an early work of Copley.

Description.

The portrait represents a young woman, about twenty years of age, three-quarters length, nearly full front, her head turned slightly to her right. She stands before a vine-draped masonry wall, on a projection of which her right hand rests, while her left hand loosely holds a flower which resembles a purple aster. To the spectator's right the background shows a road winding down to a river, sea, and hills, with a clouded sky above, all painted in low tones. She is handsomely dressed in a mauve-pink satin gown, with very long, slender waist and full skirts. The bodice is laced by a bright blue ribbon, two knots of which appear above and below, and is trimmed with broad, handsome lace, as are her muslin undersleeves. She wears a blue ribbon in her dark brown hair, which falls in curls on either side of her neck. Her complexion is clear and fresh, her eyes dark brown. The coloring of the picture is very good, and it is a handsome and striking portrait.

The portrait was attributed to Blackburn by Perkins, and to Copley by its late owner, Mr. Frederic Amory, who bought it as a work of the latter artist a good many years ago. It certainly cannot be by Blackburn. It is possible to argue that it is an early work of Copley's, done before 1760. On the face of it, however, the picture strongly resembles Feke's work. The pose, the eyes, the landscape background, are all in his style. If the sitter can be identified as a person whom Feke might have painted it is logical to attribute the picture to him, and to date it from his Boston visit of 1748.

Size.

Height 49 inches; width 40 inches.

Ownership.

It was bought, through a dealer, a good many years ago, by Mr. Frederic Amory of Boston, who, before his death, gave it to Mr. and Mrs. Harcourt Amory, in whose Boston house it now hangs.

SAMUEL WALDO

Subject.

Samuel Waldo, born in Boston, 1695. He was a wealthy merchant, owner of an extensive grant of land on the Penobscot in Maine. He commanded a regiment at the siege of Louisburg, 1745, and for his services was promoted to the rank of Brigadier-General. His second wife was Sarah Erving, sister of Mrs. James Bowdoin. He died in 1759.

Description.

"Feke shows him — as a tall, slight, graceful, debonair figure, prominently placed against a landscape background showing in the distance across a stretch of water a walled settlement which looks much like New York as we know it from the earliest engravings. It is, however, probably intended to represent Louisburg. In the middle distance on the nearer shore is a fort in action. Waldo is richly dressed in a golden-brown [1] velvet coat and knee-breeches, with a long red waistcoat elaborately embroidered with gold braid. His powdered wig is tied with a black queue bow, his stockings are white, and his low black shoes are enlivened with large gold buckles. His dark, keen eyes are directed to the spectator and his attitude suggests one of alertness and haughty elegance. His left hand is held against his hip, while with his right he grasps a spy-glass which rests upon a conveniently placed pile of rocks. In pose the picture recalls Feke's portraits of William and James Bowdoin hanging in the same gallery and that of Charles Apthorp, recently acquired by the Cleveland Museum of Art, and although no date or signature has been found on it, it was probably painted in 1748, the same year in which these portraits are dated." [2]

It may be added that the background is a particularly interesting one. In the middle distance is a narrow sheet of water, showing the

---

[1] Since Park wrote this the portrait has been cleaned, revealing the coat as deep red, rather than golden-brown. The details and the background have also come out much more distinctly.

[2] Lawrence Park in *Art in America*, VII, 216–218.

spars of several sunken vessels. On the farther shore is the be-
leaguered town, attractively painted, at which a battery in the fore-
ground is firing. To the left is a range of hills, on the top of one of
which a cross is visible.

Date.

Probably painted at Boston, 1748. The background clearly indicates that the picture was painted after Waldo acquired his military
reputation at Louisburg. The picture has been attributed to Smibert, and inasmuch as Smibert's career as a painter did not come to
an end until about 1748, the attribution is not an impossible one.
The portrait, however, is closely associated with the portraits of
James and William Bowdoin and their wives, with whom Waldo was
connected by marriage, and, as the Bowdoin portraits are indubitably by Feke, it would be entirely natural that the same painter
should have also done the portrait of Waldo. The Waldo portrait,
furthermore, has many of Feke's mannerisms. In his critical study
of the portrait the late Lawrence Park definitely asserted it to be the
work of Feke, disputing the correctness of its "attribution to Smibert, to whose work it bears neither in palette, pose nor method any
resemblance. One has only to compare it with Smibert's full
lengths of Sir William Pepperell in the Essex Institute at Salem, the
Sir Peter Warren in the Athenaeum at Portsmouth, New Hampshire, and the privately owned portraits of William Browne and his
wife to be convinced that Smibert could not have painted the graceful, dignified figure of Waldo, for successful as Smibert was with
busts and half-lengths he was never able to master the correct pro-
portions of the full length and his uneasy attempts are distinctly
unhappy." [1]

Size.

Height 96 inches; width 59¼ inches. (Feke's largest canvas.)

Ownership.

The portrait was owned by Lucy Flucker Thatcher, by whom it was
bequeathed in 1855 to the Bowdoin Museum of Fine Arts, Bowdoin
College, Brunswick, Maine.

Exhibited.

Loan Exhibition of Portraits by American Painters before the Revolution, Copley Society, Boston, March, 1922.
    Bowdoin Museum of Fine Arts, Brunswick, Maine.

[1] Lawrence Park in *Art in America*, VII, 216–218.

Reproduced.

(1) There is in the Frick Art Reference Library, New York, a small wood-cut reproduction of this portrait, probably made about 1880. The figure is shown half-length, but the background is altered to show a panelled room.

(2) Earle, *Two Centuries of Costumes in America*. Macmillan, 1902, II, 404.

(3) *Art in America*, VII, 218.

(4) *Catalogue, Loan Collection of Portraits by American Painters before the Revolution*, Copley Society, March, 1922.

(5) *International Studio*, LXXVII, 432.

(6) F. W. Bayley, *Five Colonial Artists of New England*. Boston, 1929.

MRS. JOSEPH WANTON (Mary Winthrop)

Subject.

Mary, born September 18, 1708, daughter of John Winthrop, sister of Waitstill Winthrop of New London, and granddaughter of Governor Joseph Dudley of Massachusetts. She married Joseph Wanton, the last royal governor of Rhode Island. She was buried February 28, 1767, in the Wanton vault, Chilton Burying-ground, Newport.

Description.

The figure is set in a painted oval, nearly full front. It represents a woman thirty to thirty-five years of age. She wears a blue watered-silk dress, cut low in front, with white lace around the bodice. An old-rose silk cloak is thrown over her shoulders. The beautiful face is lighted from its left side, the head slightly tilted, with dark eyes and hair, a curl of which falls over the left shoulder. The background is dark on the left half of the picture and lighter on the right, contrasting with the light and shaded sides of the face.

A bunch of gay flowers was added in the front of the bodice after the picture was given to the Redwood Library. Mrs. Maud Howe Elliott in an article entitled *Some Recollections of Newport Artists* in the *Bulletin of the Newport Historical Society* for January, 1921, states that this corsage bouquet was added by Miss Jane Stuart in 1859 by order of the directors of the Redwood Library.

Date.

Probably painted in Newport not much later than 1740.

Size.

Height 30 inches; width 25 inches.

Ownership.

The Redwood Library, Newport, the gift of Angelica Gilbert Gardner. Miss Gardner was a great-granddaughter of Mrs. Wanton's through the latter's daughter Elizabeth, who married Thomas Wickham, whose daughter Elizabeth married Walter Gardner. Miss Gardner died in 1844, and the Redwood Library acquired the portrait either by gift or bequest from her.

Exhibited.

Redwood Library, Newport.

Reproduced.

(1) A poor copy of this portrait now hangs in the building of the Massachusetts Historical Society, Boston, as a loan from the Winthrop family. It shows Mrs. Wanton without the corsage bouquet and was therefore presumably painted before Miss Stuart's decoration was added to the original portrait, although it might have been done later if the copyist knew the bouquet to be an addition. Perhaps it is the copy made by Miss Jane Stuart referred to in the following vote of the Directors of Redwood Library:

"December 12, 1864. Permission was given Miss Jane Stuart to take to her house the portraits of Governor and Mrs. Wanton, so long as it may be necessary for her to copy them." (*Redwood Library Annals*, p. 247.)

(2) W. Updike, *History of the Church in Narragansett*, 2d edition.

Bibliographical References.

Publications of the Rhode Island Historical Society, New Series, III, No. 2, p. 83.

PHILIP WILKINSON

Subject.

Philip Wilkinson, merchant, born in the North of Ireland about 1710. Emigrated to Newport before 1736, as his first wife died after reaching America and he married Elizabeth Freebody as his second wife on April 26, 1736. He was a captain in the Newport Artillery Company, and a pew-holder in Trinity Church. He died in 1782.

Description.

Wilkinson is depicted sitting in a high-backed mahogany chair, three-quarters front, his left shoulder toward the spectator, his face turned nearly full front. He wears a white curled wig and is handsomely but soberly dressed in a gray coat, gray knee-breeches, pearl-gray stockings, and white neckband and ruffled shirt, which shows through the partly unbuttoned long black waistcoat.

His left hand rests upon his leg; his right lies upon a table covered with a blue-green cloth, upon which stands a pewter inkstand with a white quill pen. An open letter is partly hidden by his right arm. The background is a dull brown but above the table an opening shows a small full-rigged ship of the mid-eighteenth-century type, putting out to sea. He has a full, florid, and not very attractive face, brown eyes and red eyebrows. He looks like a choleric person who has lived high. He appears to be in his late thirties. The label on the picture ascribes it to Smibert, but Smibert had gone to Boston to live long before this portrait could have been painted. On the other hand, as Wilkinson was forty years old in 1750, this might well be one of Feke's latest works. The manner in which the costume is treated, the thin painting, the low pearly tones, all are in Feke's style. The arrangement of table, papers, pewter inkstand, and quill pen is closely similar to that shown in the portrait of Charles Apthorp, as is also the treatment of the coat and waistcoat. The Apthorp portrait was painted in Boston in 1748. Feke found the same accessories appropriate to the portrait of a Newport merchant painted about the same time. The face is not painted in Feke's usual manner, but perhaps this red-headed Irishman represents a type with which the painter was not particularly sympathetic.

Date.

Undated and unsigned: presumably painted in Newport about 1750.

Size.

Height 50 inches; width 40 inches.

Ownership.

Redwood Library, Newport, gift of Catherine V. Allen.

Exhibited.

Redwood Library, Newport.

Reproduced.

W. Updike, *History of the Episcopal Church in Narragansett,* 2d edition, 1907, I.

MRS. CHARLES WILLING (ANNE SHIPPEN) (No. 1)

Subject.

Anne, daughter of Joseph and Abigail Shippen, born in Philadelphia, August 5, 1710; married, January 21, 1730, to Charles Willing, who had emigrated to Philadelphia from Bristol, England. He was Justice of the City Court in 1747, mayor of Philadelphia in 1748 and 1754, dying in the latter year. Mrs. Willing died June 23, 1791.

Description.

The subject is shown standing, three-quarters length, three-quarters front, with her left shoulder to the spectator, her face turned left nearly full front. She is a dignified, robust, rather portly matron, handsomely dressed in a very full gown of olive and light gray brocade of a very large flowered pattern, with white lace around the bodice, and lace undersleeves showing below the elbow. She wears a white cap which covers most of her dark hair. The curl falling to one or the other shoulder which appears in most of Feke's portraits of women is absent in her case. Her right hand rests upon the stone plinth of a column, her left hand holds a closed fan.

The background is dark on the spectator's right, opening at the left to a vista showing a hill, trees, and sky, painted in subdued tones. The picture appears to have been repainted above the right forearm, and about the right side of the subject's bosom.

Date.

Signed and dated "R. Feke Pinx, 1746" (on the edge of the masonry plinth beneath her right hand).

Size.

Height 50 inches; width 40 inches.

Ownership.

This must have been the picture which Mr. J. Francis Fisher reported to Dunlap, and which the latter listed as that of Mrs. Charles Welling in his three-line mention of Feke in *History of The Arts of Design in America* (see Appendix A). Mr. Fisher did not give the name of the owner, but the portrait was then or soon after in the hands of Mrs. Willing's grandson, Dr. Charles Willing of Philadelphia. His widow exhibited it, with other portraits, at the Loan Exhibition of Historical Portraits, Pennsylvania Academy of Fine Arts, December 1, 1887–January 15, 1888, and it is included as No. 470 in the *Catalogue* of that exhibition, where it is attributed to Benjamin West, although Feke's signature is easily discernible. Fragments of the label pasted on the back of the frame at the time of the exhibition are still in place. The portrait afterwards passed to Dr. Willing's nephew, Edward S. Willing; thence to the latter's daughter Alva, Lady Ribblesdale, and is now owned by her son, Mr. Vincent Astor.

Reproduced.
Anne H. Wharton, *Salons Colonial and Republican*. Lippincott, 1900.

MRS. CHARLES WILLING (Anne Shippen) (No. 2)

Description.
This portrait, which has not been definitely located, appears to be a variant of that listed as Mrs. Charles Willing, No. 1. The figure, so far as can be judged from photographs, is a close replica, except that the fingers of the right hand are in a slightly different position and seem to rest upon a table or masonry wall rather than on the plinth of a column, and that the face is not quite so lifelike. The background, however, is quite different, and rather more pleasing than in No. 1. The foliage behind the subject's head is more abundant, and the vista to the left shows nearby foliage and a distant lake and hill. The photographs would indicate that this portrait is in somewhat better condition than No. 1. A small photogravure of it is printed in *Hannah Logan's Courtship*, ed. A. C. Myers, Philadelphia, 1904, and comparison with the photogravure of No. 1 in *Salons Colonial and Republican* discloses the differences between the two versions.

The fact that the portrait has not been located and that its existence is assumed on the evidence of photographic reproductions might lead to the surmise that it is one and the same picture as No. 1, but that the background and accessories have been repainted and the fingers of the right hand altered. That such is not the case, however, seems clear for the following reasons: First, the reproduc-

MRS. CHARLES WILLING (No. 1)

tion of No. 1 in *Salons Colonial and Republican* antedates by four
years the reproduction of No. 2 in *Hannah Logan's Courtship*, so
that the theory that the picture has been repainted requires one to
believe that an older photograph was used in the later book. Second,
it is improbable that the less pleasing background of No. 1 should
have been painted over the more pleasing one of No. 2. Third, although there is some evidence of the retouching of No. 1 above the
right forearm, and along the lace which lines the right side of the
bosom, the rest of the background and the masonry upon which
Feke's signature and the date are painted show no signs whatever of
repainting, and the signature appears to be genuine. That it has not
been added in recent times is also proved by the evidence of J.
Francis Fisher who cites the portrait as signed and dated.

A careful comparison of a good photograph of No. 2 with the
original painting of No. 1 seems clearly to indicate that No. 2 is a
contemporary variant, presumably painted by Feke himself, either
in 1746 or during his later visit in 1750.

Ownership.

In *Hannah Logan's Courtship* No. 2 is said to belong to Edward S.
Willing of Philadelphia, so that at the beginning of this century Mr.
Willing seems to have owned both versions of the portrait. Both
seem to have passed to his daughter Alva, Lady Ribblesdale, who in
August, 1924, supplied Mr. Thomas B. Clarke of New York with a
photograph of No. 2, and wrote of it as "a copy," stating that it was
in storage in New York. It has not been traced further.

MISS (ANNE) WILLING (So-called)
MISS (MARGARET) WILLING (So-called)

These two portraits, representing two young women whose identity
is quite uncertain, can best be discussed together.

That to which the name of Anne Willing is now attached represents
a young woman, sitting, nearly full front, with her face turned a little
to her left. She has dark brown eyes and hair and a fresh complexion,
and wears an old-rose satin dress with white undersleeves and ruffles.
The sleeves are caught up at the inside of the elbow with silver pins,
and in her bodice is a brooch with pearls in the centre and pale blue
stones on either side. She holds a dark brown leather book, closed, in
her hands, her right elbow resting on a stone wall, over the edge of

which grasses fall. The background is dark at the right, with a faint vista of trees and clouds to the left. The portrait is unsigned and undated. Its height is 49 inches, width 39 inches. It seems certain that this is the portrait listed as No. 471 in the *Catalogue of Loan Exhibition of Historical Portraits*, Pennsylvania Academy of Fine Arts, December, 1887–January, 1888. It is therein entered as "Miss Willing? Anonymous."

The portrait to which the name of Margaret Willing is now attached seems clearly to be a companion piece of the above, though it is the finer picture of the two. It represents a handsome young woman of about twenty, standing, three-quarters length, half-front, her left shoulder to the spectator, her intelligent and attractive face turned to her left, nearly full front. She has dark brown hair and eyes, and full, rosy cheeks. She is dressed in a blue-green satin gown, with crystal buttons, the sleeves caught up with similar buttons or pins. About her waist is a silver cord with hanging tassels. Her dress has white undersleeves, a white ruffle about her neck, and a rose-colored underskirt, and there is a triangular rose-colored insert, edged with silver, at her breast. Her right hand rests upon the carved base of a dark gray column, while her left hangs at her side holding loosely a flower, apparently a small peony. About the column is draped a dark crimson curtain, and to the right is a second column, the space between being dark brown. This portrait also is unsigned and undated, and is 49 by 39 inches. It is doubtless the same as that listed as No. 472 in the *Catalogue of Loan Exhibition of Historical Portraits* of the Pennsylvania Academy of Fine Arts, December, 1887–January, 1888. It also is there entered as "Miss Willing? Anonymous."

The problem presented by these portraits arises from the fact that, if they represent Anne and Margaret Willing, who were the younger daughters of the Mrs. Charles Willing whom Feke painted in 1746, they cannot be the work of Feke, because Anne was not born until 1750 and Margaret until 1753, and Feke had been long dead when they reached the age of the women shown in these portraits. On the other hand, if the portraits are by Feke, painted not later than 1750, they cannot represent any of Mrs. Charles Willing's children.

The present owners accept a late and uncertain family tradition that the pictures do represent Anne Willing and her sister Margaret, the latter of whom married Robert Hare in 1775, and tentatively attribute them to Copley, dating them from the early seventeen-seventies. That the tradition is a late one is indicated by the fact that when the widow of the Dr. Charles Willing of the last century exhibited the portraits forty years ago at the Loan Exhibition of Historical Portraits at the Pennsylvania Academy of Fine Arts, she was evidently uncertain as to the identity of the subjects, entering each only as "Miss Willing?" On the death of Mrs. Willing the pictures passed to Dr. Willing's sister, Mrs. Hare, presumably on the supposition that one of them represented the Margaret Willing who was the ancestress of the Hare family. What was only a supposition has become a tradition, and the attribution to Copley is the result of his being the only painter whose career fits the required dates.

There are, however, grave difficulties in accepting this identification of the subjects of these pictures, and the accompanying attribution of the pictures to Copley. In the first place the costume is not that of the seventeen-seventies but of the seventeen-forties. In the second place the manner in which the portraits are painted is not at all that of Copley at the height of his powers, whereas in every detail it resembles the work of Feke in many of his portraits. In the third place the picture of Margaret Willing (so-called) resembles to an extraordinary degree the portrait in the Historical Society of Pennsylvania which is there listed as that of Mrs. Clement Plumstead. The dress in the two portraits is practically identical, and the countenance of the sitters so similar as to suggest that if the two pictures do not represent the same individual, they at least show two members of the same family. Finally both portraits resemble the portrait of Mary McCall's mother, Mrs. George McCall.

The conclusion seems inevitable that the portraits of Anne and Margaret Willing (so-called) do not represent those persons, but two members of the same family as that to which Mrs. Clement Plumstead (so-called) belonged. Perhaps the best explanation is that all three young women were daughters of George McCall and his wife Anne Yeates. That couple had a large family, including several daughters who would have been of the right age to be thus depicted by Feke in either of his two earlier visits to Philadelphia. Their son Samuel McCall left no male issue, but his daughter Anne (Nancy) married Thomas, eldest son of the Mrs. Charles Willing whom Feke painted in 1746. Portraits of members of the McCall family of an earlier generation might thus easily have passed into the Willing family, and their identity, like the name of the painter, might have been forgotten by later generations.

While the foregoing is highly conjectural it does seem clear that the portraits are the work of Feke; that therefore they cannot represent the Willing sisters; and that the identification of the subjects as members of the McCall family offers at least a plausible hypothesis.

The portraits are now owned by the estate of J. I. Clarke Hare, at Radnor, Pennsylvania.

NOTES ON OTHER PICTURES BY FEKE OR ATTRIBUTED TO HIM

In the foregoing Descriptive List the following pictures have not been included:

(1) "The Judgment of Hercules" (see pp. 59–63) which Feke certainly painted but which is known only from the comment of Dr. Alexander Hamilton.

(2) The portrait called "Rev. Heysham." This picture was picked up by the Ehrich Galleries in New York in 1928. It had recently been relined and put on a new stretcher, on which was written in red crayon "Rev. Heysham, aet. 19, Robert Feke." No information was available as to the history of the picture, the authority for the inscription, or the identity of the subject. It represents a not very pleasing youth, in a white wig, brown coat, and pleated shirt with plain neckband, and wrist-bands fastened by silver buttons. The face is tolerably well modelled, but the figure is rigid and lifeless. The picture certainly bears small resemblance to Feke's later work. It is, however, just possible that the inscription represents an authentic tradition, in which case the picture must be regarded as one of Feke's early attempts at portraiture, dating perhaps from his visit to New York in the early seventeen-thirties.

(3) A portrait of "An Unknown Woman holding Wild-flowers." This picture was picked up in 1928 by Mr. Alexander A. Kelley of New York, who thought it might be the work of Feke. It represents a young woman with dark hair and a fresh complexion, dressed in pearl-gray silk, seated and holding flowers in her lap. Its history is unknown, and it has few if any of the characteristics of Feke's work.

(4) The portrait sometimes called that of Judith Bowdoin Flucker, in the Bowdoin Art Gallery, attributed to Feke by some persons. Lawrence Park, in his pamphlet on *Joseph Blackburn*, has identified the portrait as probably that of Hannah Waldo, second wife of Thomas Flucker, probably painted by Blackburn in 1755.

(5) The portrait called "Portrait of a Lady," reproduced in *The International Studio*, November, 1923, vol. LXXVIII, No. 138, p. 154, under the heading of "An American Old Master in London," with an unsigned statement attributing it to Feke. No information is given as to the identity of the subject, where the portrait was found, or whether there is any reason to suppose that it was painted in America. It bears no marked resemblance to Feke's work, and the costume seems too late for his period. If the picture was painted in this country it is more likely to be the work of Blackburn.

CHRONOLOGICAL LIST OF EXTANT PORTRAITS

NOTE. The year can be given with entire assurance only for those few pictures which are signed and dated. The years given for the undated portraits are in parentheses as being conjectural. In the case of the undated Boston portraits it is assumed that they were painted in 1748. The undated Philadelphia portraits which cannot be definitely assigned to 1746 may have been painted either in that year or in 1750. Pictures known to have been painted by Feke, but probably or certainly not now extant, are bracketed. Portraits doubtfully attributed to Feke are followed by a question mark.

(1725?)	The Early Self-Portrait
(1732) (Painted at Oyster Bay?)	"Phiany" Cock
(1733?) (Painted in New York?)	"Rev. Heysham"?
Between 1735 and 1740) (Newport)	Rev. Nathaniel Clap?
(Before 1740?) (First Philadelphia visit)	Tench Francis, No. 1
	Mrs. Tench Francis, No. 1
	Mrs. George McCall
(1741) (First Boston visit)	James Bowdoin II, No. 1
	Isaac Royall and Family
(1740–44) (Painted at Newport)	"Pamela Andrews"
	Mrs. Joseph Wanton
	John Gidley, Jr.
	["The Judgment of Hercules"]
	The Unknown Man with a Spaniel
1745 (Painted at Newport)	Rev. John Callender
	Rev. Thomas Hiscox
1746 (Second Philadelphia visit)	Tench Francis, No. 2
	Miss Williamina Moore
	Mrs. Charles Willing, No. 1 (and No. 2)
(1746)	Mrs. Tench Francis, No. 2
	Benjamin Franklin
(1746 or 1750) (Second or third Philadelphia visit)	William Peters
	Mrs. William Peters
	Miss Mary McCall? (Mrs. William Plumstead? so-called Mrs. Clement Plumstead)
	William Plumstead
	Mrs. James Tilghman, No. 1 and No. 2
	Miss Anne Willing (so-called)
	Miss Margaret Willing (so-called)
(1746? or 1750?) (Painted at Hemstead, Long Island?)	Josiah Martin
	Mrs. Josiah Martin

(1747) (At Newport, between the second Philadelphia and the second Boston visit, or

(1749) Between the second Boston and the third Philadelphia visit)

John Channing, No. 1
Mrs. John Channing, No. 1
[John Channing, No. 2]
Mrs. John Channing, No. 2
Ebenezer Flagg
Mrs. Ebenezer Flagg
Gershom Flagg III
Isaac Stelle
Mrs. Isaac Stelle
Mrs. Tweedy
Philip Wilkinson

1748 (The second Boston visit)

Charles Apthorp
Mrs. Charles Apthorp
Robert Auchmuty, II
James Bowdoin II, No. 2
Mrs. James Bowdoin
William Bowdoin
Mrs. William Bowdoin
Oxenbridge Thacher

1749
(1748) (The second Boston visit)

Mrs. Oxenbridge Thacher
Miss Ruth Cunningham
Gershom Flagg IV
Mrs. Gershom Flagg
Col. Thomas Goldthwait
Ralph Inman
Mrs. Ralph Inman, No. 1 and No. 2
Mrs. Benjamin Lynde
John Rowe
Mrs. John Rowe
Richard Saltonstall
Stephen Sewall
Mrs. Barlow Trecothick
Mrs. John Vinal?
Samuel Waldo

(1750) (The third Philadelphia visit)

Thomas Hopkinson
Miss Richea Meyers
William Nelson?
Mrs. William Nelson?
Edward Shippen, Jr.
Joseph Shippen
(And perhaps others of the undated Philadelphia portraits)

(1750) (Painted at Newport, prob- The Late Self-Portrait
ably after the third Philadel- Mrs. Robert Feke
phia visit)

PRESENT LOCATION OF PORTRAITS

DISTRICT OF COLUMBIA
Washington
    Thomas Hopkinson

ILLINOIS
Elgin
    Unknown Man with Spaniel

MAINE
Brunswick
    James Bowdoin, No. 1
    James Bowdoin, No. 2
    Mrs. James Bowdoin
    William Bowdoin
    Mrs. William Bowdoin
    Samuel Waldo

MASSACHUSETTS
Belmont
    Robert Feke, Early Self-Portrait
    Gershom Flagg IV
    Mrs. Gershom Flagg

Boston
    Mrs. Charles Apthorp
    Robert Auchmuty
    Mrs. John Channing, No. 2
    Thomas Goldthwait
    Ralph Inman
    Mrs. Ralph Inman, No. 1
    Mrs. Ralph Inman, No. 2
    Mrs. Benjamin Lynde
    Mrs. John Rowe
    Mrs. Barlow Trecothick
    Mrs. John Vinal

Cambridge
    Benjamin Franklin
    Isaac Royall and Family
    Stephen Sewall

Chestnut Hill
    Richard Saltonstall

Lexington
    John Rowe

Milton
    John Channing, No. 1
    Mrs. John Channing, No. 1

NEW JERSEY
Madison
    Tench Francis, No. 1
    Mrs. Tench Francis, No. 1
    Mrs. James Tilghman, No. 1

NEW YORK
Lawrence, L. I.
    Josiah Martin
    Mrs. Josiah Martin

New York City
    Miss Ruth Cunningham
    Ebenezer Flagg
    Mrs. Ebenezer Flagg
    Gershom Flagg III
    Miss Williamina Moore
    Oxenbridge Thacher
    Mrs. Oxenbridge Thacher
    Mrs. Charles Willing, No. 2

Rhinecliff
    Mrs. Charles Willing, No. 1

OHIO
Cleveland
    Charles Apthorp

PENNSYLVANIA
Bryn Mawr
    Mrs. Tench Francis, No. 2
    Edward Shippen, Jr.

PENNSYLVANIA (*continued*)
Jenkintown
Tench Francis, No. 2

Media
"Phiany" Cock
Philadelphia
Dr. Phineas Bond
Miss Richea Meyers
William Peters
Mrs. William Peters
William Plumstead
Miss Mary McCall? (Mrs. William Plumstead? — Mrs. Clement Plumstead, so-called)
Radnor
Miss Anne Willing (so-called)
Miss Margaret Willing (so-called)

RHODE ISLAND
Newport
Rev. Nathaniel Clap?
John Gidley
Rev. Thomas Hiscox
Isaac Stelle
Mrs. Isaac Stelle
Mrs. Joseph Wanton
Philip Wilkinson
Providence
Pamela Andrews
Rev. John Callender
Robert Feke, Late Self-Portrait
Mrs. Robert Feke
Mrs. Tweedy

VIRGINIA
Richmond
William Nelson
Mrs. William Nelson

INDEX

INDEX

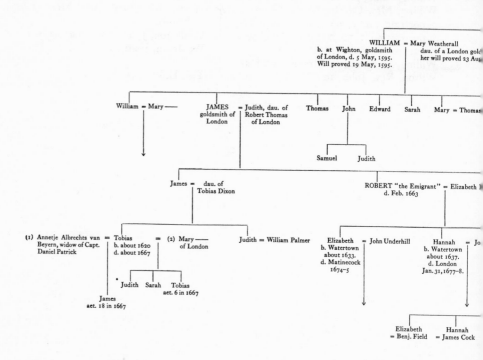

RT FEKE (The Painter)

JAMES FEAKE of Wighton, Norfolk (16th century)

James = Parnell ——   Edmund   Simon   Robert

Bourneford   James   William   Margaret   Judith   Ann   Parnell   Ann et als.   Numerous descendants   James

p   Alice

= Elizabeth Prior   Robert = ?   Sarah
d. Feb. 25,   bapt. New Amsterdam   bapt. New Amsterdam
1701–2   17 July, 1642   14 April 1647
d. Flushing, 1668?

BERT "the Preacher" = Clemence Ludlam,   Sarah   Martha   Abigail   Deborah
b. Matinecock,   b. 1684,   = John Carpenter   = Josiah Coggeshall   = Thomas Whitson
22 June 1683   d. Aug. 8, 1770
d. Oyster Bay,
April 1, 1773

Henry   ROBERT "the Painter" = Eleanor Cozzens   John   Charles   Deborah = James Cock   Sarah   Elizabeth
b. Oyster Bay, 1705?   b. Newport,
d. Barbados? 1750?   Nov. 15, 1718   Levinah (Phiany), et als.
m. Sept. 23, 1742
d. Aug. 6, 1804

Horatio   Phila   = John Townsend   Sarah   = John Thurston   Charles
?   b. 1744   b. about   b. about   b. 1750
a   d. Mar. 22, 1803   1746?   1748?   d. Apr. 25,
d. Mar. 15,   d. before   1822
1802   1772

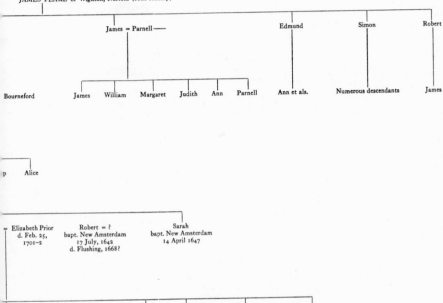
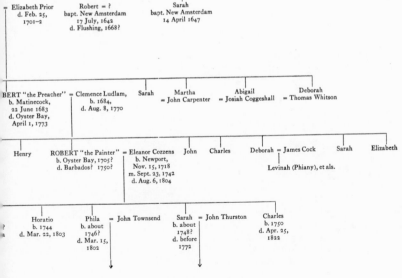